IN THE COMPANY OF PARTNERS

IN THE COMPANY OF PARTNERS

Business, environmental groups and sustainable development post-Rio

David F. Murphy and Jem Bendell

First published in Great Britain in 1997 by

The Policy Press
University of Bristol
Rodney Lodge
Grange Road
Bristol BS8 4EA

Telephone (0117) 973 8797
Fax (0117) 973 7308
e-mail: tpp@bris.ac.uk

British Library Cataloguing in Publication Data
A catalogue record for this book is available from the British Library

ISBN 1 86134 017 6

Cover design: Qube, Bristol.

The Policy Press works to counter discrimination on grounds of gender, race, disability, age and sexuality.

Printed in Great Britain by Hobbs the Printers Ltd, Southampton.

Contents

Acknowledgements

We would like to thank everyone who replied to questionnaires, gave interviews and provided us with written material. Without your invaluable contributions, this book would not have been possible.

A number of other people provided guidance or support throughout the writing and production process. We would like to say a special thanks to: David Mathew, Gill Coleman and Alex Cutler at New Academy of Business; Mark Gilden, Andy Moore and Bill Oates at EcoSourcing International; and Dawn Pudney, Julia Mortimer, Sue Hayman and Vicky Price at The Policy Press.

Various people commented on the original book proposal, draft text or provided guidance. We would like to express our warm appreciation to: John Elkington of SustainAbility; Malcolm McIntosh, Social and Environmental Management Consultant; Tom Davies, Sue Barrett and Bernard Lane, University of Bristol; Jo Smith and Bill Adams, University of Cambridge; and Francis Sullivan and Mike Sutton at WWF-International.

We would also like to acknowledge the assistance of the Economic and Social Research Council, the Social Science and Humanities Research Council of Canada and the University of Bristol which provided research funding for some of the material in the book.

Finally we would each like to thank our families for their ongoing support.

Foreword

John Elkington

[John Elkington is Chairman of SustainAbility Ltd and of The Environment Foundation, and a Member of the Business in the Environment Advisory Group and of the EU Consultative Forum on the Environment. He is also co-author of a recent two-volume report for the United Nations Environment Programme (UNEP), *Engaging stakeholders.*]

In the company of partners is a timely book on a subject which is rapidly rising up the agenda of the sustainable development community and of a growing number of company boards. New forms of partnership are evolving in every sector of the global economy, involving complex mixtures of government, non-governmental, business and other assorted actors. The trends underlying and increasingly driving such partnerships are well described in the following pages.

In the process, David F. Murphy and Jem Bendell make a number of references to work we have done in such areas as the interfaces between business and consumers, between companies collaborating in the growing range of 'green business' or sustainable development networks, and between companies and campaigning groups. Governments, whether regulating, enforcing or encouraging the evolution of voluntary partnerships along the lines of the Dutch industry covenants, also play a fundamentally important role. But few types of partnership are as challenging for business as those some companies are beginning to develop with their erstwhile enemies, the non-governmental organisations (NGOs).

Given this fact, the growing number of such partnerships can be seen as a direct, powerful indicator of the pressures for change. And, to help set the scene, it is perhaps worth exploring some of the trends – and some of the drivers – in more detail.

Mix sodium and water and you are guaranteed an explosion. Put business people together with people from campaigning groups, or other NGOs, and the last couple of decades have taught us to expect an even more violent reaction. Yet, in September 1996, Greenpeace held its first conference tailor-made for business people, attracting a capacity audience. So what is going on? And what can both sides expect to gain in the process?

In the old days, the answer was blindingly clear. Mainstream NGOs wanted money. Whether the funding was for core costs, campaigns or other initiatives, the nature of the deal was clear. Give us money and we will splash your name over some appropriate surface. Some NGOs developed huge corporate sponsorship departments dedicated solely to hunting down deep-pocketed corporate donors.

Fine, as long as it lasted. But then two things happened in parallel. First, companies became more discriminating. They began to insist on a bigger PR bang for their sponsorship buck. And they wanted their benefits in the form of an enhanced reputation with selected audiences. As a result, some of those NGO corporate sponsorship departments became almost indistinguishable from mainstream advertising or PR agencies.

The second shift was driven by NGO needs. They found them-selves managing increasingly large projects and budgets. Their staffs mushroomed and demanded better employment conditions. They found they needed the same kind of people, project and financial management skills in which business was rich. So downsizing companies seconded managers to NGOs, often as a way of easing them into retirement, and NGOs appointed people from business to their boards and top management posts.

Not all of these transfers worked. More than a few business managers – and some of those actively head-hunted – were fish out of water when it came to managing NGOs. But enough of these grafts 'took' to ensure that NGOs remain interested in finding new ways to access the human resources and skills available within their business partners.

Now we are entering a new phase in the evolution of business–NGO relations, involving strategic alliances between companies and selected NGOs. In fact, exactly the sort of strange alliance that Greenpeace pioneered in its Greenfreeze campaign with companies like Calor. One likely outcome: mutual reprogramming of mindsets.

Earlier in 1996, SustainAbility had been asked to investigate the growth of such alliances worldwide, working alongside BP. In the news that year because of alleged misdemeanours in Columbia, BP actually has a long track record of working with NGOs. The company's board needed to decide whether it should develop a strategic alliance with one or more NGOs. And, if so, with whom and to do what?

We surveyed over 60 environmental NGOs wordwide and followed that up with interviews of 40 selected NGOs and companies that had already developed strategic alliances. These included companies as diverse as BT, General Motors and McDonald's, and, indeed, the project unfolded against a background of increasing collaboration between companies and NGOs, among them WWF's link with Unilever on sustainable fisheries.

As the environmental agenda broadens to incorporate sustainable development, with its triple bottom-line (economic prosperity, environmental quality and social equity) NGOs are realising the key role that business can – must – play in forging workable solutions. At the same time, growing numbers of businesses are seeking to move beyond confrontation to forge more productive relationships with NGOs.

The convergence of these trends creates an opportunity for new forms of partnership, but also raises an interesting new issue. Once, many business people thought there were too many NGOs for comfort. If current trends continue, however, we will see a shortage of credible NGOs willing and able to work alongside business. Thus, companies that lead their competitors in forging strategic alliances with key NGOs could enjoy a strong 'first mover' benefit.

Over 85 per cent of our respondents believed that partnerships will increase over the next five years, and that NGOs should get involved in more company partnerships. Even so, confrontational styles of NGO–company relationships are expected to continue and several factors could reverse the trend towards collaboration. As a result, we expect that both companies and NGOs will need to grapple with the internal schizophrenia within their own organisations.

NGO interest in partnerships reflects a fundamental shift in their thinking about the role of business. They reported a clear shift from problem-focused to solution-focused advocacy. This shift is accompanied, indeed driven, by a gradual disillusionment with government as a provider of solutions. Industry is also losing confidence in government and sees NGOs having much higher levels of credibility.

Less positively, there are factors that could well reverse the trend towards cooperative forms of NGO–company relationships, swinging the pendulum back towards confrontation. Despite their interest in working more closely with industry, NGOs fear loss of integrity and identity from being (or being seen to be) coopted. Some of the NGOs interviewed will return to core advocacy (as they are already doing in the USA) if environmental laws come under attack, believing that laws underpin cooperative relationships.

However, closer working between NGOs and the world of business seems inevitable and, in many respects, desirable. These strange alliances will demand extraordinary vision and new political and management skills from people who in the past have found it much easier to simply lob bricks at each other. Now they are being asked to build together and if the approach works, they will need to accept shared responsibility for both the ends and the means. If, on occasion, they fail, as many experiments do, we need to recognise that even failures should be celebrated if we learn from our mistakes. Readers of *In the company of partners* will be well placed to avoid at least some of those mistakes. But, more importantly, they will be better informed about when it makes sense to form partnerships – and how they can best be developed and sustained.

List of acronyms

API	American Petroleum Institute
BATNEEC	Best Available Techniques Not Entailing Excessive Costs
BCSD	Business Council for Sustainable Development
BP	British Petroleum
BPEO	Best Practicable Environmental Option
CAP	Community Advisory Panel
CASA	Clean Air Strategic Alliance
CCPA	Canadian Chemical Producers' Association
CEFIC	European Chemical Industry Council
CEO	Chief Executive Officer
CERES	Coalition for Environmentally Responsible Economies
CPPA	Canadian Pulp and Paper Association
CSA	Canadian Standards Association
CSD	Commission on Sustainable Development
DDT	Dichlor-diphenyl-trichlorethane
DIY	Do-It-Yourself
EA	Environmental Advantage
EC	European Commission
ECOSOC	Economic and Social Council
ECRA	Ethical Consumer Research Association
EDF	Environmental Defense Fund
EEB	European Environmental Bureau
EHS	Environment, Health and Safety
EMAS	Eco-Management and Audit Scheme
EMS	Environmental Management System
ENDS	Environmental Data Services
EPA	Environmental Protection Agency
EPE	European Partners for the Environment
ESC	Endangered Seas Campaign
ESI	Eco-Sourcing International
EU	European Union
FAO	Food and Agriculture Organisation

FoE	Friends of the Earth
FSC	Forest Stewardship Council
GATT	General Agreement on Tariffs and Trade
GDP	Gross Domestic Product
GGT	Global Guardian Trust
GNP	Gross National Product
HMSO	Her Majesty's Statistical Office
ICC	International Chamber of Commerce
ICI	Imperial Chemical Industries
ICLEI	International Council for Local Environmental Initiatives
IFAW	International Fund for Animal Welfare
IFCS	Intergovernmental Forum for Chemical Safety
IIED	International Institute for Environment and Development
ILO	International Labour Organization
INEM	International Network for Environmental Management
IPF	Intergovernmental Panel on Forests
ISO	International Organisation for Standardisation
ITTA	International Tropical Timber Agreement
ITTO	International Tropical Timber Organisation
IUCN	World Conservation Union
MORI	Market & Opinion Research International
MEB	Management Institute for Environment and Business
MSC	Marine Stewardship Council
MTV	Music Television
NABG	North American Buyers Group
NCC	National Consumer Council
NEEP	National Environmental Policy Plan
NEF	New Economics Foundation
NGO	Non-governmental Organisation
NLRTEE	Newfoundland and Labrador Round Table on the Environment and Economy
NOVIB	Netherlands Organisation for International Cooperation
NDRC	National Resources Defense Council
OECD	Organisation for Economic Cooperation and Development
PETA	People for the Ethical Treatment of Animals

PCB	Polychlorinated biphenyl
POP	Persistent Organic Pollutants
PR	Public Relations
PVC	Polyvinyl chloride
QA	Quality Assurance
RAG	Rainforest Action Group
SNM	Netherlands Society for Nature and Environment
SCS	Scientific Certification System
TAC	Total Allowable Catch
TFAP	Tropical Forestry Action Plan
TFW	Timber/Fish/Wildlife Agreement
TNC	Transnational corporation
TTF	Timber Trade Federation
UK	United Kingdom
UML	Unilever Merseyside Limited
UN	United Nations
UNCED	UN Conference on Environment and Development
UNCTAD	UN Conference on Trade and Environment
UNDP	UN Development Programme
UNED	UN Environment and Development Committee
UNEP	UN Environment Programme
UNICEF	UN Children's Fund
UNIDO	UN Industrial Development Organisation
WBCSD	World Business Council for Sustainable Development
WCED	World Commission on Environment and Development
WFSGI	World Federation of the Sporting Goods Industry
WICEM	World Industry Conference for Environmental Management
WRTF	Waste Reduction Task Force
WTO	World Trade Organisation
WWF	World Wide Fund for Nature (or World Wildlife Fund)

Introduction

Partnership is not the first word that comes to mind when business and environmental groups are mentioned in the same breath. Over the past three decades, most relationships between the private sector and the environmental movement have been founded upon conflict. This started to change in the early 1990s with the emergence of sustainable development, which has offered a new way of looking at environmental, economic and social problems. As a result, representatives of business and the environmental movement have in some cases begun to collaborate in the search for alternatives and solutions. Sustainable development remains an elusive concept, one which some economists and environmentalists have dismissed as an unworkable compromise. Others insist that sustainable development offers a basis for innovative responses to complex, seemingly insurmountable obstacles. One of our key arguments is that business–environmental group partnerships are one of many strategies needed to put sustainable development into practice. The emergence of the business–environmentalist partnership phenomenon in the 1990s also offers new hope for building consensus towards global sustainability. The overall purpose of the book is to provide the reader with an introduction to business–environmental group partnerships, including an analysis of how and why they have emerged, and their wider significance for business and the green movement in northern, industrialised societies. Although the book is generally optimistic in tone, we accept that the prevailing pattern of business–environmental group relationships remains adversarial and that the road to sustainable development is largely uncharted territory. We, nevertheless, believe that business–environmentalist partnerships should be embraced by both business and environmental leaders as one of many strategies for sustainability.

The road to partnership often begins with conflict. Back in 1962, Rachel Carson's *Silent spring* launched the contemporary environmental movement with an exposé on the harmful effects of pesticides upon people and their natural environments. The chemical industry responded with a scathing attack on environmentalists, branding them "a motley lot ranging from superstitious illiterates and cultists to educated scientists" (Hoffman, 1996b, p 53). Thirty years later in the lead up to the Rio Earth Summit, Stephan Schmidheiny's *Changing course* was intended as a clarion call for global business to see environmental pressures as new business opportunities. *Changing course* launched the Business Council for Sustainable Development (BCSD) and offered 38 case studies of best environmental practice, including chemical-producing companies such as Ciba-Geigy, Dow, Du Pont and Shell. Greenpeace responded with a pre-emptive attack on *Changing course* hours before its official launch in May 1992. Weeks later at the Earth Summit, it released the *Greenpeace book of greenwash* (Kenny, 1992) which castigated nine of the *Changing course* companies for their poor environmental records. From *Silent spring* to *Changing course*, relations between representatives of business and the environmental movement have for the most part remained strongly antagonistic.

The mid-1995 confrontation between Shell and Greenpeace over the disposal of the Brent Spar offshore oil installation confirmed the long-standing image of two tribes engaged in perpetual war over values, words and ideas. Following Shell-UK's decision to abandon deepwater disposal of the Brent Spar, Greenpeace-UK argued that its victory represented "a sea change in attitudes to the environment" and that "it is no longer acceptable for industry to use the seas as a tip for its industrial rubbish" (Greenpeace-UK, 1995, p 7). Shell-UK's Chairman and Chief Executive Chris Fay admitted that "the Brent Spar affair ... has been a setback for Shell-UK" but insisted that Greenpeace "gave the deepwater disposal of the Spar a symbolic significance out of all proportion to its negligible environmental impact.... This has dealt a serious blow to the cause of sustainable development" (Shell-UK, 1995, p 2).

There is another side to the business–environmental group story. The Earth Summit, despite mixed reviews at the time, has in retrospect proved to be a watershed in business relations with Non-governmental Organisations (NGOs) working on environment, development and human rights issues. Coinciding with the Rio Conference preparations and follow-up, a number of businesses and environmental groups began quietly in the early 1990s to work together to overcome some of their differences. The emergence of these new collaborative relationships is closely linked to a number of inter-related factors, including ongoing environmental group pressure on businesses to improve their environmental records, such as the Greenpeace campaigns described above, and the growing prominence of the idea of sustainable development with its emphasis upon finding solutions to both ecological and socio-economic problems. Various formal partnerships and alliances between businesses and environmental groups are starting to challenge the notion that profit making necessarily precludes environmental protection or that green campaigning by definition excludes business acumen. By combining their respective strengths whilst maintaining organisational independence, many former antagonists now find themselves in the company of partners.

Since early 1992, the World Wide Fund for Nature (WWF-UK) and some 78 wood-product retailers, suppliers, manufacturers and importers in the UK have been working together on a complex product-sourcing and certification project to promote sustainable forest management around the world. In The Netherlands, Milieudefensie (Friends of the Earth-NL), the development NGO Novib and WWF-NL are working with a wide range of private and public sector partners on a similar initiative. Other forest-related partnerships have been launched or are under development in Belgium, Austria, Sweden, Switzerland, Germany, Denmark, Ireland, North America, Japan and Australia (see WWF-International, 1997a).

In North America, an array of business–environmentalist partnerships have emerged in recent years. The fast-food market leader McDonald's and the Environmental Defense Fund (EDF) launched a joint Waste Reduction Task Force in 1990. Two years later EDF initiated the Paper Task Force, a collaboration with Johnson & Johnson, McDonald's, Prudential Insurance, Time Inc. and Duke University, which was formed to find ways to reduce the environmental impact of paper production and consumption. From Canada in 1994 came the Clean Air Strategic Alliance (CASA) which has brought together "stakeholders with diverse interests to solve [Alberta's] air quality problems on a consensus basis" (CASA, 1996, p 5).

At the European Union (EU) level, Dow Chemical has been an active participant in the European Partners for the Environment (EPE), a network of business, NGO and government decision makers founded in 1994, which employs a solution-oriented process to implement key aspects of the EU's Fifth Environmental Action Programme *Towards sustainability – programme of policy and action for the European Community in relation to the environment and sustainable development*. As part of this process, one of Dow's manufacturing sites recently hosted an EPE project on enhanced stakeholder involvement in the EU's Eco-Management and Audit Scheme (EMAS).

Business–environmentalist partnerships are growing in both number and scope. WWF-International has recently launched a partnership with Unilever Corporation, the world's largest buyer of frozen fish, to create economic incentives within the seafood industry for sustainable fishing throughout the world. Greenpeace has initiated a project with a group of major UK retailers on the environmental impact of PVC in packaging and building materials. Partnerships with business are also being initiated by other segments of the wider green movement.[1] The Fairtrade Foundation, a coalition of international development, consumer and fair trade organisations, has launched a pilot project to work with British companies to develop codes of practice to guide relationships with their Third World or southern suppliers.[2] One of the UK's leading supermarket chains, J. Sainsbury, is working with Fairtrade to assess a number of its own-brand product areas against a draft supplier's charter (see Cowe, 1996a). Athletic footwear market leaders Nike and Reebok continue to face pressure from Oxfam and Christian Aid on the child labour issue, with the NGOs demanding the adoption of new codes and independent monitoring of company trading practices. Partially in response to such criticism, the World Federation of the Sporting Goods Industry (WFSGI) announced in late 1996 that it was cooperating with Save the Children-UK, United Nations Children's Fund (UNICEF), International Labour Organization (ILO) and local groups to develop a pilot project in Pakistan to address some of the underlying causes of child labour (see WFSGI, 1996). The common thread that links these various initiatives is a new form of relationship between the business community and NGOs. While there have been formal agreements between businesses and environmental groups based upon fundraising and project sponsorship for decades, the new partnerships described above are primarily concerned with strategic and operational policy issues which have a direct impact upon core business practices. Whereas in the past business primarily supported environmental or community projects as good corporate causes, businesses now find themselves also working together with environmental groups to solve day-to-day business problems associated with sourcing, purchasing, production, manufacturing, retailing, marketing, customer relations, research and development and longer-term issues such as the sustainability of certain products and production processes. Therefore, we define business–environmental group partnerships as collaborations where environmental groups assist participating businesses primarily with internal operational issues. While there are many within the wider green movement who view such partnerships with deep suspicion, others see improved relations with the private sector as a necessary tactic in trying to change unsustainable and unjust business behaviour.

If business–environmental group partnerships are to maintain momentum and public credibility, they require effective monitoring and evaluation. First, the partners must ensure that their own internal assessments are consistent with the needs of both parties. Second, there must be opportunities for critical monitoring by a range of external stakeholders, for example, business associations, NGO networks, activist groups, local authorities, government and UN agencies, and other interested individuals and organisations.

The publication of *In the company of partners* coincides with Earth Summit II, a special five-year review by the UN General Assembly in 1997 of the effectiveness of national, regional and international implementation of Agenda 21 and other Earth Summit-related agreements and initiatives. Given Agenda 21's emphasis upon the roles of business and NGOs in the post-Rio implementation of sustainable development, we present a timely synthesis of both historical review and up-to-date analysis on the changing nature of business–NGO relations in the global environmental arena.

Chapter one provides a review of past and current thinking on sustainable development with a focus on the international policy process and lessons learned from the Earth Summit and the post-Rio period. The chapter also offers an overview of the 1997 Earth Summit II process and its evaluation of post-Rio implementation of sustainable development.

Chapter two explores the changing nature of environmental group thinking and action in the twentieth century. It suggests that the recent emergence of third-wave environmentalism provides a basis for collaboration with business.

Chapter three reviews the changing business response to environmental challenges over the past three decades. It illustrates how some businesses have moved from a defensive stance towards a more proactive response to the sustainability agenda.

Chapter four looks at the experience of partnerships between environmental groups and the timber trade, with a detailed analysis of the first such initiative – the 1995 Group, a collaboration between the UK wood-product trade and the World Wide Fund for Nature (WWF-UK).

Chapter five reviews a wide range of sustainability partnership initiatives around the world. In doing so it proposes a new framework for analysing future partnerships – the business–NGO partnership matrix. The chapter includes an in-depth look at three case studies in the chemicals, fisheries and food retailing sectors, involving Dow, Unilever and Loblaws respectively.

Chapter six considers relationships between the fast-food market leader McDonald's and various environmental groups. Despite its ground-breaking collaboration with the EDF in the USA, McDonald's continues to face considerable environmental group pressure worldwide.

Chapter seven provides perspectives on the impact, efficacy and sustainability of business–environmental group partnerships. The chapter addresses some of the common causal factors, implementation themes, costs, benefits and critiques of the partnerships described in the book. It concludes that these partnerships are indicative of a new social realism which is beginning to emerge in northern industrialised countries.

Specifically designed with the practitioner audience in mind, the Annex contains a guide to the development and implementation of business–environmental group partnerships. This guide offers concise, hands-on suggestions to assist companies, environmental groups and others interested in developing or facilitating new relationships similar to those described in the book.

Our aim is to provide a critical review of a number of examples of business–environmentalist partnerships which endeavour to put sustainable development into practice. We have tried to write *In the company of partners* in a way which balances analysis with advocacy. The structure and content of the book also represents an attempt to bridge the gap between academic study and practical advice. In this sense, we have broken with the norm of writing a book with only one specific audience in mind. Its popular format and style is intended as a means of reaching a wide range of audiences and we have tried for the most part to avoid much of the academic, technical and professional jargon associated with sustainable development, environmentalism and business. For specialist audiences, we offer brief reviews of various concepts in boxes to show how the events described in the book fit into established or emerging academic debates, or to present additional background information. We would like social science to rediscover its normative purpose and have attempted to combine critical reflection with constructive advice about a possible way forward. We anticipate that this book will meet some of the needs of practitioners, policy makers and academics interested in business–environmental group partnerships. We also hope that the experiences and perspectives presented in the book will inspire new thinking and action on the implementation of sustainable development in the twenty-first century.

Notes

[1] In this context, the wider green movement includes "groups with a broadly green, leftist or liberal agenda working to increase awareness or change policies on environment, development and/or human rights issues, and/or to implement projects which have the aim of improving peoples' living standards or protecting the environment." (see McCoy and McCully, 1993, p 65).

[2] The term 'Third World' is based upon a categorisation of the world into three geopolitical divisions on the lines of capitalist first, communist

second and 'the rest' third. With the demise of the communist bloc, we believe that this nomenclature is no longer relevant. Third World has been used interchangeably with terms such the developing, under-developed or less developed world. Given current debates within the field of development (see Chapter one), the appropriateness of the term is widely questioned. We prefer the alternative 'the South' to refer to the countries of Latin America, the Caribbean, Africa, Asia and the South Pacific. Conversely, 'the North' is used to refer to industrialised countries primarily in the northern hemisphere. The North is often subdivided into the West (such as USA and UK) and the East (namely Japan). The North–South distinction is complicated by the existence of pockets of wealth within southern countries and regions, as well as poverty within the North.

one

Facing diversity: sustainable development at the crossroads

When the Rio Earth Summit made the cover of the American edition of *Elle* magazine in June 1992, sustainable development entered the mainstream. Officially known as the UN Conference on Environment and Development (UNCED), the Earth Summit brought together representatives of 178 countries, including 117 government leaders, making it the largest political summit ever. Rio brought unparalleled media attention to a host of inter-related global issues – biodiversity, climate change, consumption patterns, deforestation, fragile ecosystems, hazardous waste, indigenous knowledge, poverty, responsible entrepreneurship and the role of non-governmental organisations (NGOs), among many others. In the months leading up to the two-week international gathering of political leaders and tens of thousands of activists, bureaucrats and business people, pop stars such as Madonna, REM, Seal and LL Cool J used MTV videoclips to lobby a reluctant American President George Bush to attend. For 12 days in June 1992, the world's attention turned to Rio. From the green jamboree on the beach to the official conference hall 30 miles away, the idea of sustainable development had suddenly arrived on the world's crowded stage. Competing political interests fought for the spotlight – the ecological, the economic, the social, the developed, the developing, the corporate, the non-governmental, and so on. When the citizens of Rio and the world looked up, they found themselves facing a microcosm of global diversity in the 1990s.

Rio may have succeeded in bringing renewed attention to an array of persistent global problems. However, most participants and analysts concluded that the overall process resolved few differences and produced little consensus about how to put sustainable development into practice. If Rio was about recognising and analysing global diversity, then the post-Rio period was expected to manage this diversity more effectively.

Implicit in sustainable development is the need for partnership between diverse interests, both present and future. In 1993, the Summit's Secretary General, Canadian industrialist Maurice Strong, argued that:

> ... [the transition to] sustainable development is not just an option but an imperative.... It requires a major shift in priorities for governments and people, involving the full integration of the environmental dimension into economic policies and decision-making in every sphere of activity.... This global partnership is essential to set the world community onto a new course for a more sustainable, secure and equitable future as we prepare ourselves for the twenty-first century.
>
> (see United Nations, 1993, p viii)

Partnership has become the cornerstone of post-Rio implementation of sustainable development. Governments and UN agencies are increasingly encouraging local authorities, community groups, indigenous peoples, private sector organisations and NGOs to implement new ways of dealing with many long-standing international, national and local problems. Multi-stakeholder approaches, bilateral agreements and other forms of collaboration are also being adopted by two of Rio's strongest antagonists – business and environmental groups. The emergence of business–environmentalist partnerships, perhaps more than any other post-Rio initiative, has demonstrated that the implementation of sustainable development is underway.

In this chapter, we provide a review of past and current thinking and action on sustainable development focusing on lessons learned from the Rio process and beyond. Our purpose here is to trace the evolution of the concept of sustainable development and to illustrate how and why it has created a context where new forms of collaboration between business and the wider green movement are now possible. The chapter also includes an overview of Earth Summit II, the UN General

Assembly's 1997 Special Session in New York to evaluate the effectiveness of the implementation of Agenda 21 and other Earth Summit-related agreements and initiatives. As two of the groups identified in Agenda 21 as being critical to its effective implementation, NGOs (including environmental groups) and business/industry continue to play major roles in the implementation of sustainable development strategies. While the major challenge of the post-Rio period remains one of managing diverse and often competing interests, Earth Summit II, nevertheless, has offered business, environmental groups and all other Rio participants opportunities to review progress five years on and to identify a better way forward.

Development roots

Although sustainable development first appeared in the late 1970s, the concept has a much deeper and more complex history. One of sustainable development's key roots is the idea of development, a broad concept with many different meanings. Perhaps most relevant to our discussion is Clive Ponting's description of development as "the process of moving from a pre-industrial society to an industrialised one" (1992, p 398). Linked to the idea of progress, development has historically been seen as both a desirable and necessary means of ensuring that basic human needs and higher living standards are met. Towards the end of the colonial period, development and progress became the twin goals of both the newly-independent states in the southern hemisphere and the new aid programmes of donor countries primarily in Europe and North America. This new era of development was launched in 1949 when American President Harry Truman presented his "bold new programme for making the benefits of ... scientific advances and technical progress available for the improvement and growth of underdeveloped areas" (in Sachs, 1992, p 6).

For much of the post-colonial period, development has been linked to economic growth based upon modernisation, industrialisation and the growing influence of global corporations. In 1972, Indira Ghandi, then Prime Minister of India, criticised development's pursuit of affluence for its tendency "to overshadow all other human considerations" and identified this aspect of development as "the basic cause of the ecological crisis" (Stone, 1973, p 117). For their part, development analysts in the North have been divided roughly between those who predict ecological doom as human population outstrips the Earth's carrying capacity (Ehrlich, 1972) and those who see human ingenuity as overcoming any ecological obstacles to progress (Simon, 1981). The latter group considers population increases and economic growth as desirable whereas the former sees them as ultimately unsustainable.

By the 1980s, political leaders began to realise that development was in crisis. Under the chairmanship of former West German Chancellor Willy Brandt, the Independent Commission on International Development Issues published two timely reports (see Box 1.1). The first, *North–South* concluded that the search for solutions to international development problems was "a condition for mutual survival" (Brandt Commission, 1980, p 282). Three years later in response to worsening global economic problems and a lack of international cooperation, the Brandt Commission produced a second report, *Common crisis*, which concluded that the North–South negotiating process required new principles. Governments had to demonstrate a "willingness to accept diversity" and "on occasion to proceed ... without global consensus" (Brandt Commission, 1983, p 159). Although the North–South negotiating process had deteriorated, most political leaders continued to promote development as the primary means of bringing southern countries closer to the living standards of their northern counterparts. At the same time, the two Brandt reports reminded political leaders everywhere that certain forms of development were also major contributors to both socio-economic inequality and global environmental degradation.[1]

This period also coincided with intensive debates between academics working in the field of development studies. The various development theories of the 1960s and 1970s were being undermined as a fast-changing global economy brought new realities. The emergence of the Tiger Asian economies challenged some of the basic leftist assumptions about the exploitative relationship between the industrialised North and the so-called Third World. Socialist models of development were also in decline. In central and eastern Europe, communist countries faced growing economic and environmental crises. 'Women in Development' emerged as a new UN strategy to promote greater equity for women, but was eventually dismissed as doing little to increase women's participation in economic activities. Meanwhile, modernisation theories no longer seemed relevant with the declining role of the state and the growing reach of transnational corporations. The bottom line, though, was that world poverty was not substantially in decline. Despite a few apparent success stories in Southeast and East Asia, global free trade and large-scale industrial projects had not been able to reverse the widening overall gap between rich and poor countries. Indeed the 1980s became known as the 'lost decade of development' for much of Latin America and Africa, as well as for significant parts of South Asia.[2]

The dominant global development model of open markets and mega-projects was also being associated with the adverse environmental impacts of industrial activities in both the North and the South. In the North, the 1980s were marked by a litany of high-profile ecological disasters – acid rain and Waldsterben in Central Europe, Chernobyl in the Ukraine, the Exxon Valdez in Alaska and the depletion of the ozone layer over the two poles. In the South, the adverse effects of western-style development upon both natural environments and local cultures were profound. For example, the conversion of pastoral lands to farming and intensive cattle rearing was considered to be less efficient than indigenous practice because, although initially leading to higher production, in the medium term it proved to be ecologically unsustainable.

The cumulative result of this lost decade of development was a general questioning by development academics and practitioners of the whole idea of progress. Many argued that the concept of development assumes there is a developed ideal. As the ideal developed state is characterised as a western or northern industrial economy, development itself was criticised as a western-centric idea, and its projection on the rest of the world as a form of neo-imperialism.[3]

By the end of the 1980s, development thinking had reached an impasse. According to sociologist David Booth, "crucial real-world questions were not being addressed and the gulf between academic enquiry and the various spheres of development policy and practice seemed to have widened" (in Schuurman, 1993, p 49). To overcome this impasse, Booth urged development academics to rediscover development's diversity from the global to the local levels.[4] This has prompted attempts to redefine development in terms of social change, ecological justice, empowerment and community control.   For example, David Korten calls for a "people-centered development vision that embraces ... transformation" (1990, p 5).

Box 1.1: Building blocks for sustainable development from Stockholm to Brandt 1972-83

1972 *Action plan for the human environment:* The main output of the Stockholm Conference launched "a set of internationally coordinated activities aimed first at increasing knowledge of environmental trends and their effects on [humans] and resources, and second, at protecting and improving the quality of the environment and the productivity of resources by integrated planning and management". (Sandbrook, 1983, p 390)

1972 *The limits to growth:* Commissioned by the Club of Rome to stimulate international debate on growth and society.   Widely criticised for its apparent advocacy of zero growth economics, the report acknowledged the need for material growth in the developing world, "but warned of an unthinking pursuit of indiscriminate growth by the industrialised countries". (King and Schneider, 1991, p xii)

1974 *Cocoyoc declaration:* A Mexico meeting in October analysed environmental problems in a Third World context.   The resulting Cocoyoc Declaration highlighted "the problem of the maldistribution of resources and to the inner limits of human needs as well as the outer limits of resource depletion."   The declaration "called for a redefinition of development goals and global lifestyles". (Adams 1990, p 40)

1980 *North–South:* Subtitled 'A programme for survival', this was the first report of the Brandt Commission.   The report emphasised the mutual socio-economic interests of northern and southern countries.   It concluded with an appeal for a global emergency programme to avert disaster in the poorest countries.

1980 *World conservation strategy:* At the initiative of IUCN, a process was launched in October 1977 to develop improved mechanisms for global conservation action.   UNEP provided funding and WWF-International also lent its support to the project.   Although the final version published in March 1980 included reference to population and food issues, the strategy was "essentially a document on nature conservation". (McCormick, 1989, p 165)

1983 *Common crisis:* Subtitled 'North–South cooperation for world recovery', this was the second Brandt Commission report. Its purpose was to provide a means of improving global cooperation and avoiding a full-scale economic collapse. *Common crisis* emphasised the fundamental problem of financing the global recovery.

Environmental roots

The other historical face of sustainable development is that of modern environmentalism. The modern concept of the environment can be traced to nature preservation groups which emerged in the nineteenth century primarily in Great Britain and the USA. Contemporary environmental awareness in western industrialised countries is, however, more often associated with the public response to increased pollution in the post-World War II industrial boom and the publication of Rachel Carson's *Silent spring* in 1962. Carson's revelations about the harmful effects of DDT and other chemicals created such a public outcry that the use of DDT was eventually banned throughout the North.

Another defining moment for the idea of the environment came in 1969 when Apollo XI transmitted images into people's homes of "a small and fragile ball" on the edge of a vast universe. This image proved to be a catalyst for the movement to conserve and protect our vulnerable planet Earth (see Sachs, 1992, p 26).

Ten years later James Lovelock's *Gaia: a new look at life on Earth* was published. Lovelock's theory of Gaia (named after the Greek goddess of the Earth) transformed our small blue planet, metaphorically, into a living organism which behaves as if it is "a single, self-regulating entity in which life forms and the environment continually interact to create the conditions necessary for life to exist" (M. Brown, 1992, p 67).[5] Fuelled by the idea of a living Gaia and growing evidence of the adverse ecological effects of industrial development, concern for the environment grew rapidly in the 1980s. There was a proliferation of new pressure groups and older established organisations experienced huge increases in membership (Cairncross, 1991).[6] By the end of the 1980s, the environment had risen near the top of the political agenda in western industrialised countries.

A more comprehensive review of modern environmentalism, including its historical, philosophical and theoretical roots is provided in Chapter two.

The emergence of sustainable development

In parallel with the evolution of concepts of development and environment, sustainable development slowly began to emerge in the 1970s. Maurice Strong, who also headed the 1972 UN Conference on the Human Environment in Stockholm,[7] provided an initial framework for sustainable development in a post-conference reflection:

> [T]he environment issue cannot be conceived in narrow defensive or parochial terms, but in the possibilities it opens up to bring new energies, new perspectives, and a new will to the resolution of the fundamental imbalances and conflicts which continue to afflict mankind. For the developing countries, environmental considerations add a new dimension to the concept of development – involving not merely the avoidance of newly perceived dangers, but the realization of promising new opportunities. For the richer nations, it provides a dramatic illustration of the new interdependencies which the technological society has created, and new reasons for a deeper and sustained commitment to a more equitable sharing of its benefits with the developing world. Thus, there can be no fundamental conflict between development and environment; they are integral and indivisible. (in Rowland, 1973, p x)

Strong's post-Stockholm vision of an interdependent world where development concerns are compatible with "all the elements which sustain life on this planet" (Rowland, 1973, p x) launched two decades of debate about how best to make development more sustainable.

Sustainable development was first used as a term sometime in the 1970s following the Stockholm Conference.[8]   Various individuals and organisations have been given credit for introducing sustainable development into the public domain, yet the originator of the term remains in dispute.[9] An earlier version is the term ecodevelopment which emerged out of Strong's efforts to bring together international environment and development concerns in the post-Stockholm period.

The Nairobi-based UN Environment Programme (UNEP) played an important role in advocating ecodevelopment in the late 1970s.[10] Although ecodevelopment appeared to reconcile basic human needs with ecological protection, the concept did not immediately take off. Former IUCN Secretary General, Sir Martin Holdgate, believes that the idea failed to gain wider recognition because nobody "could understand what ecodevelopment meant. The eco prefix [was] not immediately transparent."[11]

Sustainable development, an updated version of eco-development, gained considerably more attention in the 1980s. The decade began with the publication of the *World Conservation Strategy* in 1980 by the International Union for the Conservation of Nature and Natural Resources (IUCN)[12] with financial support from another major environmental group the World Wildlife Fund (WWF)[13] and also from UNEP. The overall purpose of the strategy document was "to stimulate a more focused approach to the management of living resources and to provide policy guidance on how this can be carried out" (IUCN et al, 1980, p vi). The document identified the sustainable utilisation of natural resources as one of its three priority requirements for global conservation. Twelve specific areas of action were identified for sustainable utilisation, including, for example, the need to allocate timber concessions with care and to manage them to high standards.

The strategy's concluding section was entitled 'Towards Sustainable Development' and surmised that the underlying causes of underdevelopment and environmental degradation were linked to related global factors. While the *World Conservation Strategy* provided the basis for many environmental group campaigns and programmes in the 1980s, it failed to promote partnership with NGOs advocating for more equitable socio-economic development. Another major limitation was its lack of attention to the social and political obstacles to effective implementation of sustainable development (see Adams, 1990; Reid, 1995).

Our common future

Sustainable development came into popular usage with the publication of *Our common future* in 1987. This best-selling report was the major output of the World Commission on Environment and Development (WCED), an independent body established by the UN in December 1983 to investigate the underlying causes of environment and development problems and to develop "a global agenda for change". Chaired by Norwegian Gro Harlem Brundtland, the so-called Brundtland Commission included ten members from northern countries and twelve from southern nations.

Our common future defined sustainable development as "development that meets the needs of the present without compromising the ability of future generations to meet their own needs.... It contains ... two key concepts ... the essential needs of the world's poor ... should be given overriding priority; and the idea of limitations ... on the environment's ability to meet present and future needs" (WCED 1987, p 43). The Brundtland Commission saw sustainable development as a framework for the integration of policies for environmental protection and socio-economic development. *Our common future* invited all interest groups "to join forces, to identify common goals, and to agree on common action" (McCoy and McCully, 1993, p 6). The report concluded with a call for immediate follow-up action culminating in "an international Conference ... to review progress made and promote follow-up arrangements that will be needed over time to set benchmarks and to maintain human progress within the guidelines of human needs and natural laws" (WCED, 1987, p 343).

By the end of the 1980s, sustainable development had emerged on the international policy agenda as the new big idea. Sustainable development brought together global environmental sustainability, the development needs of the world's poor and powerless, and the economic well-being of communities and countries everywhere. This attempt to integrate widely divergent interests was the cornerstone of both Brundtland and the Rio process which followed. Critics of sustainable development include those who view it as a scheme for sustained growth within the prevailing industrial model which they believe devalues nature (see Nikiforuk, 1990). One of sustainable development's main strengths, nevertheless, lies in its potential to provide a basis for "partnership to develop joint policies and strategies" (Dauncey, 1989, p 46; see also Box 1.2).

Box 1.2: Partnership and sustainable development

In northern, industrialised countries, the word 'partnership' has tended to be used primarily to describe a profit-making business relationship between two or more people where the partners jointly provide the financial capital and share both control and profits. In recent times, partnership has also entered into common usage as a neutral term to describe a romantic relationship between two individuals (ie, the partners) who may or may not live together.

Over the past three decades, social scientists in different disciplines have been analysing new forms of partnership and collaboration which are emerging in a range of organisational settings. In the face of upheavals associated with economic and technological change, a growing number of businesses are adopting collaborative strategies such as joint ventures and research and development consortia with academic institutions and other companies. With the rise of privatisation and deregulation in the 1980s, local governments in the UK and Europe have been increasingly working in partnership with private sector interests. These public–private partnerships are now seen as "the most acceptable and required form of local governance, and will remain so into the 21st century" (Stewart and Snape, 1996, p 5). Also in the 1980s, NGOs working in different sectors and geographical regions began to speak of each other as partners.

Feminist writers such as Riane Eisler envision "a new integrated partnership politics that factors in matters that have been largely ignored in most analyses of how to move to a humane future" (1996, p 565). Organisational behaviourist Barbara Gray describes this new collaboration as "a process through which parties who see different aspects of a problem can constructively explore their differences and search for solutions that go beyond their limited vision of what is possible" (1989, p 5). The catalyst is usually a complex problem which organisations have been unable to resolve alone. Management specialist Sandra Waddock notes that partnerships often emerge when a problem is so broad in scope that it requires "the interaction of many interdependent actors for [its] resolution" (1991, p 487).

Sustainable development emerged in the 1980s as a new organising concept which integrated a wide range of complex, global issues related to environmental protection and socio-economic development. According to Frances Westley and Harri Vredenburg the Brundtland Commission report offered sustainable development as: "a new problem domain ... in which both environmentalists and business were clearly stakeholders" (1991, pp 71-72).

The Rio process

The Earth Summit would not have taken place without many years of exerted pressure by environmental groups upon governments, particularly in Europe and North America. With sustainable development and other environmental issues near the top of political agendas in most northern industrialised countries, the UN General Assembly called for a global meeting to "devise strategies to halt and reverse the effects of environmental degradation in the context of increased national and international efforts to promote sustainable and environmentally sound development in all countries."

The UNCED or Earth Summit was subsequently scheduled for June 1992 to coincide with the twentieth anniversary of Stockholm. For the UN and its member states, the Earth Summit was also a response to worsening North–South socio-economic disparities and related global environmental degradation. This was a key factor in both the selection of Rio as a strategic southern venue and the adoption of a broader agenda than in 1972.

Despite Rio's lofty ambitions, expectations for the Earth Summit varied widely. Some environmental groups used Rio as a media opportunity to argue that the summit represented the "last chance to save the planet". Others accepted that action by governments and international institutions at Rio needed to be augmented by action at the community level. In this context, political leaders and their representatives needed to be supported and compelled to act by individuals and citizens' groups. The predominant message from the environmental movement to the conference organisers, was, however, that "the world is running out of space and time" (IUCN et al, 1991, p 165).

The International Chamber of Commerce (ICC), on behalf of its 7,500 member companies and associations, wanted the UN and its member states to ensure that the conference gave "full attention ... to understanding the scientific and economic aspects of environmental issues and to implementing market-oriented approaches". Furthermore, the ICC wanted delegates to recognise that multilateral environmental agreements could have adverse impacts upon trade and economic growth (see Willums and Golüke, 1992, p 18). The other major business perspective was articulated by the Business Council for Sustainable Development (BCSD), which emphasised the essential role of economic growth in sustainable development and argued that the summit should consider a combination of economic instruments, regulatory mechanisms and private sector voluntary initiatives. The business response to sustainable development before and after Rio is explored in detail in Chapter three.

Expectations of government representatives for Rio were largely influenced by political priorities at home. Writing in *The New Yorker* just days before the official conference opened, John Newhouse described the summit's North–South divide as follows:

> [T]he rich societies of the industrialised North want everyone to begin being sensible about the environment; the people of the Southern latitudes maintain that those who polluted the environment en route to great prosperity are really asking the less well off to take steps that will keep them that way. We will play the environment game, the developing countries say, only if the developed world greatly expands its aid that it provides us. (1992, p 64)

Although most northern governments opposed the idea of a linkage between environment and development when the proposed summit was first discussed in 1989 Japan backed southern governments' insistence on equal billing for their socio-economic development concerns.

Media coverage of the actual conference largely focused on irreconcilable North–South divisions. A sample of newspaper headlines painted a picture of chaos, confusion and despair:

> Earth Summit comes down to money (June 3)
>
> Rio talks clogged by Malaysia forest plan (June 8)
>
> Summit is falling apart (June 9)
>
> Chaos reigns supreme as leaders take to stage (June 12)
>
> Good intentions doomed by gulf between rich and poor (June 15)
>
> Earth Summit trips over high hurdle (June 16).[14]

Box 1.3: Sustainable development from Brundtland to Rio 1987-92

1987 *Our common future:* This was the main report of the World Commission on Environment and Development. The Commission was expected to "re-examine the critical issues of environment and development, and formulate innovative, concrete and realistic action proposals."

1991 *Caring for the Earth:* A joint effort by IUCN, UNEP and WWF produced this follow-up to the 1980 *World Conservation Strategy.* Subtitled 'A strategy for sustainable living', its stated aim was "to help improve the conditions of the world's people" by seeking commitment to "the ethic of sustainable living" and by integrating conservation and development efforts.

1991 *Agenda Ya Wananchi:* This 'citizens' action plan for the 1990s' was the major output of the Paris Roots of the Future global NGO conference organised by the Nairobi-based Environment Liaison Centre International. Agenda Ya Wananchi advocated citizen involvement in building a new world. The document was presented to governments at the Earth Summit and was seen as a lobbying tool beyond Rio.

1992 *Changing course:* This book was the BCSD's official report for the Rio Summit. Its purpose was "to present a global business perspective on sustainable development and to stimulate the interest and involvement of the international business community" (Schmidheiny, 1992, p xix). Some 50 business leaders contributed to this consensus report.

1992 *Agenda 21:* Adopted at Rio, Agenda 21 is a framework to make development socially, economically and environmentally sustainable. It provides UN agencies and member states with the tools to develop coordinated international and national strategies for sustainable development. Agenda 21 states that such strategies should be developed in partnership with civil society.

As the conference drew to a close, however, Paul Lewis of *The New York Times* offered a more balanced reflection on the Rio process:

> The Earth Summit ... has given the world the first real glimpse of the kind of global diplomacy that is becoming possible now that the cold war is over. But the conference has also shown how difficult negotiating worldwide solutions to worldwide problems is likely to be.... The summit agreement that was approved today has already been denounced by some groups as weak

– as "business as usual" and "as a failure to set a new direction for life on earth," as Friends of the Earth called it today…. But for many, the accord is important mainly as the start of a process that could eventually change the way the world approaches economic growth and the challenge of underdevelopment in the southern hemisphere, shifting the basis of all new aid and investment toward environmental sustainability. (1992, p A1)

The participation of environmental groups and other NGOs also proved to be significant, as Martin Khor of the Malaysia-based Third World Network reminds us:

[Rio] succeeded in legitimising the environmentalists' crucial concerns … [and] forged new and stronger links between Northern and Southern groups, between development and environment activists. It would now be difficult for environmentalists to stick to wildlife issues or population, without simultaneously addressing international equity and global power structures … [Rio] has also given legitimacy to the cause of environmental protection in the South. (1992, p 4)

The London-based International Institute for Environment and Development (IIED) added that for NGOs, "Rio represented a push forward, a raised profile, and an added recognition by governments and international organisations" (Holmberg et al, 1993, p 19).[15]

For business, Rio heightened awareness about corporate environmental policy and management initiatives such as the ICC Business Charter on Sustainable Development and the BCSD *Changing course* report. Despite Greenpeace and the efforts of others to dismiss these contributions as 'greenwash', the presence and influence of global corporate leaders in the Rio process was considerable. Two hundred foreign executives attended the ICC Industry Forum in Rio. According to the ICC's Nigel Blackburn, Rio confirmed that business had an essential role in cooperating with government and international aid agencies on large-scale investments in environmental improvements such as superior technology, improved infrastructure and greater energy efficiency

(Centre for Our Common Future, 1992, p 6). In its post-Rio analysis, IIED argued that "the long-term result of the [business] presence in Rio ... may be a growing willingness by business to participate in such gatherings, and also a growing willingness by governments to accept and encourage that participation" (Holmberg et al, 1993, p 16).

Whereas NGOs such as Greenpeace-International, Oxfam and the Third World Network were highly critical about the role of business and industry in the Rio process, others such as WWF-International, IUCN, IIED and the Worldwatch Institute were much more willing to enter into policy discussions with business about sustainable development.

Box 1.4: Official Rio agreements

- *Rio Declaration on Environment and Development:* A non-binding statement of 27 broad principles to guide for sustainable development. The declaration recognises environmental protection as part of socio-economic development and gives priority to the needs of developing countries.

- *Agenda 21:* A non-legally binding blueprint to clean up the global environment and to promote sustainable development. This 800-page document was adopted by consensus after developing countries withdrew their demand for specific commitments of aid from developed nations to fund its implementation.

- *Convention on Biological Diversity:* A legally binding treaty that requires inventories of plants and wildlife and plans to protect endangered species. It also obliges countries to ensure equitable distribution of benefits from the use of biological diversity.

- *Convention on Climate Change:* A legally binding treaty that aims to stabilise greenhouse gases in the atmosphere at levels which will minimise impacts upon the global climate system. The convention recommends cutting emissions of carbon dioxide, methane and other greenhouse gases associated with climate change.

- *Statement on Forest Principles:* A non-legally binding document that recommends that countries assess the impact of economic development on their forests, and take steps, both individually and with other countries, to minimise the damage. Earlier negotiations for a convention failed.

After Rio

Since Rio, a number of high-level UN conferences have been held which have close links to the goals of both the Earth Summit and Agenda 21. The achievement of sustainable development depends upon a more integrated response within the UN system and in collaboration with governments, NGOs, business and other actors from the global to the local level. Accordingly, the UN has responded with a series of inter-related conferences which have continued and in many cases deepened the sustainable development debate. Since 1992 there have been six major conferences in this regard:

- International Conference on Population and Development, Cairo.

- World Conference on Human Rights, Vienna.

- World Summit on Social Development, Copenhagen.

- Fourth World Conference on Women, Beijing.

- Habitat II, The City Summit, Istanbul.

- World Food Summit, Rome.

Nitin Desai, Under Secretary-General for the Department of Policy Coordination and Sustainable Development describes the connections between Rio and these six conferences:

> The search for consensus on global co-operation links these economic, social and environmental conferences together in an international policy dialogue that seeks to define a more integrated and holistic strategy for human development and welfare. Although each of these conferences tackles development from a slightly different perspective and offers something unique ... they all build on and reinforce each other in significant ways. (Desai, 1994, p 1)

Many have criticised these conferences as global 'talk shops' which resolve little and which add unnecessary complexity to the idea of sustainable development. Others believe that such international gatherings are a necessary part of the process of clarifying and deepening our understanding of sustainable development, particularly as it applies to different sectors, issues and target groups.

Box 1.5: UN Commission on Sustainable Development

At its first organisational session in June 1993, the commission developed an extensive review and reporting process to involve all actors recognised in Agenda 21 and any others deemed appropriate. Environmental groups made substantial contributions to on-the-floor debates and participated in "informal negotiations specific policies and initiatives" a trend which was sustained throughout the subsequent sessions (Dodds and Bigg, 1997). Some 350 NGOs were represented at the 1993 session. Business representation was "dominated by those with interests likely to be damaged by the full implementation of the Rio agreements" (Roddick, 1994, p 7). The oil and nuclear industries were particularly active. "Green industries such as the renewables, water sanitation, etc [were] noticeably absent."[16]

The 1994 session included the following agreements among others:

- emphasis on the importance of continuous exchange of information on practical experience gained by countries, organisations and major groups;

- support for the ongoing work on the elaboration of realistic and understandable sustainable development indicators that can supplement national reporting;

- development of innovative ways of working ... including means by which information can be shared and the expertise of a wide range of actors could be sought. (Dodds and Bigg, 1997)

Other conclusions of the second session were less optimistic, including issues such as inadequate Agenda 21 financing and environmental technology transfer, and the adverse effects of existing consumption patterns upon sustainable development.

The 1995 session established an Intergovernmental Panel on Forests in an effort to improve upon the Forest Principles agreed at Rio. Other major outcomes of the 1995 session included an analysis of consumption and production patterns and an agreed timetable for the preparation of sustainable development indicators.

The 1996 session proved to be a disappointment in comparison with 1995 given that much of the time was spent discussing the parameters of the five-year review of progress since Rio. The 'Day in the Workplace' session hosted by representatives of business and trade unions was singled out as one of the positive outcomes of the session. The 1996 session also concluded that while "eco-efficiency is a promising strategy for policy development, it is not a substitute for changes in unsustainable lifestyles of consumers" (Dodds and Bigg, 1997). The 1997 session – which was open-ended to allow for the full participation of all States – was devoted to preparations for Earth Summit II.

The UN Commission on Sustainable Development

In parallel with the various UN conferences outlined above, a new UN body has been coordinating international policy dialogue on sustainable development. Chapter 38 of Agenda 21 recommended the establishment of a high-level Commission on Sustainable Development "to ensure the effective follow up of the [Rio] Conference, as well as to enhance international cooperation and rationalize the intergovernmental decision-making capacity for the integration of environment and development issues" (UNCED, 1992, p 275). When the 47th session of the General Assembly met in December 1992 to review the Rio agreements, member states passed resolution 47/191 which detailed the terms of reference for the new commission. The Commission on Sustainable Development (CSD)[17] was defined as a functional body of the Economic and Social Council (ECOSOC).[18]

In addition to its official mandate identified above, many governments and NGOs saw the new commission as a mechanism for completing Rio's unfinished business. In practice, this meant that the commission was expected to coordinate the efforts of all actors identified in Agenda 21 in order "to build on each other's successes and learn from each other's failures" (Aydin, 1994, p 2).

Since June 1993, the commission has held five formal sessions culminating in the April 1997 meeting which also served as the final preparatory session for Earth Summit II, the Special Session of the UN General Assembly to review progress since Rio. For a review of the main outcomes of the sessions to date see Box 1.5 above.

General assessments of the commission's work to date vary. The so-called policy entrepreneurs,[19] particularly members of government and UN agency delegations and some major group representatives, are generally upbeat about its achievements. They believe that the commission has deepened many of the policy debates of Rio. Others, particularly major group representatives, have found the commission process tedious with little in the way of tangible outcomes. As one business delegate bluntly states:

> *Many of us feel that the CSD is not particularly effective. The meetings are boring and have a lot of inertia. They seem to be covering areas which are being covered elsewhere and they're going through the motions as it were. I think the CSD*

> *ought to be able to take a step back and say: What*
> *was it supposed to do but has not done very well?*
> *Given that all the other processes are going on*
> *within the conventions and the other insti-tutional*
> *arrangements, is the pace of activity since Rio fast*
> *enough? Are there issues which are not being dealt*
> *with properly? Can we stimulate those*
> *governments which are slower in producing their*
> *action plan? Can we stimulate them to do more?*
> *Can we give those sorts of signals?*

Other major groups have also been critical of the commission and other aspects of the official post-Rio process. The London-based UN Environment and Development Committee (UNED-UK), a forum for major group dialogue and collaboration on post-Rio matters has organised various workshops and conferences since Rio.   At the 1995 UNED-UK Annual Conference *Sustaining developments since the Rio Summit*, the following points were among the conference's main findings:

- Government has withdrawn from a number of essential policy areas to do with sustainable development.

- National government is devolving responsibilities to local authorities, with neither the power nor the resources to carry them out.

- The main point of sustainability has been missed – the need for common goals and cooperation ... among those respons-ible for economy, environment and social equity at national and local level.

- The Biodiversity and Climate Change conventions have produced more meetings and reports but little else.

- The CSD ... is largely a discussion forum as well, where governments describe what could or should be done to further sustainability, but make no commitments.

- There is fragmentation ... among the NGO community.... [T]o solve sustainability problems we have to learn to talk to each other (see McInery, 1996, pp 33–35).

Given that most of the UNED-UK Conference participants were representatives of the nine major groups identified in Agenda 21, it is not surprising that there was strong criticism of the role of governments in implementing sustainable development. The conference findings, however, also reveal a deeply-held feeling among most major groups that governments are failing to provide the necessary policy frameworks for sustainable development. Barbara Bramble of the National Wildlife Federation in the USA and a major player in the post-Rio process argues that governments:

> ... must contribute to and not interfere with international consensus on solutions to global problems no nation can handle on its own.... This role is essentially to facilitate the work of others. It would, indeed, be a loss of power. (in McInery, 1996, p 36)

If the Commission on Sustainable Development, other UN agencies and national governments were to take on board the "serious application of Agenda 21" it would mean "the end of business as usual". As Bramble asserts, "real change will only come when ... the whole business of government" adopts and integrates the principles and recommendations embodied in Agenda 21.

Major group implementation

Whereas most governments continue to resist necessary policy changes, major groups are creating a growing body of practical experience with the implementation of sustainable development. A detailed review of this extensive work is beyond the scope of this book. We offer here a brief overview of various post-Rio initiatives by major groups to emphasise the importance of partnership in the implementation of sustainable development. Agenda 21 identified "the need to activate a sense of common purpose on behalf of all sectors of society" and asserts that "the chances of forging such a sense of purpose will depend on the willingness of all sectors to participate in genuine social partnership and dialogue" (UNCED, 1992, p 230). Among the nine major groups specified in Agenda 21 as key actors in the shaping and implementation of policy alternatives, NGOs and business have emerged in the post-Rio period as both competitors and partners along the road to sustainable development.[20]

Examples of environmental group, business and other major group initiatives in the post-Rio period are provided below:

- World Wide Fund for Nature is the world's largest independent conservation organization, with more than five million supporters and a global network of 24 national organizations, five associates, and 26 programme offices. WWF-International has been involved in the Rio process – from the first preparatory meeting in August 1991 through to the Earth Summit and beyond to the consecutive sessions of the CSD. The organisation has participated in every intersessional and CSD session and as a result has formed a strong working relationship with UN staff and delegates. Each year WWF-International produces concise position statements on the issues tabled at the CSD, offering decision makers action and policy recommendations illustrated with projects and case studies. The CSD has provided important opportunities for advancing WWF's existing programme of work at the national and international levels, including on trade, biosafety and chemical safety. Rio continues to provide a useful banner under which the organisation can further develop its policy and fieldwork based on an integrated approach to environment and development issues and their inter-relationships. The Rio process has led to formal and informal partnerships with other major groups, for example, with industry on energy efficiency centres in Eastern Europe and with other NGOs on Local Agenda 21 and preparations for Earth Summit II. (Source: C. St Laurent, WWF-International)

- World Business Council for Sustainable Development (WBCSD) is a coalition of 120 international companies committed to the environment and to the principles of economic growth and sustainable development. The Geneva-based successor to the BCSD has members in 33 countries, representing more than 20 major industrial sectors. One of its main goals is to promote closer partnership between sectors. The World Business Council's strategy and activities in the post-Rio process are as follows:

  1. The Earth Summit endorsed eco-efficiency as the way forward for business to collectively contribute to sustainable development. At the Business Council, eco-efficiency is the

centre of the work programme, and is the fundamental concept underlying its activities. The council defines eco-efficiency as the process of producing more from less; reducing waste and pollution, and using less energy while meeting the demands of consumers.

2. From the Rio Conference, a number of programmes the WBCSD has followed up include introducing mechanisms to internalise environmental costs; looking at the development of an open multilateral trading system recognising that trade and protection of the environment are not contradictory; developing innovative methods of production and management to use the world's resources efficiently.

3. To help advance the process of eco-efficiency, the council and member companies have worked closely with governments in the North and South; in partnership with environmental campaigners; and communities. The council believes that business is changing to meet emerging social and market trends in which it influences, and is influenced by, change. (Source: A. Holmes, WBCSD)

- International Network for Environmental Management (INEM) is a German-based global federation of non-profit national and regional industry associations, promoting and fostering environmental management and sustainable development. The INEM network comprises 24 member and affiliated business associations and nine cleaner production centres in 27 countries on five continents. INEM's major post-Rio programme is Industry 21, the first private sector initiative for the implementation of the business-related aspects of Agenda 21. Industry 21 included the Global Environmental Management Survey which compared the state of environmental management around the world. Industry 21 encompasses 13 other programmes and projects. INEM has collaborated with intergovernmental organisations such as the Organisation for Economic Cooperation and Development (OECD), and EC; UN bodies such as the CSD, UNEP, UN Development Programme (UNDP) and UN Industrial Development Organisation (IDO); standard-setting bodies such as the International Organisation for Standardisation (ISO); and business associations such as the World Business Council and ICC. (Source: T. Davis, INEM)

- International Council for Local Environmental Initiatives (ICLEI) serves as the international environmental agency for local governments that have direct environmental management responsibilities. Formally associated with the International Union of Local Authorities, the Toronto-based ICLEI aims to build and serve a worldwide movement among its constituency of 240 local governments and their associations to achieve and monitor tangible improvements in local and global environmental conditions through cumulative local actions. ICLEI supports the Local Agenda 21 process with technical assistance and networking. Local Agenda 21 is a process whereby community-level, sustainable development strategies are developed by local authorities in cooperation with citizens, local organisations and private enterprises. Chapter 28 of Agenda 21 requested all local authorities to develop their own Local Agenda 21 by the end of 1996. A recent ICLEI survey found that more than 2,000 local authorities worldwide have already done so. (Source: J. Walker, ICLEI)

Earth Summit II: June 1997

Earth Summit II, the UN General Assembly's Special Session held in June 1997, was conceived to review progress on the implementation of Agenda 21 and the other Rio Agreements since 1992. Earth Summit II has offered an opportunity to reflect on both the accomplishments and the shortcomings of local, national and international efforts to promote sustainable development. The summit has helped to revitalise the global sustainability agenda as we face the new millennium.

Governments and relevant regional and subregional organisations were asked to report on progress achieved since Rio. Contributions were also welcomed from the following: hemispheric, regional and subregional conferences on sustainable development; relevant organisations and bodies of the UN system; and the Conferences of the Parties or other regulatory bodies of the Framework Convention on Climate Change, the Convention on Biological Diversity and the Convention to Combat Desertification, as well as the regulatory bodies of other relevant instruments and the Global Environmental Facility. The importance of major groups participation in the process was also emphasised.

The Secretary-General's report contained a comprehensive evaluation of the progress achieved since Rio in the implementation of Agenda 21 and related outcomes at all levels, as well as recommendations for future actions and priorities. This report was tabled at the April 1997 Session of the Commission on Sustainable Development and included the following:

- concise reports which include appraisals of progress achieved in specific sectoral and cross-sectoral areas;

- country profiles which provide a succinct presentation of progress made and constraints encountered in implementing Agenda 21 at the national level, compiled on the basis of national information received and in close cooperation with the governments concerned;

- major and emerging trends and issues within the context of Agenda 21 and related outcomes of the Rio Conference in the area of sustainable development, including the environmental impact of activities that are extremely hazardous to the environment, taking into account the views of states; and

- recommendations on the future role of the Commission on Sustainable Development in the follow-up to the outcome of the Rio Conference and related outcomes, building on experience gained since 1992.

UNED-UK identified the following substantive issues for Earth Summit II based upon various reports from major groups and official sources:

- strengthen the integration environment and development;

- place greater emphasis upon poverty and unemployment;

- address unsustainable patterns of production and consumption;

- implement comprehensive ecological tax reform;

- achieve 0.7 per cent of Gross National Product (GNP) directed to overseas development assistance;

- evaluate market-based instruments such as environmental cost accounting;

- negotiate a code of conduct and compliance measures for transnational corporations;

- establish an Intergovernmental Panel on Financing Sustainable Development;

- improve the accountability and representation of the inter-governmental process of the Commission on Sustainable Development;

- enhance government regulation and global governance (see Bigg and Mucke, 1996).

Above all, the effective implementation of Agenda 21 and the other Rio agreements depends upon the collaboration of individuals and groups "who understand what sustainable development means in their everyday lives ... and who are both able and willing to participate in shaping a sustainable future" (Bigg and Mucke, 1996).

Sustainable development at the crossroads

Sustainable development remains a powerful, yet elusive, concept in the post-Rio period. Between and within communities, social movements, governments, NGOs, businesses, industry associations, academia and numerous other groups worldwide, there are many definitions and interpretations of sustainable development. Certain segments of the environmental movement continue to dismiss sustainable development as a contradiction in terms, whereas others have embraced it as a new way of putting environmental and social issues on the public policy and corporate agendas. Many government, NGO and UN aid agencies have adopted sustainable development as the basis for new technical assistance programmes to address the worsening socio-economic conditions of the world's poor and related environmental degradation. Within the business community, sustainable development has been used both as a strategic planning framework for environmental management and as a public relations term to enhance corporate image.

The academic community remains largely divided between those who regard sustainable development as a "basically flawed" concept (Beckerman, 1995, p 126) and those who believe that "it invites us to give practical support to the values of social equity, human worth and ecological health" (Reid, 1995, p 235). In between these two extremes, Bill Adams acknowledges sustainable development's "eclecticism and inconsistencies" and yet recognises that it has helped raise awareness about "significant problems and real issues" (1993, p 218). Adams elaborates further on sustainable development's conceptual appeal and calls for practical implementation:

> Sustainable development is a flag of convenience under which diverse ships sail, and it is this catholic scope that goes a long way to explain its power and popularity as a term.... [It should embrace] micro and macro scale, from peasant to transnational corporation, from field to bio-sphere.... [It needs to be] lodged in practice, within the daily realities of people's lives. (1993, pp 218-19)

While many researchers and practitioners continue to call for a universally agreed definition, there is growing acceptance that the meaning of sustainable development is evolving. Clearer and perhaps fewer definitions of sustainable development may emerge from the world of practice in the coming years (see Box 1.6).

We believe that sustainable development has become a new organising principle, perhaps an emerging, positive myth, which has the potential to bring together diverse and often competing causes. The mythic quality of sustainable development lies in its capacity to clarify the Earth's complexity and facilitate commitment to new collaborative models. Lending support to this argument, Joseph Campbell believes that "the only myth that is going to be worth thinking about in the immediate future is one that is talking about the planet, not the city, not these people, but the planet and everybody on it" (1988, p 41). The emergence of the sustainable development myth may indeed be an important catalyst for the formulation and implementation of creative and effective responses to many of the overwhelming challenges presented in Agenda 21 and the other Rio agreements.[21]

Box 1.6: Key elements of sustainable development

Sustainable development is both a change process (ie, developing sustainability) and a key organising principle, similar to concepts such as social justice, human rights and equity. We believe that less time should be devoted to finding an ideal definition and more to exploring the opportunities and risks which sustainable development presents. Sociologists Tade Aina and Ade Salau see sustainable development as a paradigm which contains "different currents while sharing a broadly similar platform on methodology, philosophy, epistemology, ideology, politics and practice." They believe that sustainable development is based upon a set of key elements which constitute a shared platform. These include:

- ecological integrity and sustainability;

- equity and distributive justice at all levels (global, national, community, household and intergenerational);

- socially-relevant economic productivity and technological development;

- popular participation and collective autonomy;

- prevalence and institutionalization of human and democratic rights. (1992, p 3)

Sustainable development challenges us to understand and act upon ecological, social, economic and political issues in an integrated manner.

An emerging consensus between pragmatists within both the environmental movement and the business community indicates that sustainable development must promote solutions to social, environmental and economic problems from the local to the global level. As part of this attempt to identify solutions, a growing number of environmental groups are entering into agreements with business to implement pilot projects which promote sustainable development in a wide range of industrial and service sectors. The rest of the book elaborates on how and why these new relationships have emerged in recent years.

The experience of Rio and beyond indicates that sustainable development has reached a crossroads. The process of finding solutions will still include conflict, however the partnership road to sustainability requires greater emphasis upon dialogue and listening than in the past. In order to be able to resolve conflict between people with quite different interests, the various stakeholders in the future must begin to work together and learn to value human, cultural and biological diversity as central tenets of sustainable development. Many contentious issues will remain unresolved; competing interests will continue to promote different agendas. The challenge for business and environmental groups, nevertheless, is to learn how to work together more effectively. If Rio was about struggling with diversity, then the post-Rio period provides an opportunity to embrace diversity as a key implementation strategy for sustainable development.

Notes

[1] Gustavo Esteva offers a more damning critique of development. He calls it "a devaluation of [people's] skills, values and experience in favour of a growing dependence on guidance and management by bureaucrats, technocrats, educators, and development experts" (1992, p 138).

[2] In 1990, the World Bank insisted that "the 1980s did not, in fact, reverse the overall trend of progress" and yet conceded that "the setbacks of the 1980s fell heavily on particular regions ... in Sub-Saharan Africa and Latin America incomes fell ... and the incidence of poverty increased." See World Bank (1990) pp 1-2. With the exception of the initial positive perceived impacts of the 'Green Revolution', there was significant political unrest throughout South Asia. David Korten argues that "the development industry ... is in a state of disarray.... Development has become a big business, preoccupied more with its own growth and imperatives than with the people it was originally created to serve" (1990, p ix).

[3] This perspective is anti-developmentalism and equates development with the project of modernity. Modernity has been the organising principle for nation states since the Enlightenment of the eighteenth century, when science and rationality began to achieve reverential respect. Such arguments have fertile ground from which to draw ideas, including sociological analyses of forced consumption (Hirsch, 1977) and supply-led demand (Gorz, 1989). Other examples can be found in development theories about the exploitation of peripheral areas (Wallerstein, 1974) and the creation of underdevelopment by industrialised countries (Frank, 1967).

[4] Booth argues that development needs a new research agenda based upon academics doing a much better job of investigating and explaining the different experiences with development in the 1990s.

[5] However, Lovelock's Gaia thesis implies no consciousness on the part of the Earth.

[6] Membership in six leading UK environmental groups rose from 1.7 million to 3.8 million between 1981 and 1990. In the USA, membership for seven major environmental NGOs went from 5.3-9.5 million between 1980 and 1990.

[7] The Stockholm Conference had a definite northern bias. According to Adams (1990) the impetus "came from the developed world, and the initial focus was on the environmental problems of industrialization." Only eight of Stockholm's 109 Recommendations for Action dealt with the problem of development and environment (p 37).

[8] Andrew Knight, a specialist in UN reform sees the most positive outcomes of Stockholm as: Earthwatch (an early warning surveillance system); Infoterra (a decentralised information clearing house); World Environment Day; and the Nairobi-based UN Environment Programme (UNEP). However, UNEP is seen as being one of the UN's least effective and poorest agencies (Adams, 1990). And Knight calls Stockholm's achievements only "incremental changes" (Ghosh, 1992, p A10).

[9] David Reid (1995) identifies the following candidates: Eva Balfour, founder of the Soil Association, Wes Jackson, the American geneticist, and the London-based International Institute for Environment and Development (IIED).

[10] Wolfgang Sachs describes eco-development as "an approach to development aimed at harmonizing social and economic objectives with ecologically sound management, in a spirit of solidarity with future generations" (1979, p 113). Key features of ecodevelopment included: meeting basic human needs; the importance of participation; and the role of appropriate technology. Eco-development implied qualitative growth as opposed to zero growth and advocated initiatives such as low energy consumption, recycling and ecological land use and human settlement planning (see Adams, 1990, pp 51-56).

[11] Interview with Sir Martin Holgate, 1 October 1996. From this point on all unreferenced quotes are from interviews or personal communications with the authors.

[12] Now known as the World Conservation Union.

[13] Now known as the World Wide Fund for Nature, except in Canada and the USA where the original name continues to be used.

[14] Post-Rio analysis in specialist environmental or NGO publications was equally despondent. *The Ecologist* referred to "The Earth Summit Débâcle". *Greenpeace Business* condemned the "Rio fiasco". The UK Green Party's *Real World* summed up the Rio process with a leading question: "Wrong Agenda, Wrong Outcome?" Post-Rio environmental books also mocked the Earth Summit process with provocative titles such as Joni Seager's *Earth Follies* (1993) Pratap Chatterjee and Matthias Finger's *The Earth Brokers* (1994).

[15] Another view of the Rio process is offered by Chatterjee and Finger (1994). They argue that NGO interests were coopted through their participation in the process. By mobilising for Rio, NGOs were legitimising an agenda dominated by governments, UN agencies and transnational corporations.

[16] Personal correspondence from J. Roddick, 23 August, 1994.

[17] The CSD has 53 members who are drawn from UN member states. Seats are allocated as follows: Africa (13); Asia (11); Eastern Europe (6); Latin America/Caribbean (10); and western Europe/North America (13). Membership rotates with one third up for election each year. Elections are conducted through the UN regions. The CSD Secretariat is located within the Department for Policy Coordination and Sustainable Development in New York, and has a staff of less than two dozen.

[18] One of the principal UN organs, ECOSOC is responsible for coordinating the specialised agencies, several autonomous intergovernmental organisations, functional and regional commissions, sessional and standing committees, and expert, ad hoc and related bodies. See Riggs and Plano (1988) pp 40-44.

[19] Regular participants in international conferences and meetings who in some cases have developed powerful identities as global policy actors separate from the official organisational affiliation. Another interpretation of policy entrepreneurs sees them as individuals and organisations who formulate and implement policies to fulfil their own agendas or to justify their own survival rather than concentrating on identifying and assessing the utility or acceptability of their work to intended beneficiaries who are often excluded from the international policy process.

[20] The other major groups identified in Agenda 21 are: women, youth, indigenous peoples, local authorities, trade unions and workers, farmers and the scientific/technological community.

[21] Murray Edelman challenges the dominant interpretation of myth as untruth or unreality: He calls it "an unquestioned belief held in common by a large group of people that gives events and actions a particular meaning ... [and] a particularly relevant form of symbol in the emergence of mass political movements" (1971, p 53). For anthropologist Mary Douglas, the rituals associated with myth provide valuable "mediating institutions" (1970, p 19).

two

Towards partnership: a history of environmental group thinking and action

At the Rio Summit, business and environmental groups were invited to the conference table with national governments to discuss the future of the planet. By involving these often adversarial groups, Rio planted the first seeds of cooperation which we have seen grow over subsequent years. Although some believe that NGO involvement was largely cosmetic and it was business that really shaped the summit agenda (Chatterjee and Finger, 1994), the conclusions contained in Agenda 21 established the need for cooperation between governments and all non-state actors in the pursuit of sustainable development. Even though Agenda 21's version of sustainable development contained numerous contradictions, its call for global partnership has not gone unheeded. As noted in Chapter one, increasingly major groups such as business, NGOs and local governments are collaborating to implement various aspects of the action programme outlined in Agenda 21.

Accordingly environmental groups have begun to develop strategies and campaigns which give a new priority to the pursuit of practical solutions. What we are observing in the post-Rio period is a new form of partnership, concerned with environmental or ethical aspects of the internal operations of the business partner. These partnerships have not yet received the attention that they deserve, with media coverage on environmental issues continuing to focus on conflict. For example, the Shell–

Greenpeace stand-off over the deep-sea dumping of the Brent Spar oil container was the major international environment story of 1995, closely followed by the international outrage at Shell's involvement in Nigeria, after the execution of environmental activist Ken Saro-Wiwa had brought attention to the plight of the Ogoni. Meanwhile, and beyond the media view something of major significance to our economies and the environment has been progressing behind boardroom doors: dialogue and partnership between business and environmental groups.

The rapid growth in the number of business–NGO collaborations in western countries in the 1990s suggests that there are some underlying factors providing an economic and political context within which partnerships can flourish. To understand the nature and significance of these factors it is useful to examine the history of environmental group action, the history of business responses to environmental challenge and, significantly, businesses' and campaigning groups' changing views of each other.

Chapter three examines the changing business response to the challenge of sustainable development. Chapters four to six catalogue the changing, if still diverse, relationships between business and environmental groups in the wood product, chemical, seafood, supermarket and fast food sectors. In this chapter, we review the development of western environmentalism as demonstrated by the changing outlook and tactics of environmental groups. In doing so we describe the emergence of third-wave environmentalism in the post-Rio period, which is increasingly characterised by partnership with business.

The waning of the greens?

By the end of the 1980s, the environment had become the new hot political issue. The evidence was overwhelming: Greens with 15 per cent of the vote in the UK European election, environmental groups experiencing a quadrupling of membership (Cairncross, 1991) and green consumer books becoming bestsellers overnight.[1] The forests were dying, the seas being emptied, the rivers poisoned and people were getting angry. There was a strong belief that something had to be done. But has anything changed? With most people apparently more concerned with day-to-day economic concerns, is it possible that the green thing was just a pastime of the credit-boom society?

There was a lot of media hype, but the real problems have not gone away and neither has action on environmental issues. Today's world still has the same problems of deforestation, species extinction, global warming, over-fishing, ozone depletion, poverty and famine, among many others (Brown, 1995). A recent Food and Agriculture Organisation (FAO) study estimates the rate of tropical forest loss at 170,000 square kilometres per annum, (Rietbergen, 1995) while WWF-International has reported a major decline in the quality of temperate and boreal forests (Dudley et al, 1995). Scientists estimate that the planet is already losing 50,000 species annually, or about 140 each day (Flavin and Young, 1994), while 300 of the world's top climate scientists on the Intergovernmental Panel on Climate Change now report that global warming is upon us, with industrial emissions contributing to a 1°F warming of the planet over the past century.

Box 2.1: World Wide Fund for Nature-International

Founded in 1961, WWF is the world's largest non-governmental international conservation organisation with 28 affiliate and associate national organisations around the world. It has more than five million international supporters, including over 200,000 in the UK. From its original focus on the conservation of flora and fauna, WWF has broadened its analysis in recent years to encompass social dimensions of environmental protection and degradation. Its global mission statement for the 1990s commits WWF 'to conserve nature and ecological processes by: preserving genetic, species, and ecosystem diversity; ensuring that the use of renewable natural resources is sustainable both now and in the longer term; promoting actions to reduce pollution and the wasteful exploitation and consumption of resources'. WWF's ultimate goal is to stop, and eventually reverse, the accelerating degradation of our planet's natural environment, and to help build a future in which humans live in harmony with nature (WWF-International, 1994). An organisation-wide evaluation completed in 1993 prompted WWF to focus future activities in three priority areas: forests, freshwater ecosystems, and oceans/coasts. WWF-UK's income fell by more than £3 million to £18.9 million between 1989 and 1992. There was also a 10 per cent drop in membership during this period. By 1997 they were experiencing the best growth in new members since the late 1980s.

In addition to these well-described problems, there are warning signs of new crises which may develop over the next ten years and beyond. In the seas we have the collapse of fisheries, the bleaching of coral reefs, phytoplankton blooms, demise of sea urchins, mass mortality of seals and dolphins and cancer in fish. On land we hear news of the feminisation of nature and the decline in sperm counts, with compounds such as those found in PVC accused of mimicking the effects of female hormones. We are also warned of increasing ecosystem stress, where all the different pollutants and pressures may, one day, work together to throw ecosystems into a new and unstable state unsuitable for human life.

We can safely say, therefore, that the environment was not a fad of the 1980s. The mass popularity of environmental issues at that time was just one expression of a social movement which has been developing for over a hundred years and continues to develop in new ways today. The roots of modern environmentalism reach deep into the nineteenth century and counter-reactions to the Industrial Revolution. Looking at the development of the western environmental movement in the twentieth century illustrates the development of ideas and actions in response to changing environmental challenges and a changing social, political and economic context.

Today there remain many different types and typologies of environmentalism, and many different ways to be 'green'. Various writers have attempted definitions of environmentalism: some differentiate political approaches to the environment (Box 2.2), others differentiate ideological approaches to the environment (Box 2.3), others differentiate philosophical approaches to the environment (Box 2.5), and others mix these approaches. Ecosocialism, ecoliberalism, ecocentrism, biocentrism, ecological humanism, ecoegalitarianism, ecomodernism, post-modern ecologism, ecofeminism, radical greens, reformist greens, light greens, deep greens – it is difficult not to become engulfed in a quagmire of categories.

Despite the very different strands of green thought which continue to have influence, we believe it is possible to outline a progression in environmental thinking and action, with certain perspectives emerging, maturing and gaining ascendancy over time. For ease of comprehension, we describe organised environmentalism as developing in three waves:

- the first wave of habitat and wildlife conservation beginning in the early 1900s, based on a preservation ethic;

- the second wave of lobbying for legislation and regulation beginning in the late 1960s, based on a holistic ecological ethic; and

- the third wave of market-based approaches beginning in the mid-late 1980s, based on a solutions ethic which also embraces socio-economic concerns.

Each wave of organised environmental group action has reflected the relative importance of different attitudes to our environment, its value and our relationship with it. A discussion of these waves shows how there is greater potential today than ever before for environmentalists to take a positive and collaborative stance towards the business community.

First wave environmentalism

The turn of the century witnessed the first wave of environmentalism.[2] A residue of the romantic movement, which had championed a return to nature in the wake of the industrial revolution, the early environmental movement focused on the pains of industrialisation and on the need to conserve nature. In Britain, popular writers of the period such as Dickens described the environmental degradation accompanying industrialism. These popular critiques never properly reached the political agenda and there was little direct political activity concerned with pollution problems. The first stirrings of organised campaigning came not from the industrial cities but from rural Cumbria, England. Residents of the Lake District began to protest at the use of the lakes as reservoirs for the expanding urban centres.

Whereas these kinds of group were of little consequence at the time in the UK and Europe, in the United States similar groups were more powerful: "[Under] Theodore Roosevelt, the conservation movement was one of the strongest political forces in the nation" (Enloe, 1975, p 175). It was in the USA where the deep-set concept of 'wild nature' as a threat to human settlement gave way to a new and romantic depiction in which the wilderness experience was celebrated. In the west the frontier was on the verge of closing and on the eastern seaboard natural landscapes were rapidly disappearing as urban growth proceeded. As Charles Adams wrote in the *Naturalist's guide to the Americas* (1926), the wilderness, like forests, was once a great hindrance to our civilisation; now it should be maintained because society cannot live without it (in McGrew, 1993). The case for wilderness preservation was taken on by a clutch of new conservation organisations from the Sierra Club (founded 1892) to the Wilderness Society (founded 1935). Preservation was the key word – nature was to be protected in an unchanging state in order to be enjoyed as a separate aesthetic 'thing'. The expression of this view of nature was the establishment of National Parks such as Yellowstone, which served to fence off areas of natural wilderness from the growing occupancy by humans. This physical separation of humans and nature was indicative of the mental separation of the human and the natural world. Aesthetic environmentalism was an outlook that separated humans from nature, for coexistence between people and the environment was not properly considered at this time.[3] While this first wave of environmentalism ultimately failed to dislodge the existing economic view, it nevertheless left behind a number of achievements: bird sanctuaries, national parks, wilderness trails, conservation organisations and, above all, "an ethic which stated that nature had more than simply a functional value" (Hannigan, 1995, p 115).

Second-wave environmentalism

The second wave of environmentalism can be identified as beginning in the late 1960s and early 1970s. It was at this time that environmentalism became politically significant in industrially-advanced societies. This coincided with the prolonged period of post-war economic growth and the birth of vibrant counter cultures and social movements, such as the black, gay and women's rights movements. At this time environmental groups proliferated and environmentalism became a distinct ideology with ecocentrism as its philosophical basis: a philosophy that starts from a concern about non-human nature and the whole ecosystem, rather than from humanist concerns (Box 2.5). This outlook fundamentally challenged the dominant values and structures of industrial society, as it rejected the continual striving for economic growth, materialism and the subjugation of humans to technology.

Box 2.2: Political approaches to the environment

Traditional left–right politics has shaped a certain amount of debate on environmental issues. Accordingly two schools of environmental thought can be defined as ecoliberalism and ecosocialism.

Ecoliberalism holds a belief in pluralist democracy and the market. Therefore ecoliberals are reformist rather than radical. Although some would argue that they sit outside the left-right conception of politics, David Pepper (1996) believes they are inherently right-wing through their allegiance to the concept that free choice is exercised through the market system "When it comes to policies, they often try to adapt the existing system advocating eco-taxes, pollution charges and codes of conduct for industry". Most green economists can be considered ecoliberals, and most do not support any fundamental critique of capitalist democracy as the structure at root of our environmental problems (notable exceptions being Paul Ekins and Herman Daly). Not surprisingly then it is the ecoliberal outlook that has been most widely embraced by business, government, even NGOs and the wider public.

Conversely, "ecosocialism ... [looks] ... particularly to the structural features of capitalism to explain why there are ecological problems today" (Pepper, 1996, p 33). It identifies our current environmental problems as the natural outcome of our present capitalist system. Rejecting the arguments of ecoliberals, they contend that "solving environmental problems is more than a matter of technical fixes and reformist management of the same social and economic system" (Pepper, 1996, p 8). Ecosocialism is borne out of left-wing political thought. Ecosocialists argue that we can only achieve an environmentally sustainable society by securing social justice and that a concern for nature is meaningless without a concern for human rights. Moreover the way to social justice is to change the way we organise our production, particularly the way ownership of production is allocated. Centralised, commonly-owned production is seen as the only way to control our impacts on the environment and achieve a sustainable balance between human consumption and nature. This belief in the need for a comprehensive administrative structure to organise a sustainable society sets ecosocialists apart from other greens.

Neither ecoliberals or ecosocialists question their utilitarian view of nature, and the philosophical assumptions such a position suggests. Neither do they question their assumption of 'progress' and 'development', and as such are very northern and industrial in their outlook. This is their fundamental weakness and other greens question these assumptions (Box 2.3).

Box 2.3: Ideological approaches to the environment

In the last ten years post-modernism has gained popularity in the academic world, providing new perspectives on what we value as knowledge (phenomenology) and as worthwhile or good (our ideology). It has allowed the 'modern' to be thrown into relief and analysed more critically. Using this theoretical cleavage between the modern and the post-modern, we can identify two distinct ideological approaches to the environment: ecomodernism and post-modern ecologism.

Ecomodernism is, arguably, industry's discourse on the environment. It describes an ecological switch of industrialisation that considers the maintenance of the existing resource base. It adds an environmental dimension to the development path but does not allow that dimension to radically alter it. It does not represent a break with the past and the existing economic and social structures but a continuation of it, being essentially modernist in its outlook. To the modernist, progress is the organising principle of human society, and is seen as synonymous with development, which is understood as economic development and economic growth.

Post-modern ecologism provides a different perspective, questioning whether Gross Domestic Product (GDP) is really economic growth, whether economic growth is really economic development, whether economic development is really development, whether development is really progress, and whether progress for its own sake is really desirable. Can GDP really be economic growth, when an oil spill, plane crash or even a war can make more money change hands and add to GDP? No. Is economic growth really economic development when it is based on an assumption of continual expansion in a finite globe? No. Is economic development really development if the most important things to develop in our lives are love and respect? No. So, is continual development really progress, when we might be happy just the way we are? No. Finally then, is progress per se actually progressive? Probably not.

Post-modern ecologism suggests we disregard continual economic development as the organising principle of society. For the post-modern ecologist, the organising principle for society is sustainable development. The watchwords of this outlook are empowerment, community, security and creativity.

Cynics dismiss these attitudes as unrealistic. They are confused with the romantic view of nature that is described as ecocentrist (Box 2.5). Although many ecocentrists do share the views of post-modern ecology (and vice-versa), they should not be confused. Post-modern ecologism does not necessarily identify nature as central but rather questions our current assumptions about human civilisation. *and marketing*

Environmentalism.   *within it.*

This environmentalism was holistic, seeing the world as an interconnected whole, a fragile globe floating in space. The image of the Earth from space became a strong symbol, illustrated by the use of an Apollo XI mission picture on the cover of the preparatory report for the UN Conference on the Human Environment at Stockholm in 1972. An emphasis on the whole rather than the partial also shaped the political outlook of the emerging campaign groups: comprehensive legislative change was required and was to be achieved by campaigning through the political system.

There are a number of different views on why environmentalism became such a widely-held identity in the 1960s and early 1970s. Some argue that the growth in environmental consciousness at this time was a direct result of a degrading environment, although most sociologists prefer a more complex explanation. Often described as the new middle-class thesis or post-materialism thesis, Ronald Ingelhart (1977) has argued that as the post-war generation experienced greater affluence their concern for the non-material became more pronounced, the environment being one of those concerns. Consequently the new environmentalism was located in the new middle classes that were developing at the time (Cotgrove and Duff, 1981). J. Hirsch and R. Roth (1986) have suggested that state politics systematically marginalises certain concerns because they are either of no relevance, or a challenge to both big business and government.[4] They identified this as the reason why movements expressing these grievances grow outside the mainstream political system.

All of these factors played a part in the growth of the second wave of environmentalism, coupled with the growth of ecology as a respected and often normative science. In the early 1970s ecologists increasingly began to step outside their role as scientists to become major contributors to the environmental debate, following the pioneering work of Rachel Carson in the early 1960s. In her book, *Silent spring*, Carson (1962) brought the concepts of food chains, the web of life and the balance of nature into the common vocabulary for the first time. Using ecology as the explanatory glue she brought together a variety of human/nature relationships into one environmental crisis. The new power of the imagery of ecology was such that even a new left-wing environmentalist British magazine of the time called itself *The Ecologist*.

Other key texts which helped shape the movement were Garett Hardin's *Tragedy of the commons* (1968), The Club of Rome's *Limits to growth* (Meadows et al, 1972) and Fritz Schumacher's *Small is beautiful* (1973). *Limits to growth* specifically concluded:

> If the present growth trends in world population, industrialisation, pollution, food production, and resource depletion continue unchanged, the limits to growth on this planet will be reached sometime within the next hundred years. The most probable result will be a rather sudden and uncontrollable decline in both population and industrial capacity.

In other words, billions of people are going to die very horribly sometime in the next century. This message made a significant impact in the media at the time, with the *New York Times* running a front page headline "Mankind Warned of Perils in Growth" and *Time* magazine describing the collapse of civilisation as "a grim inevitability if society continues its present dedication to growth and progress" (in Bailey, 1993). This in turn helped reinforce western public perceptions of an imminent crisis and in turn catalogued a wave of protest and direct action.

The early 1970s saw the newly-formed Friends of the Earth (FoE-UK) harass the largest mining company in the world so that it abandoned its proposal for a huge copper mine in the Welsh National Park of Snowdonia. Other high-profile campaigns included: FoE-UK's dump of 1,500 non-returnable bottles on the doorstep of the drinks manufacturer Schweppes; the first Greenpeace-International anti-nuclear demonstrations off the Muroroa Atoll; and their first anti-whaling mission which set out from Canada with a crowd of 23,000 seeing them off. These events were a new form of protest, peaceful yet confrontational, often witty while at the same time making a recognisable and serious point. The enthusiasm of the time meant that campaigners like Teddy Goldsmith, did "genuinely believe that if politicians were alerted to what was happening to the planet, they would do something about it" (Pearce, 1991, p 13).

Box 2.4: Friends of the Earth

Founded in the USA in 1969 as an off-shoot of the Sierra Club, Friends of the Earth (FoE) was established in the UK in 1971. From its inception, FoE has led major campaigns against nuclear power, industrial pollution and many other controversial environmental issues. While the organisation has always had a global, long-term focus, it has maintained a commitment to decentralisation. The international organisation has remained a network of autonomous and varied groups which share a common name and compatible goals. In the UK it has about 100,000 national members and additional regional supporters. This represents a major fall in members and donations since the late 1980s. FoE-UK has responded by restructuring its departments to place more emphasis on the health and social implications of environmental problems.

Unfortunately, apart from a few regulatory measures such as the import ban on fur coats, politicians did not do enough about it. Despite this, the emergence of second-wave, modern environmentalism did have a number of effects on western society. Besides mobilising public opinion and influencing political debate, environmentalists also contributed to the institutionalisation of environmentalism within the state apparatus. Both the United States and Britain witnessed the creation of the Environmental Protection Agency (EPA) and the Department of the Environment, respectively, in the early 1970s (Enloe, 1975).

Third-wave environmentalism

The late 1980s saw the popularisation of environmental issues and a heightened profile for them on the international political agenda. In many western countries membership of environmental organisations rose by 600 per cent in five years, to a point where environmental group membership in the UK outstripped that of the political parties – over four million by 1993. With this new popularity, environmental groups became better funded and more powerful and the focus of organised environmental group campaigning began to shift towards finding and implementing solutions and an examination of market mechanisms as a potential vehicle for achieving this. This is third-wave environmentalism and is characterised by an increasingly more pragmatic view of the role of environmental campaigns in bringing about societal change. During the late 1980s and early 1990s a flood of environmentalists left campaigning groups to work as consultants, such as Peter Wilkinson (former director of Greenpeace-International) and David Bellamy (a popular English botanist and conservationist). These professionals could be described as 'environmenticians' who are 'post-environmentalist' to the extent that they moved beyond protesting and towards practical action. As the 1990s progressed, the major environmental groups began to embrace the new, pragmatic, view. WWF has positioned itself as a 'solutions organisation', and in 1994 Dr Claude Martin, its international director, remarked that "the time for protest alone is over – if, indeed it ever existed.... Conservationists today must develop practical solutions to environmental issues."[5] In 1996, Peter Melchett, Director of Greenpeace-UK, stated at a conference of senior business managers that the new environmental struggle is to put solutions into practice, and his organisation continues to explore new green product developments, working with industry to design new refrigerators, solar panels, and so on.

It appears that the large environmental organisations have been undergoing a major shift in their priorities, activities and image. This new positioning and presentation of environmental group policy and practice, although still in the process of development, is a very necessary response to the challenges facing the organised environmental movement at the close of the current millennium. We believe it is this development which has allowed collaboration with business and industry to be seen as a valid tactic for today's environmental groups.

Factors behind third-wave environmentalism

In the late 1980s most environmental groups experienced a huge increase in their income. The call from these groups had been "Help! Wake-up!" and people had responded with donations, filling the coffers of those various groups that had secured a few minutes on prime-time television. Now campaigners had a new responsibility: to use the money to bring about changes. Whereas in the 1970s and 1980s environmental groups had the task of identifying, describing, promoting and lobbying for legislation on environmental issues, in the 1990s they had to rise to new opportunities and responsibilities.

Box 2.5: Philosophical approaches to the environment

To philosophers, ideological debates on the environment are mere family quarrels, and political debates mere sibling scuffles when compared to the philosophical debate of the human's place in the universe. Should we assume we are at the centre of the universe? Can we do anything else?

Most environmentalists profess a nature-centred view of the world, seeing humans as part of the natural universe, not above it. Some take this further and resist the view that humans are more 'valuable' than other aspects of nature. Sometimes called ecocentric, biocentric or deep-green, this perspective wishes to recapture the sacredness of nature so that, for instance, trees are seen as gods and it is a sin to fell them. This is the intrinsic value of nature, extended by Richard Nash to suggest that "rocks, just like people, do have rights in and of themselves. It follows that it is in the rock's interests, not the human interest in the rock, that it is protected" (Nash, 1977). With roots in paganism, Amerindian spirituality, and 'Noble Savage' cultures, ecocentrics advocate a 'future primitivism' where people live naturally in a reinstated wilderness (Merchant, 1992). This view appears incompatible with global governance, business and most NGOs. It is also wonderful fodder for green-bashers who portray all environmental types as a 'long-haired loony-lefty brigade'.

The ecocentric view is not only impracticable but flawed. We, as humans, value nature. It is impossible for us to do anything else but value nature from a human perspective. It is also flawed to view the ecocentric perspective as 'deep green'. Focusing on personal philosophies and lifestyle, it ignores any structuralist analysis of society's problems. Marxists criticise deep ecology for being shallow because it does not place at the centre of its analysis the economic structures of society without which the cultures and belief systems cannot be understood (Pepper, 1996). Homocentrism is the opposite philosophy of nature and the environment, placing humans at the centre of creation. If applied fundamentally then this perspective can be destructive as it can inform a very utilitarian view of nature which when wedded with a materialistic conception of human need can override emotional and spiritual concerns for the environment. The sacred groves in northern India or the aboriginal valleys in Australia may have less material utility than a hydroelectric dam but are they any less valuable?

The kind of debates described in Boxes 2.2, 2.3 and 2.5 go round in circles. What implications do they have for saving and improving environments, whatever the motivation? Very little. We believe that reconciliation of very different political analyses, ideologies and philosophies can be found at the operational level. This may then provide some insights into an approach which embraces our environment, our society and human existence (Box 2.6).

To start with, in many developed countries, industry, governments and the public, have been turning to the wider green movement for ideas and solutions. The dilemma facing environmental groups has therefore been whether to hold out for a radical change in society, or to work incrementally towards achieving their environmental goals. To choose the former would leave environmentalists open to criticism as part of a blame culture, whereas to choose the latter would allow more constructive action. On the one hand an engagement with the traditional enemy may help to implement localised sustainable development as well as facilitating a breakdown of the antagonistic positions of the past and the fostering of greater understanding. On the other hand, engagement runs the risk of compromising ecological principles and the loss of independence. There are differing views within the environmental movement as to which route is best, but the dominant practice in third-wave environmentalism is one of cooperation and partnership, backed up by radical grassroots protest to keep environmental issues in the public eye.

The move away from a blame culture towards a solutions culture is also the result of something we call 'public cry-wolf fatigue'. Environmental groups are in the public-attention market, having to compete for the sympathies, and charitable giving, of the public. This explains why so many organisations have adopted scare tactics in their campaigns. While effective in the short term this strategy is unsustainable in the longer term. Environmental groups can not continue to say the Earth is going to die tomorrow, when 'tomorrow' is the next day, week or month for individuals – and in the West environmental problems will take far longer than this to reveal themselves fully. In other words, the West's perception of the environment can best be understood in terms of incremental change. This means that, for the human conception of time, environmental catastrophes will appear gradually. Take, climate change for example, where a one degree rise per 50 years will be catastrophic for ecosystems but not necessarily catastrophic for many people in the foreseeable future.

This is not to say disasters are not happening – environmental degradation is having severe consequences for people in southern countries, and even in the North pollution has been linked with deaths from respiratory and other health problems. Anger, dismay and a sense of urgency are very real and valid feelings to hold about environmental, social and ethical issues but such feelings are often overwhelmed by day-to-day issues of doing one's job, studying for exams or running a household.

In response, third-wave environmentalists are developing a solutions culture and attempting to tap new emotions to receive the desired response. While public fear remains a key emotional target of campaigning groups aimed at increasing awareness, it is now viewed as an inadequate strategy for increasing public participation in solutions. Today environmentalists increasingly look to generate public participation by targeting the emotions of creativity, compassion and responsibility.

In addition to these internal dynamics of the environmental groups, it can be argued that the development of third-wave environmentalism has been driven by factors external to the environmental movement. Today the 500 top companies in the world control 25 per cent of the planet's output, in GDP terms, a situation which led UNEP Secretary-General, Elizabeth Dowdeswell, to assert that "the market is replacing government as the key determinant influencing our society".[6] The shifting balance of power from government to transnational business with the process of globalisation must be recognised as a significant factor shaping the outlook of many environmental groups.

The continuing development of the global market, with increasingly mobile capital and industry, has served to weaken the power of national governments to set their own policy agenda. In today's global market if a transnational corporation does not favour the policies of a certain government it can choose to locate elsewhere. Similarly, if the international money markets anticipate this reaction from a number of transnationals then confidence in a country's economic performance and therefore it's currency may decline. Together these factors can produce increasing unemployment and prices, creating a recipe for recession. In light of this, governments are locked into a process of competitive deregulation. Although environmental groups have been campaigning for greater regulation, governments are increasingly loath to do so.

Indeed, continuing deregulation by governments is the new economic and political context within which environmental groups must operate. In the UK, North America and continental Europe, recent years have been characterised by a 'rolling back' of the state where regulations have been progressively removed and public expenditure slashed.[7] In addition to the global economic down-pressure on regulation and tax, the prominence of laissez faire economics has been a significant factor working against the adoption of new environmental legislation. To the laissez faire economist, regulating the level of pollution requires monitoring and enforcement which in turn requires undesirable government expenditure, while fiscal measures such as environmental taxes are seen to distort the market and lead to inefficiency.

In addition to these economic constraints on the political process, in most developed countries politics has undergone a process of self-emasculation. In countries where avoiding bad press is the major concern for political parties, adventurous ideas do not receive the attention they deserve. Recent arguments for centrist policies by politicians in the USA, Britain and throughout Europe suggest that politics may be able to move beyond the categories of left versus right, monetarism versus Keynesianism, social intervention versus liberalism and perhaps focus more on sustainability issues and solutions. However, if the new politics focuses increasingly on media management, with one sound bite versus another sound bite and one personality versus another personality, it will provide an unfavourable context for difficult political issues to be debated and legislation to be proposed.

Just as the door to achieving environmental security through the democratic process has been closing, a new door has opened for the environmental movement: the boardroom door. The changing response of business to the environmental challenge and the increasing recognition of corporate social responsibility has meant that business leaders are increasingly listening to and engaging with environmentalists. This change in business culture is a key factor in the emerging forms of third-wave environmentalism as well as providing the business culture from which partnerships with environmental groups can be forged. A comprehensive analysis of this changing business response is provided in Chapter three.

As an aggregate of our individual activities as consumers, business should be accountable to our society's wills and desires. Therefore in business lies the cause of, and some solution to, our environmental problems. As such, business is now being seen as a very valid target group for campaigning activity by environmentalists – and not necessarily antagonistic forms of campaigning.

Figure 1: The three waves of environmental group thinking and action

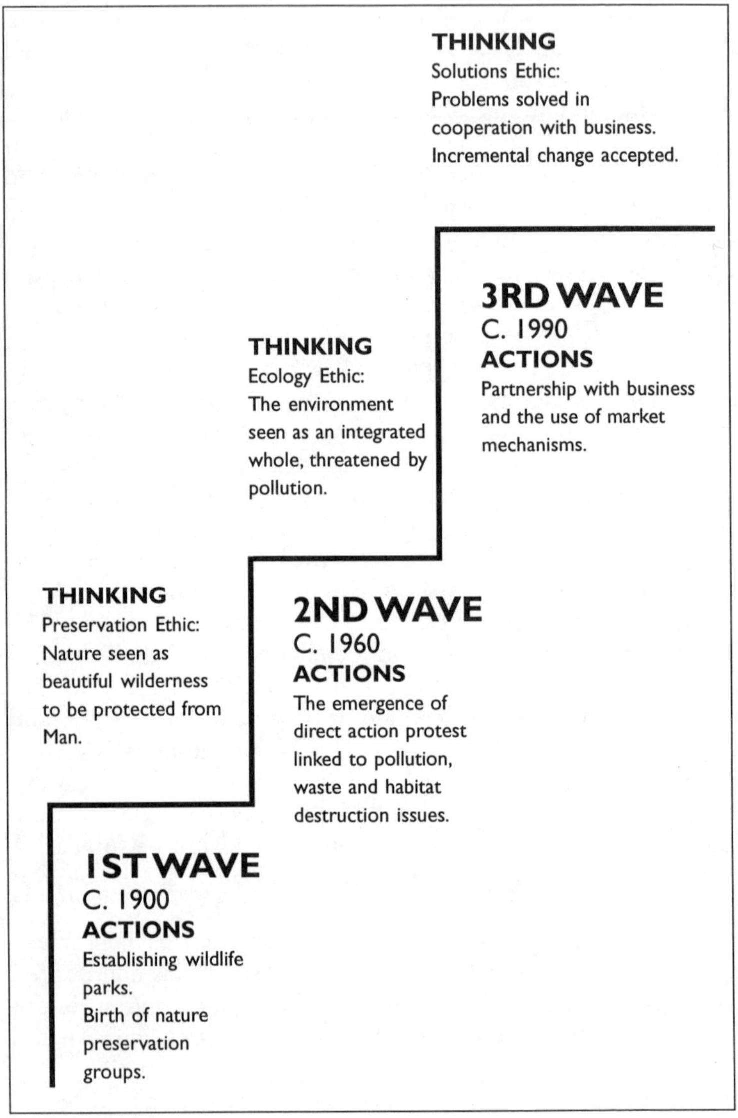

THINKING
Solutions Ethic:
Problems solved in
cooperation with business.
Incremental change accepted.

3RD WAVE
C. 1990
ACTIONS
Partnership with business
and the use of market
mechanisms.

THINKING
Ecology Ethic:
The environment
seen as an integrated
whole, threatened by
pollution.

THINKING
Preservation Ethic:
Nature seen as
beautiful wilderness
to be protected from
Man.

2ND WAVE
C. 1960
ACTIONS
The emergence of
direct action protest
linked to pollution,
waste and habitat
destruction issues.

1ST WAVE
C. 1900
ACTIONS
Establishing wildlife
parks.
Birth of nature
preservation
groups.

Obstacles to the third wave

The rise of pragmatic models of environmentalism has not been a smooth and comprehensive process. A number of legacies from the formative years of environmental groups present obstacles to the development of third-wave environmentalism. Environmental groups have always been concerned with defining, communicating and campaigning on 'issues'. This leads to a situation where, in defining areas to 'work on', environmentalists have been more likely to invest time and money in a new 'issue' rather than on a potential 'solution' which could use support. This reflects the reliance of environmental groups on the mass media for communicating their message. Moreover, the mass media has become the mechanism of delivery for many campaigns. This is a necessary result of the way our society is organised yet it presents a number of restrictions. First, other communication methods such as direct liaison with the various stakeholders involved in a particular process have not been given adequate attention. In the case of relations with business this has slowed liaison with city investors and analysts, company directors and so on. Such liaison requires a specific set of skills which were not developed in the area of media relations. Second, as the media has become the primary campaign agent, environmental group campaigns have been judged on their media success. Because of this media dependency, the media representation of campaigns increasingly becomes the reality of the campaigns. Such a situation has supported environmental groups in looking for new issues rather than looking to implement solutions, thereby restricting the transition from exclusively a blame culture to a solutions culture.

Although crucial, attention from the mass media should be rejected as the be-all and end-all of environmental group campaigns; instead it can be viewed as a useful mechanism in a far broader project of environmental group activity. In addition media work should not only focus on problems. Campaigning groups require a reformulated media message for the new millennium, a message which says "the old issues have not gone away – but all of us can do something about them, and do something now". We believe that partnerships with business and industry, such as those outlined in Chapters four, five and six, with their emphasis on finding and implementing solutions and empowering the public to make a difference may increasingly be seen at the forefront of this new, third-wave, environmentalism.

Pitfalls of the third wave

Environmentalism today is not as clear cut as it once was. As a movement of opposition it was easy to know what environmentalism stood for – by what it was against. Unless there is very clear thinking and open debate the development of pragmatic models of environmentalism may lead to the fragmentation of the environmental movement and the kind of infighting that will do little to bring positive change. Some of these pitfalls are discussed here.

First, environmental issues are by their very nature interdisciplinary. Over the years environmental groups have had to address the scientific, economic, social and cultural aspects of any one issue. With increased resources environmental groups have been able to develop pools of expertise in specific areas. Unfortunately increasingly specialised campaigning has, in many cases, led them to become more disjointed. It is not uncommon for one unit of an environmental group to be unaware that something very relevant is being pursued by another unit. Similarly, coordination with other environmental groups is often lacking. This lack of coordination can be disempowering as it allows the broader view of the social and economic foundation of our environmental problems to be neglected. Therefore forums for communication are essential to bring together different environmental groups working on related issues.

Specialisation is just one aspect of the 'new professionalism' of environmental groups. The professionalism that is associated with the third wave is arguably a necessary response to the increased income, power and responsibility of environmental groups. However, it has some major implications for the organisational culture of environmental groups. As leading environmental groups such as Greenpeace and WWF have grown they have required more accountants, fundraisers, administrators and so on. Increasingly, therefore, new employees may join with little ideological commitment to the issues involved, yet find themselves in positions of strategic importance after a number of years of service. In a similar way professionals with no background in charitable work are increasingly – and necessarily – employed to implement environmental group policies and programmes. Over time these professionals can assume positions to directly influence policy and strategy. The problem is that in the near future environmental groups may have people in top management with no fundamental ideological commitment to environmental issues. These people may have more in common with company directors than their charitable donors or the people whose environments they are meant to be protecting.

One should remember that environmentalism is not just a technology to be devised, developed and implemented. It is much, much more. The more that people in environmental groups become accustomed to a high salary, high standard of living and moving in business circles, the more likely it is that they will lose touch with grassroots campaigners and their concerns.

Cooperation or cooptation?

The development of third-wave environmentalism in western countries in the 1990s is needed for us to find the road to sustainability. By facilitating communication between previous adversaries it is helping to move the debate forward and allow practical actions to be taken on the environment. But at what expense? Some would argue that the environmentalists were right all along, and we do not have the time to hold lengthy negotiations about partnership, consensus, practicality and so on. If the Earth *is* going to die tomorrow then valuable time shouting about it is being wasted as those who should be doing the shouting are now sitting in boardrooms 'consulting'. These concerns are articulated by Mark Dowie (1995b) who proposes a rebellion against pragmatic models of environmentalism and a "fourth wave" of grassroots protest and action. For third-wave environmentalists to assuage such concerns they must be able to deliver results in the shorter term.

A wider view

The preceding description of the changing nature of environmentalism is exclusively the western experience. The story can be very different in nations of the South, where environmental campaigners are not always given the respect that would allow their views be heard and where some are even denied the basic rights of nourishment and education that would facilitate their engagement in debate over the use and abuse of their lands. In Nigeria, Indonesia, Brazil and other countries, confrontation between campaigners and national elites is still typical. Whether environmentalism will develop in Japan and the Tiger economies of the East in the same way it is developing in the West is debatable. The modest evidence of environmental concern in eastern industrial countries suggests there is a long way to go before environmental awareness becomes a force significant enough to have a bearing on their economies and societies.

Box 2.6: Where we are coming from

A number of different environmentalisms have been described in Boxes 2.2, 2.3 and 2.5. We have our own environmental philosophy, ideology and politics and hope that by spelling this out here we may avoid some misunderstandings about 'where we are coming from' in writing this book.

Our philosophy is one of 'ecohumanism'. We wish to extend our human values to nature, while recognising fully that these values can only ever be human-derived and human-centred values. We prefer to extend our values to nature for pragmatic and altruistic reasons. First, if we pollute or degrade ecosystems then this lowers their capacity to provide resources for us (a material pragmatism). Second, we get emotional, even spiritual, satisfaction and enjoyment out of nature in a relatively undegraded and unrepressed state so that, for example, we are uncomfortable with the idea of factory farming animals, and it is our discomfort on account of the animals that is a compelling reason not to do it (non-material pragmatism). Third, we are concerned for the most vulnerable in our world who tend to suffer the worst effects of environmental degradation (altruism). Put simply, we should steward nature in an attempt to foster human happiness, welfare and equality.

Ecohumanism shares the middle ground between the egocentric and ecocentric outlooks described by Carolyn Merchant (1992). We believe it provides philosophical grounding for the conclusions and recommendations of this text, as it attempts to bring together the left and the right, the radical and the reformist, in the environmental movement.

Our ideology is post-modern ecologism, congruent to that outlined in Box 2.3. We reconcile this with a pragmatic politics of incremental change that works within the system, as we believe that transformation is more likely to come from within the system than without. We develop some of these ideas further in Chapter seven.

Contemporary perspectives on the environmental movement

Three main strands of thought are emerging in the political and economic milieu that surround the environment issue. One point of view is that the environment "ain't so bad after all" and that the greens are just scaremongers who rip us off for donations and favour trees over jobs. Another point of view is that typified by the phrase "we are all environmentalists now", which embraces the environmental issue as a significant one but which can be solved by the present economic and political structures with a little application of green technology and taxes. A third strand of thought is that the environmental movement has been coopted by the powers that control the world's political and economic system, through the establishment of business-run pseudo-green groups, the granting of minor concessions to campaigners and a general greenwash of business-as-usual. It is into this context we launch our analysis of business–environmentalist partnerships. Before proceeding further let us review these contemporary perspectives on environmental thinking and action.

The anti-environmentalists

One of the more (in)famous protagonists of the American Wise Use Movement, Ron Arnold, believes environmentalists to be evil megalomaniacs who "invent environmental threats in order to recruit members and make money", and goes on, "environmentalism is a new paganism that worships trees and sacrifices people" (Krakauer, 1991, p 114). His goal is "to destroy, to eradicate the environmental movement" (Rowell, 1996, p 14). Arnold is not alone in his thoughts, with a major development of anti-environmentalist opinion emerging in the early 1990s in North America and Europe. Most anti-environmentalist organisations are funded by those industries who are the target of environmental campaigns and increasing environmental legislation, while their 'foot soldiers' are those who work in the industry and whose jobs are threatened. These economically motivated arguments have been distilled into more considered thought by 'contrarian' writers such as Ronald Bailey, Richard North, Wilfred Beckermann and Stephen Budianski, as well as self-styled optimists such as Greg Easterbrook.

The contrarian argument is twofold. First, they argue that the environment is not so bad after all. By pointing out that the world still has plenty of mineral resources, that it could feed twice its population, and that the rate of population growth is decelerating, they argue that ecological problems are either non-existent or easily solvable, with a bit of economic growth. In *Life on a modern planet: a manifesto for progress*, a book partly financed by the corporation ICI, North cites the "pretty tolerable – if not quite perfect – safety of almost everything we eat and drink" as almost intuitive evidence of how great things are (Lean, 1995, p 21).

Budianski's thesis in *Nature's keepers: the new science of nature management* is that humanity has always modified nature and the only sensible course is to go on modifying it for the maximum benefit. Although this is an accepted position by most mainstream environmental groups, he defines his as a counter-green thesis, portraying greens as those who see nature as "pristine" and something which should not be meddled with. While true of the environmentalism in the 1920s this is a misjudged analysis of contemporary environmentalism. Similarly, Beckermann wishes to "blow the whistle on the greens", and expose their thinking as scaremongering. In a complete rehash of the old growth/no-growth or boomster/doomster debate of the 1970s, he argues that the idea of growth being harmful and small being beautiful is, simply put, "stupid" (Beckermann, 1995). Julian Simon had that argument sown up in the early 1980s when he insisted that the human brain was the ultimate renewable resource which would solve all material obstacles to continued human existence: necessity being the mother of invention (Simon, 1981). The question since then has been what happens to people in those times of necessity and whether it is desirable to innovate because we have to rather than because we want to or, more simply, is something good to do just because it is achievable?

Easterbrook says he is an optimist. He believes that no matter how hard we try, nature is so huge and robust that human impacts will only ever be ephemeral. The implication is that we should concentrate on issues of social justice rather than those to do with ecology. This echoes the despairs of Beckermann who wishes we would spend more time worrying about 'real' issues such as poverty, disease, homelessness and so on. Both demonstrate a misunderstanding of the modern environmentalism we have described as 'third wave'. Environmentalism today is increasingly about environmental justice. 'Eco' or 'green' are now banners for a diverse range of ideas and concerns which are not being adequately dealt with throughout the world. Who will suffer when sea levels rise? Citizens of rich nations who can afford sea defences? No. Who suffers from toxic waste disposal? Citizens of rich nations who ship it to the developing world for 'storage'? No. Who will suffer from increasing food prices as climates change? Yes, you've got it, the poor.

Environmentalism is a different vision of life which embraces a variety of different concerns. By recognising the inter-connectedness of individuals and society and society and the environment, third-wave environmentalism is entirely compatible with sustainable development and embraces social justice as a cornerstone of environmental concern, "for the planet for the people", as FoE-UK so aptly puts it.

Unfortunately these anti-environmentalist attacks seem to fall well short of a comprehensive critique of the environmental movement. Rather than focusing on issues relating to the new power of environmental groups such as accountability, transparency, and democracy, they provide dated caricatures of environmentalists and argue from the fossilised positions of the past.

The ecomodernists

A powerful line in current thinking on the environment is ecomodernism (see Box 2.3). Ecomodernism is a perspective that treats the environment as another technological problem to be overcome in the pursuit of progress. To the ecomodernist, pollution is an economic opportunity for prevention and clean-up technologies and certainly not an indication of fundamental problems with the current economic system. Put crudely, environmental problems can be solved by spending some cash on them. Recently described as "ecological modernisation", it "indicates the possibility of overcoming the environmental crisis without leaving the path of modernisation" (Spaargen and Mol, 1992, p 330).

What differentiates ecomodernists from progressive business managers making laudable attempts at improving the environ-mental performance of their business is that ecomodernists believe they have all the answers. The implication is that campaigners can pack up and go home because business has everything under control.

The green backlash

The conspiracy theory. And with all conspiracy theories very enticing and with significant elements of truth. The green backlash to the ecomodernists and anti-environmentalist contrarians has been championed by authors such as P. Chaterjee and M. Finger, Andy Rowell and Richard Welford. Welford argues that the emerging dominant paradigm in green thought has been created by and for business, who are effectively "hijacking environmentalism" (Welford, 1997). In a critique of the motivation of ecomodernists and the paucity of their vision, he identifies confusion over, and fear of, real alternatives as the reasons for the growing dominance of the ecomodern perspective:

> Uncertainty over alternatives ... only adds weight to the more certain strategy of ecomodernism. It supports the culture of continuity of the past rather than change. In the face of this, the cultural arrogance of industrialists becomes incredible. They rely on telling us the "way things are" and "this is the way things are done around here". They decry beliefs and feelings because they find them dangerous and threatening. They seek to end the normative discourse through aggressive attacks on anyone who does not fit into their model of the economy and society. The frame of reference of such industrialists is, of course, the continuation of business-as-usual. This is not surprising since this is where they perceive their own interests lie. They are willing to take on marginal changes to business-as-usual and therefore tolerate (or even occasionally embrace) ecomodernism, but radical, creative thinking is not on the agenda. (Welford, 1996b, p 21)

These thoughts are reminiscent of the ideas of various social critics who have long claimed that social and political debate itself is constrained within an industrialist, or modernist, paradigm (see Box 2.2). It is a theory of the incorporation of the environmental movement into industrial society and the marginalisation of radical green thought.

Reflecting on this new business influence on the environmental movement, Chatterjee and Finger feel that the new order is slowly creating a global management elite that is coopting the strongest people's movements, the very movements that brought the crisis to public attention. Focusing specifically on the Earth Summit, they argue that:

> ... the [Rio] process has divided, co-opted, and weakened the green movement. On the one hand [Rio] brought every possible NGO into the system of lobbying governments, while on the other hand it quietly promoted business to take over the solutions. NGOs are now trapped in a farce by which they have lent support to governments in return for some small concessions on language, and thus legitimised the process of increased industrial development. (Finger and Chaterjee, 1992, p 2)

We would add that if this process is occurring then business and government are not the only driving forces, but also the newly-institutionalised NGOs themselves as they become big, cumbersome and self aware – in the sense that they become increasingly concerned with their own sustainability rather than that of the environment (or see the two as one in the same thing – the deadliest mistake to make).

In his enthralling book *Green backlash: the global subversion of the environmental movement*, Rowell charts the growth of anti-environmentalist arguments, sponsored largely by business and government (Rowell, 1996). He describes the growth of well-funded anti-environmentalist bodies who take on green names such as 'Wise Use', while their sole aim is to use fear and prejudice to debunk environmental arguments, even harass and harm environmentalist themselves. There is certainly something in these arguments and we are conscious of the possibility that if mismanaged business–environmentalist partnerships will only support the growing falsehoods of anti-environmentalism and ecomodernism. Yet we hope for a different outcome as history teaches us that the cooptation of social movements can be a two-edged sword, as typified by the mainstream political gains of the workers', women's and black rights' movements.

A new consensus of social realism?

The different outcome we hope for is one which would build upon an emerging consensus. It is a different strand of thought identified – not in the literature – but in the minds of some of the people who are behind the partnerships we describe in Chapters four to six. It is the new consensus between idealistic managers and pragmatic environmentalists that incremental change can be found together in the short term, without losing sight of the fact that in the long-term sustainability will require major social, economic, political and cultural changes. We call this the new social realism.[8] The ideas embodied in the Real World Coalition book, *The politics of the real world* (Jacobs, 1996) can be seen in this context. Social realism uses the language of classical economics to put across a quite radically different view of societal organisation. As it has not been distinguished from other perspectives until now, the social realist consensus is dangerously close to ecomodernism for some. If it is not to be usurped by the ecomodernist view, then we must acknowledge that the new consensus offers no easy answers, that it is experimental and requires us to face diversity – and embrace it.

Notes

[1] Take for example, *The green consumer guide* by John Elkington and Julia Hailes, which shot to the top of the bestseller list only two weeks after its release in 1988.

[2] We do not deal with the environmental consciousness of pre-industrial societies in this text.

[3] This view informed a number of harmful conservation policy decisions in colonial lands, where pastoral peoples had lived within "wilderness" for thousands of years. When, in East Africa, colonials began to observe the affects of their hunting on populations of elephants, lions and so on, they fenced off areas and drove the native Maasai out from newly formed parks. Although the pastoralists were as natural as the wildlife, northern first-wave environmentalism saw nature as apart from humans, something to be protected for its beauty and its naturalness, rather than

for a broader notion of the interconnectedness of humans and their environments.

[4] A related, yet different argument is put by Jurgen Habermas (1979), who has described the growth of new social movements as a reaction to the extension of capitalism and the state into more and more aspects of our personal lives.

[5] This quote is from a speech at the 1994 WWF-International Annual Conference in South Africa.

[6] From a speech at a UNEP Conference, Massachusetts, USA, October, 1995.

[7] This policy has been exported to countries of the South through International Monetary Fund (IMF) Structural Adjustment Policies (SAP).

[8] The term social realism was first used to describe the writings of Dickens and others, who decried the pains of industrialising society in nineteenth-century Europe. It has subsequently been used to describe a positivist approach to sociology. Our new social realism – described in detail in Chapter seven – has no relationship to either body of work. Rather it represents an integration of traditionally leftist concerns for the 'social' with traditionally rightest concerns for 'realism'. New social realism can also be described as 'new left', though more radical than the centrist politics emerging in the late 1990s in the US and UK.

three

Seeing the green light? The business response to sustainable development

"There's no profit to be made in the destruction of the planet. It's very bad for business", at least according to 'The Kingpin', one of cartoon superhero Spiderman's arch villains. When these words were spoken on Saturday morning television in late 1996, one could say that the idea of corporate environmental responsibility had truly arrived. As this example illustrates, the need for a positive business response to sustainable development is slowly becoming part of our cultural landscape. Related ideas such as corporate social responsibility and stakeholding are also gaining wider currency in the corporate boardroom and among senior managers.

The starting point for most businesses is usually enlightened self-interest, but the idea of sustainable development also has the potential to bring new values and ideas into the world of business. Being environmentally and socially responsible in the late 1990s means much more than anticipating demand for environmentally-preferable products; designing safer, healthier and less-polluting manufacturing facilities; or increasing recycling capacities. Today's business leaders must also concern themselves with managing technological risks; conserving non-renewable natural resources; protecting special habitats; safeguarding worker welfare in different geographical and political contexts; and providing for animal welfare; not to mention even larger sustainability issues such as climate change, biodiversity and the integrity of complex ecosystems.

The dominant business model in today's globalised economy, however, remains highly competitive and mobile. Businesses struggle to find cheaper human and natural resources in order to remain profitable and maximise shareholder value. On financial matters, executive management is legally accountable only to company owners. On environment, health and safety matters, business leaders have generally complied with laws and regulations dating back to the nineteenth century. Even when businesses and their managers follow the letter of the law, they have profited (and continue to profit) enormously from the destruction of vast quantities of the Earth's natural resources. Many workers and communities around the world have faced health risks and have often received limited economic gain as part of this process. The focus for most businesses continues to be the economic and legal bottom lines, with the notion of an ethical bottom line still very low on many corporate agendas. Beyond the world of Saturday morning cartoons, many business villains still make lots of money by plundering the planet.

In this chapter, we review the changing business response to sustainable development and more specifically to environmental matters. We begin with a brief historical review of the relationship between commercial activities, human health and the natural environment prior to the 1960s. We then proceed with a more detailed analysis of why and how the business response to sustainable development has changed over the past three decades. We suggest that there are many outstanding questions about the capacity and commitment of business to fully embrace sustainability. The chapter concludes with some general reflections on the different dimensions of the business response. Ongoing tensions between economic, ethical and public relations motives remain unresolved, and many environmental groups remain sceptical about the extent to which business can change.

We share this concern. While we acknowledge that a growing number of corporate executives and senior managers espouse green business strategies, there are many factors which limit the business response around the world. As mentioned above, one of the major limitations is the nature of the global economy where countries (and regions) compete against each other to attract investment and to take on the production costs of globally mobile corporations. David Korten argues that "a green corporation simply can't last in our unregulated market where competing companies are not internalizing their costs. If you do attempt to 'green' your business you'll soon be bought out by some corporate raiders who see an opportunity to externalize the costs and make a short-term killing" (1996, p 13).

Another factor which limits the business response to sustainable development is of equal importance. If business is to embrace wholeheartedly the sustainability agenda, then it must be willing to "to re-examine its underlying assumptions" and to define the purpose and actions of business "from the perspective of the world and society beyond its self-referential borders" (Hawken, 1994, p 9). In order to respond more creatively to the sustainable development challenge, above all business people must be willing to listen to their critics and to engage a range of stakeholders. Otherwise business will remain unaccountable and ultimately unsustainable. The net result will be an ever-widening gulf between rich and poor, the powerful and the powerless, and people and nature.

We believe that partnership is a key implementation strategy for sustainable development. Partnerships with environmental groups have the potential to help business understand why sustainable development is important for business and society. In Chapters four to six, we present case-study material which demonstrates how these new partnerships work in practice. Partnerships do not necessarily shelter business from public criticism nor do they create sustainable business organisations as the McDonald's case shows in Chapter six, however, many of the partnerships described in this book offer the possibility of alternative futures. To paraphrase Riane Eisler and David Loye, business people must learn to live with other actors in society in the mutually respectful and cooperative way required for a pluralistic, sustainable and truly democratic, or partnership world (1990, p 33).

Early responses

The problems associated with unsustainable development at the end of the twentieth century have deep historical roots. Today's globalisation and North–South socio-economic divisions can be traced to more than five hundred years of European colonial domination over much of the globe. Clive Ponting (1992) notes that the creation of the Third World began early in the fifteenth century with the arrival of Portuguese settlers on the uninhabited island of Madeira. The Portuguese replaced the forests with sugar cane plantations which required imported slave labour from North Africa.

The roots of contemporary pollution problems lie in the linked processes of urbanisation and industrialisation. Human societies have always struggled to manage their waste, however the growing populations of cities created new problems. Industrial and technological development produced new forms of pollution and introduced new threats to human health and the environment. Most of the early environmental impacts of industrialisation were localised and public concerns about adverse effects were either deflected or unheard. Ponting adds that many of the characteristics of contemporary responses to pollution were also prevalent in earlier societies:

- fatalistic acceptance of pollution as an inevitable consequence of human activities;

- authorities balking at prevention or control measures;

- lack of foresight and technical understanding;

- the problem of allocating responsibility;

- a preference for short-term local fixes rather than long-term solutions;

- and a failure of individuals or companies to take responsibility for their actions. (p 346)

Not all early corporate responses to industrial pollution were irresponsible. Nineteenth-century philanthropic industrialists such as Robert Owen and Titus Salt wanted healthy, contented workers in their factories and saw a need for various education, welfare and housing schemes to alleviate the adverse living and working conditions of the time.

Irresponsible industrialists were challenged by social critics such as novelist Charles Dickens and utopian socialist William Morris who argued that the harsh working and living conditions of British cities desperately needed improvement. Morris' novel *News from nowhere* (1891) imagined a future society which replaced exploitative and physically harmful factory work with a cooperative, sustainable model where small was indeed beautiful (see Wheeler and Sillanpää, 1997).   Other socialist writers such as Frederick Engels and Karl Marx insisted that the careless nature of capitalism would eventually lead to its demise.

Early government responses to urban environmental problems came in the form of British public health legislation from 1848 onwards which attempted to secure minimum housing standards. The first environmental legislation specifically directed at business production processes was the Alkali Act 1863.   It established the Alkali Inspectorate to inspect all manufacturing establishments "concerned with the production of substances ... which may involve the release of noxious fumes and smoke" (Bingham, 1973, p 158).

Contemporary origins of business response

Business in the twentieth century has been dominated by the idea that 'big is beautiful'.   Some of the most significant technological innovations have been Henry Ford's Model T, new products in electronics, synthetic chemicals, atomic energy and more recently information technology.   These new technologies have required new, larger-scale production patterns which have depended upon higher levels of investment (see Elkington and Burke, 1989, p 42). With business increasingly associated with 'bigness', industrial pollution of air and waterways has also increased.   Globalisation has shifted capital and production to many southern countries, bringing new forms of environmental degradation.   Twentieth-century consumers in both the North and the South have increased the worldwide demand for cars, roads, new fibres, plastics, televisions, stereos, computers, many other consumer goods and the energy they require.   This rise in consumption has contributed further to global pollution and a growing depletion of the Earth's natural resources.

A number of factors have prompted a changed business response to environmental matters in the second half of the twentieth century.   These include inter alia the role of public opinion; legislation; and environmental groups.   Below we review each of these factors in turn.

Shifts in public opinion

Growing public environmental awareness has been one of the key factors which has prompted a changed business response on environmental matters. As we noted in Chapter two, evolving social attitudes and values and corresponding consumer and environmental activism have had a profound impact on the political process in western industrialised countries over the past three decades. Some of these changes in attitude have been driven by media coverage of environmental disasters. More significantly, however, the rise of environmental awareness in the 1960s can be linked to a shift from material to non-material concerns resulting from growing levels of material affluence in the West (see Ingelhart, 1977). Other contributing factors included the rise of counter-culture values and a feeling that the planet was becoming smaller and more fragile, the latter driven particularly by the emerging communications revolution (Brenton, 1991, pp 22-23). These changes helped launch the contemporary environmental movement and also affected the markets within which business operates (see Chapter two).

Over the years public opinion research has revealed growing public concern for the environment. Whereas a public opinion survey in 1979 found that only five per cent of Americans agreed that environmental regulation "had not gone far enough" in supporting environmental protection, by 1993 the number of Americans who agreed with this statement had grown to 48 per cent (Smith, 1995, p 19).

In the early 1990s, a Market & Opinion Research International (MORI) poll of environmental attitudes across Europe found that 70 per cent of the public in France, Italy, Portugal, Spain and the United Kingdom had the strongly-held view that "companies do not pay enough attention to the environment". Within the UK, 40 per cent of industry leaders agreed that "British companies do not pay enough attention to the environment" (Worcester, in Taylor et al, 1994, pp 18-20).

At the global level, the Gallup 'Health of the Planet' survey conducted in 22 developed and developing countries just prior to the 1992 Earth Summit found "widespread concern for the environment among citizens of all types of countries." The same survey noted that in a majority of countries polled, "citizens believe that business and industry are the major cause of environmental problems" (Gallup, 1992 in UNCTAD, 1996, p 2).

The role of legislation

Historically, the business response to environmental matters throughout the world has been largely driven by legislation (Robins and Trisoglio in Holmberg, 1992, p 165). The threat of legal action is often the single most important factor. Research has also shown that many companies seek to anticipate future legislation when embarking upon new policies and programmes (Roberts, 1995, p 81). Below we review environmental regulation in three western industrialised countries – United Kingdom, USA and The Netherlands – to illustrate how environmental regulation is shifting toward more flexible approaches based upon greater dialogue with business and in some cases environmental groups.

United Kingdom: Post-World War II Britain was seen as a leader on environmental regulation with the introduction of new planning legislation in the late 1940s and the 1956 Clean Air Act. Other milestones included the establishment of the Royal Commission on Environmental Pollution in 1970 and the Department of the Environment in 1971. Sir Martin Holdgate, the first head of the British government's central unit on environmental pollution offers the following reflections on business–government relations in the early 1970s:

> *Relations with industry were interestingly varied. We had some contacts and degrees of friction with elements of industry in the early seventies, although very often they were through other departments of government that were industry's self appointed champions. The industrial position in the early seventies in the UK was very mixed. Some companies wanted to be up front on environmental questions, entered into dialogue, improved their practices. Some were dragged kicking and screaming. Some sheltered behind friendly defensive bits of government.... Industry moved, like a convoy of ships at different speeds and you had to chase the laggards up all the time.*

The British position in the early 1970s was that action would be taken only if it could be scientifically proven that action was essential. The idea of imposing additional costs on industry without such scientific proof was definitely out of the question.

For much of the period from the 1960s to the 1980s the British government was largely seen as complacent on environmental matters (see Young, 1993). Despite the introduction of a new Environmental Protection Act in 1990, the UK continues to be viewed at the EU level as a "follower" on environmental regulation (see Buitelaar, 1995). The act introduced flexible concepts geared towards the needs of business, namely "Best Practicable Environmental Option" (BPEO) and "Best Available Techniques Not Entailing Excessive Costs" (BATNEEC). Since 1996, it has been the role of the new Environmental Agency to monitor and assess what constitutes BPEO and BATNEEC. According to many environmental groups, such flexible measures weaken existing legislation and give business more power to appeal against regulatory decisions. FoE-UK argues that the government has succumbed to the "superficial attraction" of the voluntary approach which "amounts to them shifting into neutral and taking their hands off the wheel" (see FoE-UK, 1995, p 45).

USA: The early regulatory catalysts were the 1970 National Environmental Policy Act, the 1970 Clean Air Act and the establishment of the Environmental Protection Agency (EPA) in 1971. Enabling legislation guaranteed environmentalists greater influence than industry over the EPA's staffing and administrative structures. Clauses within the primary legislation ensured that the EPA had the power to impose strict compliance deadlines. For much of the 1970s, the American Congress created a form of "institutionalised confrontation" between the EPA and business. In the 1980s under President Reagan, there was a marked shift to "reactionary, laissez faire" anti-environmentalism. The Bush presidency introduced a period of transition and presented both industry and environmentalists with contradictory signals. Since 1993, the Clinton administration has attempted to build "pragmatic, cooperative relationships" between regulators and business (see Wallace, 1995, pp 112-16). For example, in early 1996 the EPA approved a policy to encourage environmental compliance by offering businesses incentives to disclose and correct violations on a voluntary basis. Cooperating companies will face substantially reduced penalties or none at all. No punitive damages will be sought in cases where violations are discovered through audits. Similar laws have already been adopted by 14 American states (see Makower, 1996).

The Netherlands: Early Dutch legislative responses included the 1970 Pollution of Surface Water Act and the 1972 Air Pollution Act which imposed strict local industrial standards. In the 1980s, the Dutch experienced new forms of pollution affecting groundwater and soil. Acid rain also emerged as a growing concern. Both the government and the general public agreed on the need for a proactive response to promote sustainable development. This resulted in the world's first comprehensive national environmental programme. The National Environmental Policy Plan (NEEP) has redefined the relationship between government and other sectors of society, including business and societal organisations such as environmental groups. In addition to specific emission reduction targets, one of the hallmarks of the NEEP is a system of voluntary agreements between government and eight industrial sectors (see Wallace, 1995).

As the above examples illustrate, most western industrialised countries have experienced a shift from 'command and control' environmental regulation in the 1970s towards more flexible approaches and a growing emphasis upon self-regulation. Many business interests continue to argue that rigid environmental regulation inhibits economic growth whereas voluntary measures stimulate growth. In order to define potential market-based alternatives, a number of businesses have begun to collaborate with environmental groups and other parts of the wider green movement.

The role of consumer and environmental groups

As mentioned earlier, the emergence of modern environmentalism in the 1960s has meant that consumer and environmental groups have gained growing prominence in the political process in western industrialised countries. Individual activists, local groups and both national and international organisations have played major roles as lobbyists for environment, health and safety legislation and regulation geared primarily towards the activities of business.

High profile consumer campaigns in the 1980s meant that by the end of the decade green consumerism was perceived by both businesses and campaign groups as a powerful new economic force. The rise of global environmental issues such as acid rain, the ozone layer, tropical rainforests and climate change have been accompanied by creative and confrontational campaigns against the policies and practices of governments and business. Consumer boycotts, direct action and other forms of market-driven pressure throughout the 1980s and into the 1990s combined to make many business leaders realise that their companies had to do more than merely comply with existing legislation.

Having identified the three main reasons why business has generally responded to environmental matters, we now review how the business response has evolved over the past three decades. We have divided the business response into three stages as follows:

- 1970s   the first stage – the pollution prevention agenda;

- 1980s   the second stage – the self-regulation agenda;

- 1990s   the third stage – the sustainability agenda.

As part of this review, we also offer examples of more recent factors which have affected the business response, particularly the Brundtland and Rio processes.

The first stage: pollution prevention

The first phase of global business environmental awareness began in the early 1970s when a number of leading companies in North America and western Europe initiated programmes aimed at reducing or preventing industrial pollution. The 3M Company was among the early pioneers with its Pollution Prevention Pays programme which had four related goals: "a better environment, conserved resources, improved technologies and reduced costs" (Royston, 1979, p 91).

Another early environmental innovator was the Anglo–Dutch conglomerate, the Royal Dutch Shell Group. An internal Shell management information brief dated September 1969 demonstrates that the company recognised early on the growing significance of the environment as a social responsibility issue for large corporations:

> The size and wide range of Group companies' activities make the problem of environmental conservation a matter of close concern. The efforts and resources devoted to its solution ...

are part of the pattern of doing business in a way that is responsible and socially acceptable. (Shell Briefing Service, 1969, p 8)

In order to formalise its commitment to environmental issues, Shell introduced its first official policy on environmental conservation in December 1969 (Box 3.1). The policy statement was prepared by the Shell Committee for Environmental Conservation in the central offices and approved by the managing directors. The policy requirements emphasised themes such as legal compliance, research and forward planning. Shell's policy statement restricted the need for external cooperation to governments, local authorities, other industries and professional groups.

Box 3.1: Original Shell environmental policy requirements

- Treat with care all materials that may cause pollution.

- Comply with all regulations framed by government to safeguard water, air and soil.

- Prevent nuisance by wastes, light and noise, and also provide additional protection where practical.

- Encourage, support and conduct research to minimize pollution.

- Make available to others new conservation techniques they develop.

- Cooperate and, when necessary, take the initiative with governments, local authorities, other industries and professional bodies in establishing practical measures that will reduce potential pollution arising from their own operations or the use of their products.

- Keep these authorities and the general public well-informed on what the company intends to do or is doing.

- Try to foresee future environmental requirements and provide for them in their long-term planning. (Royal Dutch Shell Group, 1969, p 1)

Figure 2: The three stages of business response to sustainable development

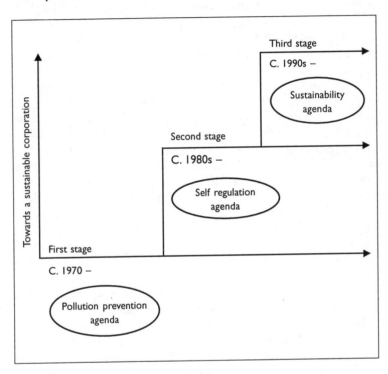

Early business responses to environmental management concerns were for the most part limited to large global corporations, particularly in the petroleum and chemicals sectors. Dialogue with environmental groups was largely restricted to site-level consultations about the potential environmental risks associated with new factories, mines, drilling operations, pipelines and refineries (Royston, 1979).

For much of the 1960s-1980s, however, the overall business response to environmental matters was largely defensive and confrontational. The American chemical industry is a case in point. The 1960s began with mild interest in environmental matters and an anti-regulatory stance. The industry insisted that it had the expertise to handle pollution issues itself. By the late 1960s, the industry asked governments for regulatory clarity but continued to promote self-regulation as the best option. In the 1970s, there was increased confrontation between the industry on the one hand and environmental activists and the US government on the other. Increased regulation was judged by industry to be too restrictive and unfair with companies preferring to invest in anti-pollution measures and clean-up activities (Hoffman, 1996b).

The confrontational stance described above was also a theme of one of the first business books about environmental management. In *The environmental factor: an approach for managers*, D.J. Davison (1978) argued that most people believe that business managers have an overriding responsibility to protect society as much as possible from potential environmental risks. Davison also observed that managers have a key role to play in resolving conflicts of interest within society about environmental matters. Underlying Davison's argument, however, was the belief that managers have the expertise to make appropriate environmental decisions and were best placed to challenge the "extreme propositions" of their opponents. This approach offered little hope of dialogue or partnership with environmental groups.

A more critical analysis of the business response to the environment is offered by environmental management specialist Michael Royston in his book *Pollution prevention pays*. Royston noted that business usually becomes accountable to society for its actions only after conflict begins. Furthermore Royston revealed that many business leaders see "a basic contradiction between the corporate objectives and the social responsibility of the enterprise"

(1979, p 41). The alternative offered by Royston linked managerial success to environmental analysis and action:

> [O]nly through proper concern about the environment and the avoidance of pollution [can] the modern manager ... meet the classical and basic criteria for successful management.... The modern manager realizes that in a complex world in which many different considerations guide his decisions, he is expected to get the best results from a system containing diverse and often seemingly contradictory factors.... It is only by viewing himself and his enterprise as part of the total system which includes the enterprise, the communities in which it is working and the common environment which links them both, that it will be possible for the manager acting on behalf of the enterprise to discharge his responsibilities to its various stakeholders. (pp 42-54)

Many of Royston's ideas were well ahead of the general business response to environmental matters at the time and indeed for much of the following decade. Aside from the groundbreaking work of relatively few pioneering companies, most managers in the 1970s and for much of the 1980s demonstrated only limited environmental concern. Royston's suggestion that business should embrace a holistic environmental strategy in collaboration with its many stakeholders represented little more than a distant dream.

The second stage: self-regulation

The need for a more proactive and integrated business response to environment and development issues was one of the key conclusions of *Our common future* (WCED, 1987) as we noted in Chapter one. The so-called Brundtland Report recognised that "the sources and causes of pollution are far more diffuse, complex and inter-related – and the effects of pollution more widespread, cumulative and chronic – than hitherto believed" (p 211). Brundtland called for a strengthening of measures to reduce, control and prevent industrial pollution and promoted the idea of sustainable industrial development. In addition to government leadership, Brundtland urged industry to "accept a broad sense of social responsibility and ensure an awareness of environmental considerations at all levels" (p 222). Brundtland also emphasised the need for company-wide and industry-wide policies related to resource and environmental management, incorporating compliance with all legal requirements.

To reiterate one of our key arguments in Chapter one, the Brundtland Report's call for sustainable development created:

> ... a new problem domain ... in which both environmentalists and business were clearly stakeholders. When the environmental crisis was reconceptualized so that the demands of development and the need for economic growth needed to be balanced with the need to expand or at least preserve ecological resources, the issue was defined as one of common concern to business and environmental groups alike. The concept of sustainable development reframed the issue to make collaboration among businesses, environmentalists and governments a vital aspect of problem resolution. (Westley and Vredenburg, 1991, pp 71-72)

Although many radical green groups dismissed sustainable development "as an ideological cover for business" (Westley and Vredenburg, 1991, p 72), many mainstream environmental groups began to insist that working with business was necessary to negotiate the new sustainable development agenda.

Business did not immediately embrace the Brundtland challenge. At the height of public environmental awareness in 1990, *The Economist*'s Frances Cairncross estimated that no more than 200 companies worldwide had made environmental performance one of their top concerns. Despite the emergence of new ideas such as sustainable development, most corporate responses were considered reactive and unsystematic. The result in most cases was "end-of-pipe" solutions which did not fundamentally change production processes and products. The lack of holistic strategies meant that corporate waste was often transferred from one medium to another (eg, water to land) (see Robins and Trisoglio, 1992).[1]

Around this time, however, growing numbers of global companies in various polluting industries began to develop a greater sense of corporate environmentalism. A number of industry associations ranging from chemicals and petroleum to automobiles and banking established self-regulating, corporate codes of conduct (see UNCTAD, 1996). Many of these codes and guidelines first appeared between the publication of *Our common future* (1987) and the adoption of the Earth Summit's Agenda 21 (UNCED, 1992), with a proliferation following Rio.

The International Chamber of Commerce (ICC) published an environmental statement as far back as 1965. However, it was not until the mid-1980s in the aftermath of the Union Carbide disaster in Bhopal, India that the first formal corporate codes of conduct emerged. Perhaps the first such code was the Canadian Chemical Producers' Association's (CCPA) Statement of Policy on Responsible Care, which was backed up by Guiding Principles and six codes of environmental management. The European Chemical Industry Council (CEFIC) adopted its own version of Responsible Care in 1987 while in 1989 the UK Chemical Industries Association followed suit.[2]

The Exxon Valdez disaster of 1989 led to the formation in the USA later that year of the Coalition for Environmentally Responsible Economies (CERES) and the adoption of a voluntary code of conduct known as the Valdez Principles (later known as the CERES Principles). CERES is a membership organisation that includes representatives of national environmental organisations, social investment leaders, public interest groups and unions. The CERES Principles established an environmental ethic with criteria by which investors and others could assess the environmental performance of companies. Companies are invited to endorse the principles as a voluntary code of conduct.

The petroleum industry then responded with a number of self-regulating alternatives. In 1990, the American Petroleum Institute (API) launched its Environmental Mission and Guiding Principles, and the UK's Institute of Petroleum followed suit in 1992 with its Model of Safe Practice in the Petroleum Industry. Also in 1992, the API introduced Strategies for Today's Environmental Partnership, an umbrella programme (based upon the chemical industry's Responsible Care), encompassing industry-sponsored environmental initiatives and individual company programmes.

During the 1989-92 period, Shell International played an important role, first in the development of the ICC's Business Charter on Sustainable Development which was launched in 1991, and then in the ICC's participation in the Rio Conference. Agenda 21 contains no fewer than 32 provisions "pertaining specifically to transnational corporations (TNCs) or of direct relevance to TNC operations" although very few require specific TNC commitments on environmental matters (see UNCTAD, 1996, p 2). UNCTAD, nevertheless, considers Agenda 21 to be "an appropriate benchmark against which to evaluate ... progress in achieving global goals set for environmental improvements." Unlike voluntary industry or NGO codes, Agenda 21 was adopted by governments through a democratic and participatory process which included major group representation from both business and NGO communities.

Many of the voluntary, industry-association codes have, however, stimulated considerable environmental awareness and action within various companies and industry sectors. The major criticism of these codes is that there has been almost no independent assessment of implementation to date. The UK Chemical Industry Association's initial three-year report on Responsible Care (1990-93) acknowledged that the programme "was not functioning in accordance with its aims" with only 57 per cent of firms submitting returns for all three years (see Welford, 1995, pp 36-37). The association's 1996 report *The UK indicators of performance 1990-95* reveals a marked increase in the total number of returns, from 252 in 1990 to 392 in 1995. Nevertheless, Welford's assertion that many chemical companies "treat Responsible Care as a smokescreen" (p 37) cannot be refuted without independent, third-party evaluation of site-level implementation.

With the exception of CERES which includes environmental groups as members, most environmentalists have been highly critical of voluntary codes. Whereas CERES Principles' signatories must agree to undertake an annual self-evaluation of progress in implementing principles, the ICC does not require signatories to the Business Charter on Sustainable Development to actually implement the charter's principles. On the other hand, CERES' signatories also must agree to complete an externally created CERES report for public dissemination.

Despite its good intentions, even CERES has recently faced criticism. Andrew Hoffman argues that successive redrafts of the CERES Principles reveal "a merger of environmental and business interests" and that this has "lead many environmentalists to think that the principles have been diluted to insignificance" (1996a, p 63). He nevertheless acknowledges that "the changing landscape of corporate environmentalism bears CERES's mark" (p 61). As the first independent mechanism for evaluating corporate environmental performance, it could be argued that CERES was also a catalyst for much of the current impetus for third-party certification schemes which evaluate environmental performance standards, such as the Marine Stewardship Council (see Chapter five), or environmental management systems such as ISO 14,001 and the EU's Eco-Management and Audit Scheme (EMAS, Box 3.2).

A recent UNCTAD study on corporate environmental reporting and voluntary codes reveals that, "by far the strongest trend is towards industry- or firm-set targets and standards ... [with] a minority push for externally-set targets, external auditing and public reporting" (1996, p 38).

The UNCTAD study also notes that "a great deal of emphasis ... is on improvements in relative corporate performance rather than against absolute thresholds." The study also raises questions about the overall focus on adherence to approaches and standards rather than "the actual environmental impact of [company] operations" (pp 86-87).

Of crucial importance, UNCTAD concludes, is the need for "environmental improvements to be measured against externally defined benchmarks of sustainable environmental practice, such as Agenda 21" (p 87). Furthermore, UNCTAD sees "a major role for national regulation and international governance in setting frameworks for corporate environmental activity, and assessment and monitoring, to ensure that industry moves toward global sustainable development" (p 87).

Quite apart from whether business complies with state regulation or adopts voluntary codes of conduct, many business leaders still have an antagonistic attitude towards environmental groups. This remains a major impediment, which prevents many businesses from moving to the third stage of the business response to sustainable development – the sustainability agenda. Kunio Yonezawa of the Japanese Global Guardian Trust (GGT) believes in confronting environmental groups and projecting a corporate rendition of sustainable development:

> Now that the world's communist movement has gone, I think the only one circulating around the world is the extremist environmental movement of Greenpeace and the like. It's a world political party which has encroached into the political core of Anglo-Saxon-led countries like the UK, Australia, etc. (in Rowell, 1996, p 368)

Such extremist demonisation of greens, so reminiscent of the reactions of business leaders to the protests of the 1960s and 1970s, is not restricted to the head of the GGT. The GGT is one example of the many green business networks which have proliferated in the 1990s.

Many of these new organisations have played important roles in promoting corporate environmental responsibility, yet most are linked to existing industry or trade associations whose purpose is to defend member company interests. Such industry associations have tended to limit dialogue and collaboration to member companies and government agencies. Environmental groups and other NGOs (eg, trade unions) have been traditionally seen as the enemy and in many cases still are as Yonezawa's comments above illustrate.

Many environmentalists accuse such organisations, rightly or wrongly, of greenwashing – a "massive advertising and publicity effort, whose costs to industry have been estimated at about a billion dollars a year" (Helvarg, 1996, p 14). Specialist marketing and public relations companies such as Burson-Marsteller, the world's largest, are hired by businesses and trade associations to promote industry-backed "third-party advocacy" organisations, think tanks, research institutes and "synthetic grassroots" groups which cannot always be taken at face value. For their part, many green business groups insist that they have attempted to redefine the interests of their member companies and have used peer pressure to promote best environmental practice. As mentioned above, industry standards for self-regulation have been widely promoted. Many environmental groups, nevertheless, remain sceptical about the motives of green business groups and continue to see them as mechanisms which "block, get around and stall environmental legislation" (see SustainAbility and Tomorrow, 1994).

Box 3.2: The Eco-Management and Audit Scheme

The Eco-Management and Audit Scheme (EMAS) was established in June 1993 and invited voluntary participation by companies in the industrial sector. EMAS became open to company participation in April 1995. EMAS consists of 21 articles and 5 annexes. Article 1 of the regulation describes it as a:

"Community scheme allowing voluntary participation by companies performing industrial activities ... established for the evaluation and improvement of the environmental performance of industrial activities and the provision of relevant information to the public.... The objective of the scheme shall be to promote continuous improvements in the environmental performance of industrial activities."

Article 3 specifies how EMAS must be implemented. In order for an industrial site to be registered under the scheme, the company must:

- adopt a company environmental policy which must include commitments aimed at the reasonable continuous improvement of environmental performance;

- conduct an environmental review of the site seeking registration;

- introduce, in light of the results from the review, an environmental management system applicable to all activities at the site;

- set objectives aimed at continuous improvement of environmental performance in light of the audit findings;

- prepare an environmental statement specific to each site audited;

- have the environmental policy, programme, management system, review or audit procedure and environmental statement(s) independently examined to verify that they meet the requirements of the regulation;

- send the validated statement to the competent body of the member state where the site is located.... Once the competent body is satisfied that the site meets all the requirements of the regulation it will register the site. After registration the company must disseminate the environmental statement as appropriate to the public of the state where the site is located. (Source: Welford, 1996a, pp 68-71)

Not all businesses have embraced environmental issues purely as a public relations exercise. Many have developed more proactive policies and programmes, with the more adventurous ones establishing partnerships with environmental groups. The problem, however, is that many businesses still only support sustainable development on the basis of self-interest:

> To a corporate economist sustainable development means development that will allow his company to remain in business forever. To an environmentalist it is development that will allow the earth to stay in business forever. (Dowie, 1995a, p 235)

Such dichotomies have led Paul Hawken to proclaim that:

> ... there is still a yawning gulf between the kind of green environmentalism that business wants to promote – one that justifies growth and expansionary use of resources – and the kind that actually deals with core issues of carrying capacity, drawdown, biotic impoverishment, and the extinction of species. Business, despite its newly found good intentions with respect to the environment, has hardly changed at all. (1994, pp 30-31)

It has been more than 25 years since pioneering companies first adopted formal environmental policies. In the intervening years, leading edge companies and industries have embraced beyond compliance, self-regulating strategies. Environmental groups and other business critics remind us that the health of the planet continues to deteriorate and that business remains culpable. If the societies and communities of the Earth are to move towards sustainability, then business must respond differently.

Box 3.3: Costs and benefits of the business response

The reasons why business has adopted progressive rhetoric on environmental and social issues are varied but include factors of competitive environmental or ethical advantage. The argument is that "environmental polices ... impose new costs and generate new opportunities for industry" (Welford, 1995, p 11) and that trusting relationships with all stakeholders and a reputation for having a good environmental record gives a competitive advantage in the long term.

There are potential increased costs for above-compliance policies and programmes. Time spent on above-compliance environmental management is time taken from other profit-related activities such as marketing, product development and sales. There are real costs in administration and additional staffing. There is also the potential for increases in supplier prices due to environmental requirements, which can reduce profit margins if such costs cannot be passed on to consumers. Companies with strict environmental procurement policies may also suffer supply-chain rigidity and miss the opportunity of cheaper supplies. A fifth cost is the potential conflict between a product's environmental integrity and a product's performance. There is also the issue of unsympathetic scrutiny generated by adopting a higher profile on environmental issues.

Above-compliance benefits concern marketing potential, employee motivation, recruitment performance, risk management, supply-chain performance, waste cost reductions and efficiency savings. First, greener products can maintain product differentiation and an enhanced corporate image may promote overall sales (Roddick, 1991).

Product and company environmental credentials also have implications for risk management. Many argue that boycotts, direct action and general public distaste can be avoided if issues are incorporated into business practice (Hutchinson, 1995). Such phenomena affect product sales and may also affect share value (White, 1995). Ethical investment has been documented as a growing feature of the financial markets with companies' environmental performance and policies coming under increasing scrutiny. Some studies have found that staff motivation can be beneficially affected by a good environmental record (Schmidheiny, 1992). Finally it has been suggested that environmental assessments of supply chains can lead to improved communication and product assessment, conferring greater reliability and performance from suppliers (Hill in Taylor et al, 1994).

Towards the third stage: the sustainability agenda

As we approach the new millennium, what then are the prospects for business to move to the third stage and embrace a more ambitious agenda based upon sustainability? Within a globalised market economy, the starting point for even environmentally responsible business leaders remains one of enlightened self-interest. This helps to explain why environmental management is increasingly being seen as a strategic tool for gaining competitive advantage or merely remaining competitive in a fast-changing global marketplace. Leading companies have started to move towards a more strategic response to sustainable development which involves both costs and benefits (Box 3.3). Sangeeta Bhargava and Richard Welford describe the post-Rio period as:

> the period of strategic action.... Theories of corporate strategy are ... gradually being modi-fied to incorporate environmental problems and concerns. However, there is still relatively little debate over whether a traditional corporate strategic planning approach ... with all its financial and short-term constraints ... can actually lead us towards sustainable development. (1996, pp 14-15)

A growing number of radical business thinkers agree that business still has a long way to go before we can begin to speak about sustainable business organisations and sustainable industrial processes. Basic tensions between economics and ecology remain.

If we are serious about meeting the needs of the present without compromising the future, we believe that the business response to sustainable development must begin to move to the third stage. This means that business must work together with other sectors to build a radically new sustainability agenda which encompasses environmental protection, global equity and social justice:

> Embracing the concept of "sustainable devel-opment" is not simply an acceptance of an semantic shift from the words of "environmental protection". It is a fundamental rethinking of how our world works. It strikes at the heart of our economic and political systems and decision-

making. Making the environment a forethought not an afterthought is a radical concept. Our fundamental definition of development must [also] change. It can no longer be regarded as merely a problem of modernizing traditional societies.... It has to recognize local circumstances ... the contribution of traditional institutions and knowledge.... It has to concern itself with equity.... It has to be inherently geared toward sustainability. (see Elkington, 1996, p 3)

The major obstacle, according to Fritjof Capra and Gunter Pauli (1995), is that the quantitative and competitive aspects of business fly in the face of the qualitative and cooperative dimensions of ecology. In addition to a massive reduction in the use of raw materials, they argue that business must integrate moral, ethical and environmental issues into corporate strategy. In order to move business thinking in this new direction, Hawken proposes a fresh approach:

... a path that restores the natural communities on earth but [which] uses many of the historically effective organisational and market techniques of free enterprise.... Business must judge its goals and behaviour, not from inherited definitions of the corporate culture, but from the perspective of the world and society beyond its self-referential borders. (1994, p 9)

Such a reformulated business perspective is at the heart of *Engaging stakeholders*, a 1996 study by SustainAbility, the New Economics Foundation and the United Nations Environment Programme. Many of its key findings suggest that some of Hawken's ideas are beginning to enter the world of business thinking and practice:

- new frameworks to evaluate progress against the emerging sustainability agenda are needed;

- audiences for corporate environmental reports are broadening;

- stakeholders are increasingly using environmental reports to monitor and rank companies;

- growing pressure for mandatory, as opposed to voluntary, reporting;

- new forms of stakeholder engagement are required.

Linked to the trends outlined above, Richard Welford and David Jones (1996) suggest a wide range of sustainability principles and indicators which may provide the basis for a new business paradigm – integrating corporate social responsibility and sustainable development (see Box 3.4).

Few, if any, current businesses already meet Welford and Jones's ambitious agenda. The dominant economic paradigm of market-based capitalism – either the Anglo-American short-term shareholder model or the German long-term stakeholder model – tends to penalise or to discourage companies who may wish to adopt such a radical green agenda. Hawken, nevertheless, insists that an ecology of commerce is both necessary and possible:

> [W]e have to find an ecological, imaginative, and participative means to lessen our impact. We have to be able to imagine a life where having less is truly more satisfying, more interesting, and of course, more secure.... [W]e have to look at how our present economic system consistently rewards short-term exploitation while penalising long-term restoration.... Ecological restoration can probably be carried out more naturally and surely by smaller enterprises than by larger, unwieldy corporations. (1994, p 210)

Herein lies a major dilemma for business leaders who wish to promote sustainability in their organisations. Many global corporations are already in the process of devolving considerable responsibility for environmental and social policy to smaller business units. However, if sustainability implies the ultimate demise of large "unwieldy corporations" as Hawken suggests, then the road ahead will likely continue to be as conflict-laden and difficult as the road business has already travelled over the past three decades in its efforts to respond to environmental challenges.

Box 3.4: Agenda for change

General principles
- accountability
- transparency/openness
- education/learning

Equity
- empowerment of all stakeholders
- participation
- trading practices

Futurity
- precaution
- phase out use of non-renewable resources

Biodiversity and animal protection
- habitat and species conservation
- animal testing

Human rights
- employment policies and equal opportunities
- quality of working life
- women's empowerment and participation
- minority group empowerment and participation
- protection of indigenous peoples and land rights

Local action and scale
- community linkage
- appropriate scale
- partnership and cooperation strategies
- appropriate location

Life cycle impacts
- product stewardship
- life-cycle analysis
- product design
- product durability
- product justifiability

Source: Welford and Jones, 1996, pp 247-53.

A way forward

Although the focus of this book is on the emerging sense of cooperation and understanding between business and environmental groups, it would be cavalier to suggest that there is a broadly-based consensus in the business community either on the need for more sustainable practice or on the validity of environmental and social groups as key stakeholders and potential partners. Even ecologically aware companies recognise just how difficult it is for business to promote sustainability. For example, The Body Shop questions "the notion that any business can be environmentally friendly.... This is just not possible. All businesses involve some damage" (in Rowell, 1996, p 125).

Despite the considerable achievements of comparatively small numbers of companies, overall corporate enthusiasm for positive action on environmental and ethical issues remains limited in its intensity and scope. Many business leaders reject the idea that the social and environmental responsibilities of business must go beyond legal compliance. Many hold the view that extending a company's involvement beyond its legal obligations only serves to blur objectives and impede its ability to deliver profits.

If corporations do indeed rule the world, as Korten (1995) asserts, then which way forward? In the absence of a sudden collapse of capitalism, we will probably have to be satisfied with incremental change along the road to a more sustainable future. Greater numbers of businesses will need to change the way they operate and reduce their environmental impacts – and by introducing less damaging alternatives, in relative terms, actually help the environment. Minimising the ecological footprint of business may be a significant part of the incremental change process, but "seeing the green light" is not enough. Global corporate power needs to be more effectively controlled through enhanced state regulation and a stronger process of global governance. We also believe that moral, ethical and environmental issues need to become more fully integrated into core business practice. Those businesses which adopt new forms of stakeholder engagement will gain ascendancy in the next millennium. By engaging environmentalists in genuine partnership relationships, business people can begin to work towards a more ambitious sustainability agenda. By accepting the need for independent, third-party verification of corporate environmental

and social performance, business will be helping to build the new
frameworks needed to monitor, evaluate and reward progress
towards sustainability. In the following chapter, we illustrate how
business–environmental group collaboration in the wood products
sector has begun to find just such a way forward.

Notes

[1] A study by the International Institute for Sustainable Development
found that most large companies in the UK had allocated specific
responsibility for environmental protection.   However, most had
concentrated on "specific aspects of pollution control or waste reduction
rather than a more holistic approach." The report criticised environmental statements in UK company annual reports as "vague statements of
intent" which tended to be "selective" and rarely included "any hard
data" (IISD, 1992, pp 92-93).

[2] The main difference between the Canadian and European approaches is
that the former requires members to fulfil various reporting
requirements, while the latter only encourages annual reporting.

four

Breaking the log jam: environmental group partnerships with the timber trade[1]

> *Acting independently we don't stand a hope in hell's chance of influencing anything. We might just stand a chance if we all work together on it.... I think that we all share the same view that it is an extremely important issue and is not one that will go away if we simply turn our back on it and say we are going to ignore this.* (Mike Inchley, Do It All, UK)

> *You don't get very far when you do it on your own.... You can get very far when you do it together.* (Saskia Ozinga, Milieudefensie, The Netherlands)

Politicians talk, businesses profit, researchers research, environmentalists campaign – yet the search for solutions continues. A recent study estimated the rate of tropical forest loss at 170,000 square kilometres per annum (FAO in Rietbergen, 1993) and temperate old growth forests have also come under increasing pressure. In a recent study on the state of the world's forests Dudley et al claims:

> At the present time the world's forests face two potentially devastating threats: a loss of total area of forest in large parts of the tropical and subtropical world, and a rapid decline in the

quality of forest in much of the temperate and boreal regions. (1995, p 3)

Forests cover a large part of the Earth's surface and provide the planet with a number of essential services. Forests provide essential climatic functions and can either alleviate or contribute to global warming, depending on human impact. Forests are also incredibly species-rich, with rainforests purported to contain between 50 and 90 per cent of the world's creatures (Myers, 1992). Like pages torn out of a book before they are read, plants which could be crucial for crop development and medical research are being destroyed as we write.

Some argue that this human-perpetuated genocide of forest animals and plants is morally wrong. What is certainly wrong is the destruction of forest peoples' lands and way of life. If strangers turned up in our garden, cut down our trees and carted them off to another country, we would turn to the law to prosecute the thieves and to our insurance company to cover the costs of replanting. For most forest peoples of the world there is no insurance and no legal protection and their 'gardens' are violated week in and week out by logging companies supplying our demand for wood products.

So little has been done. Despite numerous international meetings, a set of global forest principles, a wealth of public concern and committed environmental activists, the forests continue to burn. Despite this, some people are beginning to embrace the idea of partnership, and are providing new hope for the world's forests and their peoples. In the UK, USA, The Netherlands and other western industrial countries, people in environmental groups and the timber trade are coming together in the fight to save the world's forests. What follows is an analysis of these collaborations – their origins, operation, successes, failures and futures. The main case study is the WWF-UK 1995 Group of wood-product suppliers and retailers in the UK. What started as a small bright idea in 1991 has now grown into a group worth £2.3 billion per annum in wood products and has come to be known as "one of the widest reaching environmental initiatives by a charity of all time" (Bendell and Sullivan, 1996, p 10).

The business of forests

Forests are big business. In 1990 the global timber harvest was estimated at 3.43 billion cubic metres, up from 2.93 billion in 1980 (Viana et al, 1996). With a total value over a trillion dollars per annum the timber trade is the basis of many livelihoods, from lumberjacks in North America and Scandinavia to check-out staff in do-it-yourself (DIY) stores. The DIY or home-improvement sector in the UK alone is worth almost £9 billion a year.[2]

The timber trade is deemed to bear a large proportion of the guilt for forest destruction and degradation by some commentators while others claim that its effects are minimal in relation to activities such as mining, shifting agriculture, smelting, cattle ranching and fuelwood collection. The effects of logging on the world's forests are, however, quite different in tropical and non-tropical forests.

The effects of the timber trade on tropical deforestation is hotly disputed. Frank Vanclay (1993) has determined that only four per cent of the total timber production is exported to the international timber trade while Robert Repetto and Malcolm Gillis (1988) have argued that commercial logging is the top agent of deforestation. Vanclay's analysis ignored some of the indirect effects of logging.[3] First, the volume of timber produced is far less than the area devastated in its logging, due to the damaging effects on the remaining trees by the removal of felled timber. Second, it is often only the foreign or government investors that can afford to construct roads into the forests, so that without the logging industry vast areas of forest would remain inaccessible to farmers and other agents of deforestation.[4] It is therefore unsurprising that Barbier et al (1994) found a positive correlation between industrial round-wood production and forest clearance in the tropics for the period 1980-85.

The importance of the timber trade for temperate and boreal forests is even more clear cut. Old growth, or ancient, forests in North America, northern and central Europe are being degraded by logging activity (Dudley et al, 1995). In these areas it is not conversion to non-forest land use that is the major problem but a simplification of the ecosystem into what are essentially timber factories. With increasing liberalisation in the ex-Soviet European economies, the threat of intensive exploitation of some of the oldest forests in the northern hemisphere continues to grow.

Initial responses from environmental groups

Partnership with foresters and the wood product industry has not always been a strategy for environmental groups. It was not until the late 1980s that deforestation became a business issue and not until the early 1990s that WWF-UK forest campaigners actively sought partners in the timber trade. Before then, WWF-UK, FoE-UK[5] and various Rainforest Action Groups (RAGs; see Box 4.1) pursued very different strategies in their anti-deforestation campaigns.

At the international level, FoE-UK initially targeted the International Tropical Timber Organisation (ITTO) through its official observer status at ITTO meetings.[6] A joint organisation of producer and consumer countries, ITTO differs from other commodity agreements in that its remit includes support for reforestation and policies on national timber utilisation and conservation (see Adams, 1990). After initial optimism in the 1980s FoE-UK has tended to argue in recent years that ITTO has been complacent about tropical deforestation and has avoided challenging the destructive activities of the timber industry.[7]

In addition to its international policy work FoE-UK was the first British environmental group to recognise the potential for consumer-related campaigns. FoE-UK had hundreds of thousands of members who were willing to do more than give money to FoE-UK for them to lobby at international conferences. In 1985, FoE-UK launched its Rainforest Campaign which included a consumer boycott of retailers that were selling products made from tropical timber sourced from clearcuts or non-replacement selective logging. One of FoE-UK's campaign objectives was to motivate UK and EC timber traders to adopt a code of conduct "under which they would only stock timber from concessions ... [with] a government-approved management plan which stipulates post-logging management" (Adams, 1990, p 194). Other demands included: not stocking wood from virgin forest-area plantations; labelling all wood products by country and concession of origin; and agreeing to donate one per cent of profits to a promotional fund for sustainable forest management. According to FoE-UK's forest campaigner at the time, the organisation was attempting "to find positive ways in which ... the public ... could respond to the global forest crisis in ways other than ... [funding the] limited project work by groups such as WWF." However, direct actions against the retailers of wood products were not organised by FoE-UK at this time.

The WWF-International approach during the 1985-88 period shared some common ground with FoE-UK at the international policy level. WWF-International had worked on a number of specific forest conservation projects since the 1970s.[8] WWF-International's first Forest Conservation Officer was hired in 1985 to develop tropical forest policy campaigns, principally focused on the ITTO and Tropical Forestry Action Plan (TFAP). He co-ordinated a group of six WWF campaigners from the UK, the USA, Australia, Denmark and Japan to target these and other relevant international institutions.

WWF-International's forest campaigning work was based upon a series of policy papers on tropical forest conservation. Its position was that sustainable forest management practices were needed in order to avoid future bans and boycotts. During the 1985-87 period, WWF-UK also helped fund the initial FoE-UK consumer campaign and later provided them with financial assistance for publications such as the *Good wood guide* (1988) which identified supplies of well-managed or reclaimed local timbers.

Box 4.1: Rainforest Action Groups

There are over 200 local rainforest action groups in North America, Europe and Australia, some informally affiliated with the Rainforest Action Network. However, Australian activist John Seed was the key catalyst. For Seed, political change comes through the development of locally-based radical action groups. During the late 1980s and early 1990s, Seed spent several months a year on the road. He talked to environment or student groups, encouraging them to form Rainforest Action Groups (RAGs). The early RAGs in Australia organised emotional protests, blocking ships with timber imports. RAGs later mobilised trade unions. The Victoria branch of the Building Workers Industrial Union, which covered all building projects in Melbourne, refused to use rainforest timber. British activist George Marshall brought the Australian experience to the UK in early 1991. Rainforest Action Groups in the UK have been categorised as "radical, dark green" groups whose stance encompasses concern with both the causes and effects of environmental destruction (*Green Magazine*, 1993).

Although not at the top of their campaign agendas, in the mid to late 1980s UK-based environmental groups were beginning to challenge retailers about the wood materials they were selling and their forests of origin: the seeds of deforestation as an economic and not just political issue were being planted.

Initial responses from business

The various rainforest campaigning activities of environmental groups and related media coverage had started to become a business issue. Increasing customer awareness of ethical and environmental issues and of deforestation in particular meant that a number of retailers began to consider the need to identify the sources of their wood and wood products.

The DIY retailer B&Q was one of the first to look at the timber sourcing issue. In early 1990, marketing director Bill Whiting was asked by *The Sunday Times* how much tropical timber his company imported and of what species (see Jetter, 1995). He found that much of this information was not readily available. Following some initial research on B&Q's tropical timber sources, and after the matter was discussed extensively in board meetings, the company decided to appoint an environmental coordinator – Dr Alan Knight. One of the first things Knight did was to contact UK forest campaigners with WWF, FoE and RAGs, as well as key people involved with the timber trade including suppliers. This was to be the first step in a comprehensive programme of wood sourcing research and analysis for the company.

While B&Q were still at the early stages of wood-product sourcing, Texas Homecare was claiming their wood products came from "sustainable" sources and another DIY's hardwood doors were supposedly not being sourced from "endangered areas". While such environmentally friendly claims were popular at the time, most could not be substantiated. Was this just greenwash? Were the DIY retailers taking to heart the problems with their trade in products from badly-managed forests? Even if they were, the NGOs felt a need to 'up the stakes' to bring about the necessary changes.

Box 4.2: B&Q

The first B&Q self-service DIY store opened in Southampton in 1969. B&Q is the largest UK DIY chain, in turnover, £1,464 million sales, in profits, £97 million, and in number of stores, 283 (February 1997). It has positioned itself at the centre of the DIY market, offering a wide range of products. The average size of its supercentre stores is 40,000 square feet, while its 27 warehouse stores range from 100,000-150,000 square feet. The expansion into warehouse stores is part of B&Q's strategy to increase its share of the hard end of the market (hardware, tools and construction products). Within Europe, it is amongst the top four DIY retailers. B&Q is a subsidiary of the Kingfisher Group. The total Kingfisher workforce is more than 40,000, of which more than 18,000 are employed by B&Q. The group was formed in the years following the UK management buyout of the Woolworth chain from the US parent in 1982. When 1995 results were announced in March 1996, B&Q's profits had slumped by a third from the previous year. By early 1997, B&Q's profits had rebounded with an increase of 75 per cent.

Upping the stakes – direct action against the DIYs

> The Big Six DIY superstores are major outlets of tropical timber products. As it is very difficult to distinguish between rainforest timber and wood from other areas, shoppers should boycott all timber products from these stores. (FoE-UK Press Release, 8 November 1991)

Beginning in 1991, various RAGs, FoE-UK groups, and later Earth First! groups started to take direct action against wood-product retailers. These groups organised mock chainsaw massacres outside DIY and furniture stores with protesters dressed as loggers graphically depicting the destruction of the world's rainforests. Protesters leafleted customers and delivered anti-tropical timber pledges to store managers. The most extreme protests included setting off smoke bombs inside DIY stores.

The first protests were coordinated by the London RAG. From April 1991, RAG demonstrations began to target B&Q throughout the country.[9] The RAG message was that people should "not buy tropical timber from B&Q until it can prove that it is selling timber that does not damage rainforests or the livelihoods of tribal people." Other groups were also mobilised. On 8 June, the National Liaison Committee of Diocesan Justice and Peace Groups submitted a petition to B&Q urging the company "to cease the import of tropical timbers unless these can be guaranteed to be from sustainable resources." B&Q responded to the protests by explaining the company's emerging timber policy and its preliminary discussions with WWF-UK on sourcing. According to B&Q, "agreement was not reached' yet "a useful and constructive dialogue took place" (see Knight, 1992, p 15).

RAG activists eventually reached a point where there were not enough rainforest groups to target other companies and other parts of the country. The RAG coordinator, George Marshall, contacted various local FoE groups in an effort to bring them on board. Concerned about the impact of the RAG protests on its own forest campaign, FoE-UK's office in London wrote to local FoE groups asking them to wait for its direct action campaign which was planned for the autumn of 1991.[10]

The Day of Action on 9 November mobilised local FoE groups throughout the UK to target over 100 branches of six leading DIY retailers to "Stop the Chainstore Massacre". In one weekend there were 25-30 demonstrations outside B&Q stores alone. The other DIYs were also heavily targeted (FoE-UK, 1991a). Subsequently, on 11 December, FoE-UK claimed in a press release that its protests had prompted dramatic policy developments in the DIY chains B&Q, Texas and Homebase. They reported that the three DIY retailers "have announced their intention to stop selling environmentally damaging tropical rainforest timber" (FoE-UK, 1991b).

B&Q's version of the encounter with FoE-UK differs. B&Q argued that it had attempted "to establish a constructive dialogue with FoE to discuss their concerns" but that the organisation was unwilling to listen to B&Q's position (Knight, 1992, p 15). B&Q was also concerned that FoE-UK had not mentioned in its press release that B&Q's timber sourcing policy had been adopted by the B&Q board two months before the local FoE protests began.[11] Alan Knight insists that:

> *B&Q was not seriously affected by the FoE campaign since many local groups chose not to 'do' B&Q after our managers explained our policies. Some groups actually expressed embar-*

> *rassment about not knowing the extent of our policies. They focused the attention on our competitors and this probably lead to [dialogue between the other DIYs and WWF].*

No matter the interpretation of the story, there is no doubt that the anti-DIY demonstrations proved to be highly successful and garnered considerable media and public attention. Customers began to write letters to the retailers and to confront store managers and employees with tough questions about timber sourcing. For the most part, the companies took both the protests and customer letters very seriously. In an effort to maintain pressure on the DIY retailers, demonstrations continued throughout 1992 and into 1993. RAG activist, George Marshall, illustrates how such protests also influence mainstream environmental groups and in turn their potential to work with business:

> *Strategically one of the reasons for setting up this kind of grassroots thing was actually to lobby for change within NGOs as well. My experience has certainly been that [the larger] organisations can actually become a little bit more radicalised, a little bit stronger if there's something out there.... Their concern is to be reasonable but if what's happening out there is thoroughly unreasonable, it gives them a lot more space to be reasonable in.*

The WWF-UK 1995 Group

> WWF ... believes that partnership is always preferable to confrontation. Many other NGOs do not agree.... Now is the time to prove that conservationists and industry can work together constructively.... We stand at a crossroads in our relationship between NGOs, the public and business, and this is the time for us to attempt to move forward in a spirit of cooperation. (WWF-International, 1991)

In 1991, WWF-UK presented itself to the timber trade as the reasonable option. While some environmentalists were demonstrating in DIY car parks and smoke bombing their stores, smartly dressed WWF-UK activists were willing to enter their boardrooms and talk business. The trade was being presented with a way forward – one which was to prove irresistible.

The target

In 1989 WWF-International challenged the international community to respond to the tropical rainforest crisis by establishing the end of 1995 as its target date for the world's tropical timber trade to be based on sustainable timber supplies. Only in May 1991 did ITTO respond with its Year 2000 Target for sustainable forest management.[12] A later official decision committed "ITTO members to progress towards achieving sustainable management of tropical forests and trade in tropical forest timber from sustainably-managed sources by the year 2000." With a lack of commitment and progress being observed at the international policy level, in 1990 WWF-UK decided to go it alone. The international office's 1995 target was used to launch a campaign in 1990 to ensure that all tropical wood and wood products traded in the UK would come from well-managed forests by the end of 1995.[13]

While most companies and indeed WWF-UK felt that the 1995 target was an extremely ambitious one, from the point of view of getting people motivated to take action it was considered to be the best option. From a business point of view, the 8 to 10-year timescale of the ITTO target was simply not compatible with their shorter term planning cycles. In reflecting on the early stages of the process, Francis Sullivan of WWF-UK noted that "although we had committed ourselves to a target date, we still didn't know how it was going to be done." WWF-UK wanted to get the ball rolling by getting "members of the ... wood-product trade [to] commit to the principle of taking responsibility for their supply chains and to purchase only products from well-managed forests" (1996, p 4). No one knew the financial or logistical implications of the policy at the outset and WWF-UK felt implementation details could be worked out during the course of policy implementation.

In addition, the WWF-UK commitment had wider application than that of ITTO. WWF-UK had developed a changed understanding of the issue away from a tropical rainforest focus towards all aspects of the world's timber trade. This shift coincided with greater public awareness about clear-cut logging in the old-growth forests of British Columbia, which for many campaigners had become 'the Brazil of the North'.[14]

Initially, WWF-UK attempted to collaborate with the UK Timber Trade Federation's (TTF) Forests Forever Campaign. Most of the UK trade in timber products is controlled by TTF members. WWF-UK hoped that a signed accord would get the timber trade moving on the forest issue. WWF-UK eventually realised that TTF members were not achieving what had been agreed. WWF-UK decided that it could not have its name used on "meaningless policies" and eventually withdrew from the TTF accord.

As a result of their earlier failure to mobilise the timber trade, WWF-UK's forest team became convinced that companies needed a public face in order to respond. Timber companies such as Meyer International, the largest UK timber importer, do not interface with the end users of their products. Their immediate customers tend to be wholesalers rather than individuals. WWF-UK surmised that companies which had day-to-day contact with consumers would be more likely to respond to environmental education and pressure. Accordingly, WWF-UK launched a series of annual forest seminars for wood-product retailers and suppliers in late 1990.

WWF's attempts to bring UK timber retailers, suppliers and traders on board coincided with a period of inertia and protracted negotiations at the UN level on a global forest agreement or convention. WWF-UK's precise target and specific focus on the UK market contrasted starkly with the Forest Principles document agreed at the Rio Conference in June 1992: "A non-legally binding authoritative statement of principles for a global consensus on the management, conservation and sustainable development of all types of forests" (see Chapter one). As WWF-UK's Francis Sullivan argued, "You can't just sit back and wait for governments to agree, because this could take forever."[15] WWF-UK felt certain it was right to take matters into their own hands and look to work with people and organisations who could get things done.

Figure 3: Environmental policy pressures on the wood product retailers

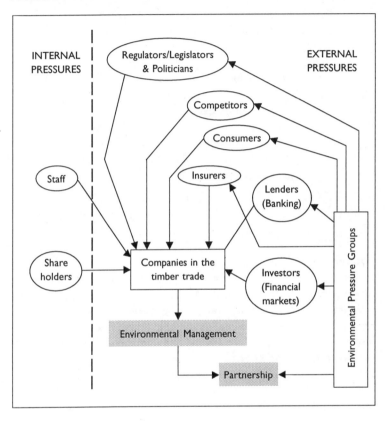

Forming a group

> *Increasingly we will see the 1995 Group of major retailers with massive clout with governments, consumers, shareholders, suppliers, and educating people as well, which I'd love to say we could have predicted back in 1991, but it wouldn't be true. This whole thing has come together by chance, and we've had to take lots of decisions ... the path has bifurcated at various places and I think that we've been fortunate that many times we've just happened to be able to take the right turn and the Group's achievement is the result.*
> (Francis Sullivan, WWF-UK)

Following the second WWF-UK forest seminar in December 1991 (entitled 'Forests are your business'), ten companies committed themselves to reaching the WWF-UK 1995 target and launched the 1995 Club as it was then called. The cumulative effects of different forms of environmental campaigning seemed to have firmly taken root in the private sector. The chainstore massacre demonstrations and resulting consumer awareness were instrumental, as was the catalytic role of WWF-UK at the forest seminars. Internally, directors of the targeted companies were worried about the public relations and commercial implications of the protests, customer letters and media coverage. Other pressures from investors, insurers and lenders were on the horizon (see Figure 3). The companies were looking for a way of solving a business problem. WWF-UK's 1995 target offered the companies a potential solution.

DIY retailers were at the top of the wood-supply pyramid. For example, B&Q has over 120 suppliers of wood products which originate from hundreds (if not thousands) of forests in over 40 countries. If DIY retailers could mobilise their timber buyers and suppliers to act on the 1995 target, then the group's impact would be felt worldwide.

With B&Q already making a public commitment to work on the timber sourcing issue, directors of competing firms felt it was important not to be left behind. The highly competitive DIY market has generally been characterised by competitors squeezing each other's margins through price wars. Now the environment was becoming a potential means of differentiating products and companies. Subsequently the DIY stores Texas, Do It All, Homebase, Great Mills and Wickes joined the group.

To join the group the companies had to agree to phase out by the target date, the sale and use of all wood and wood products not sourced from well-managed forests. Initially the companies and WWF-UK had only agreed to a target without knowing how it would be achieved. For the companies it was a fairly open-ended commitment, perhaps purposely so, as Francis Sullivan explains: "a key [in the early stages] was coming up with something that was clear enough so that the DIY retailers had a rough idea of what they were doing, but not so specific that they felt they couldn't do it."

Later WWF-UK felt it was necessary to formalise the club into a working group of companies with clear, consistent guidelines. The original requirements for membership in the 1995 Group were five in number:

- to obtain board approval to adopt the target date as company policy;

- to designate a senior executive with responsibility for policy implementation and reporting to WWF-UK;

- to provide WWF-UK with a written action programme detailing how the company would reach the 1995 target;

- to submit regular six-monthly progress reports to WWF-UK;

- to agree to the immediate phase-out from all wood products sold by the company, all labels and certificates claiming sustainability or environmental friendliness, until such a time as a credible independent certification and labelling system was established.

As part of the monitoring process, WWF-UK also agreed to respond individually to each company with comments on progress. Results from progress reports would be published in the WWF-UK's six-monthly Forests Newsletter. WWF-UK's initiative was beginning to be effective in both clarifying complex issues and facilitating a difficult process.

One of the difficult issues was manufacturers' misuse of claims about forestry management. The WWF-UK report into claims about forest management, *Truth or trickery* (1991), revealed a bewildering array of claims, most of which were either misleading or could not be substantiated. This left business in a dilemma, as Belinda Howell of Boots the Chemists recognised: "we were concerned about the plethora of confusing symbols on wood, pulp and paper products in respect of forest management. As a company we felt there was a need for a single credible system to clarify good forest management." A standard-setting body with a system for verifying product claims was therefore required.

Forest certification

Following 18 months of preparatory work, the Forest Stewardship Council (FSC) was launched in 1993. The Founding Group consisted of environmental NGOs, forest industry representatives, community forestry groups and forest product certification organisations. The FSC was formed to provide an international mechanism for promoting good forest management worldwide. Financial and logistical support was provided by both WWF-International and B&Q, among others.

The first FSC Board included two representatives from the private sector and seven from NGOs, certifiers and individual experts, a ratio which emerged following protracted negotiations. Greenpeace-International and FoE-International lobbied hard against any representation from business or commercial interests. Five of the nine board members came from the South, while four were from the North. The latter included WWF-International, the World Resources Institute and Cultural Survival. Initially a number of environmental groups disagreed with the decision concerning commercial representation on the board and decided to leave the FSC. These included: FoE, Greenpeace, Rainforest Action Network, World Rainforest Movement and ProRegenwald. However, Greenpeace, FoE and ProRegenwald subsequently rejoined.

The FSC mission statement commits members to "promote management of the world's forests that is environmentally appropriate, socially beneficial and economically viable" – language consistent with the principles of sustainable development. The FSC set up an independent forest accreditation programme to alleviate consumer confusion about environmentally friendly wood products. The FSC accreditation programme has also been seen as a means of monitoring company claims as well as their adherence to FSC principles. There are four elements to the FSC accreditation framework:

1. Ten principles of good forest management covering environmental, social and economic aspects (Box 4.3).

2. Accreditation of certifiers which inspect forest operations.

3. Flow of products from forests to consumers traced and verified by certifiers.

4. FSC logo denotes that product was sourced from an independently-certified forest according to FSC principles.

A number of environmental groups have expressed concern with the FSC and certification. Stephen Corry (1993) of Survival International criticises the use of market mechanisms for forest conservation:

> Consumers can consume even more, companies can make profits, forest communities can make an income, the environment is saved.... No one and nothing is criticised. The *causes* of rainforest destruction and the invasion of tribal peoples' lands are not addressed. This is not a panacea, a placebo or even a quick fix, it is just slow poison.

Other groups express concern not with the concept of certification but how its operation may become unduly affected by commercial interests. The German NGO Rettet den Regenwald has suggested "that the certification process might go ahead faster than the situation in the forest justifies just because there is pressure from the market."

For many environmental groups the FSC is seen as a credible part of the solution. It gains much of this credibility within the wider green movement by involving them closely in strategic decisions and not being solely reliant on income from successful certifications for its continued operation. Whereas individual certification organisations could be accused of having the potential to succumb to the will of vested interests (as these interests pay the certifiers bills), the FSC manages to perform a more independent role and therefore guarantees the integrity of the accredited certification organisations.

This system appears to be sustainable as the day-to-day operating of certification is paid for by the customer, whereas the monitoring of the standards is performed by an independent body, funded by the demand for certification (accreditation fees) and by the contributions of different sectors (eg WWF-International, the Dutch Government, B&Q plc). The sustainability of this balance of for-profit and non-profit interests is only as secure as the ability of the FSC to raise the required finance from a diverse funding base.

Whereas this set-up is welcomed by environmental groups it is of much consternation to some in the timber trade. For example, while accepting the inevitability of international timber certification, producer countries have expressed concern that the FSC initiative has been dominated by environmental groups. To some producer countries, FSC members seem more concerned with assuaging European and North American consumer concerns about tropical deforestation than the socio-economic needs of the South (see Barbier et al, 1994, p 161).

An expanding process

Although concerns exist with certification and the FSC, support for it has continued to grow at a remarkable rate. The WWF-UK 1995 Group originally focused on DIY retailers and the hardwood timber trade but now its reach has grown to cover other sections of the wood-product industry. Business people involved in the wall paper, publishing, stationery, furnishings, construction and sanitary goods trades, have all been alerted to the issue of deforestation.

The group already had 20 members by mid-1993, including major paper and pulp buyers Vymura and Boots the Chemists. By September 1994, WWF-UK realised that there was a need for someone to work exclusively on relations with member companies and they employed a group manager to monitor progress and to support those responsible for the policy in each company with technical advice.

Box 4.3: FSC principles of forest management

1. Compliance with laws and FSC principles: Forest management shall respect all applicable laws of the country in which they occur and international treaties and agreements to which the country is a signatory, and comply with all FSC principles and criteria.

2. Tenure and use rights and responsibilities: Long-term tenure and use rights to the land and forest resources shall be clearly defined, documented and legally established.

3. Indigenous peoples' rights: The legal and customary rights of indigenous peoples to own, use and manage their lands, territories and resources shall be recognised and respected.

4. Community relations and workers' rights: Forest management operations shall maintain or enhance the long-term social and economic well-being of forest workers and local communities.

5. Benefits from the forest: Forest management operations shall encourage the efficient use of the forest's multiple products and services to ensure economic viability and a wide range of environmental and social benefits.

6. Environmental impacts: Forest management shall conserve biological diversity and its associated values, water resources, soils and unique and fragile ecosystems and landscapes, and, by so doing, maintain the ecological functions and integrity of the forest.

7. Management plan: A management plan – appropriate to the scale and intensity of forest management – shall be written, implemented and kept up to date. The long-term objectives of management, and the means of achieving them, shall be clearly stated.

8. Monitoring and assessment: Monitoring shall be conducted – appropriate to the scale and intensity of forest management – to assess the condition of the forest, yields of forest products, chain of custody, management activities and their social and environmental impacts.

9. Maintenance of natural forests: Primary forests, well-developed secondary forests and sites of major environmental, social or cultural significance shall be conserved. Such areas shall not be replaced by tree plantations or other land uses.

10. Plantations: Plantations shall be planned and managed in accordance with principles and criteria 1-9, and principle 10 and its criteria. While plantations can provide an array of social and economic benefits, and can contribute to satisfying the world's needs for forest products, they should complement the management of, reduce pressures on and promote the restoration and conservation of natural forests.

Both the increasing size of the group and the fact that a number of very large companies with complex supply chains were beginning to join with only 18 months to go before the end of 1995, led the Forest Unit to revise requirements for membership. As of January 1995, the new requirements were as follows:

- Commitment to the FSC as the only currently credible independent certification and labelling system.

- Commitment to phasing out the purchase of wood and wood products which do not come from well-managed forests as verified by independent certifiers accredited by the FSC.

- Phasing out of the purchase of wood and wood products which do not come from well-managed forests and the phasing in of wood and wood products which can be shown to be from well-managed forests by 31 December 1995. In practice this means:

  1. A proportion of wood and wood products will be certified as coming from well-managed forests as defined by the FSC, by independent certifiers accredited by the FSC. The proportion of wood in this category should be demonstrably increasing.

  2. Remaining wood and wood products will come from known forests which the company has demonstrated are well-managed. Proportion of products in this category should be demonstrably decreasing.

  3. Wood and wood products which cannot be traced to known forests and/or where the quality of management is in doubt will be eliminated.

- A named senior manager will have responsibility for implementing the above commitment. Progress towards the target will be monitored via six-monthly progress reports.

- Companies may use the FSC logo when they are licensed to do so. Other labels denoting well-managed sources will not be used.

Immediately after this was agreed two of the major highstreet grocers in the UK, J. Sainsbury and Tesco, joined the group. These developments helped boost the group's turnover of wood products to over £2 billion, affecting 56,000 product lines from 2,196 suppliers and imports from 71 countries.

Tackling the problem, implementing the solution

Thus far we have charted how the WWF-UK 1995 Group began and expanded. Now we turn to consider how companies implemented the commitments they made. The first major step for each company was to develop a written action programme for submission to WWF-UK. As part of this process each company had to decide where the timber-sourcing policy would be most effectively situated. Environmental management, quality assurance, buying, and public relations or marketing were the main options. The key people upon whom action depended were the buyers and product managers responsible for the purchase of items containing wood and wood products.

The policy introduced a new and complex role for product managers and buyers, for whom product sourcing and environmental matters were not previously important. The various decisions about where to place responsibility for policy development and implementation have also influenced the extent to which buyers have seen the policy as a priority in their day-to-day work.

Some companies viewed their commitment as a Quality Assurance (QA) issue with major commercial implications. Accordingly QA departments were given responsibility for implementation, with QA managers meeting regularly with buyers to discuss environmental, product performance and price issues. In a number of cases buyers were expected to start grading all their suppliers on their environmental performance. However, very few buyers in the companies have been actually responsible for policy development and implementation. Other companies situated the policy within a new environmental department. In many cases, day-to-day implementation has been assigned to environmental or quality assurance managers often backed up by specialist technologists in timber, paper and pulp, databases and supply management.

Given that all companies had signed up to the same set of rules, it was inevitable that there would be opportunities for competitors to work together through the group. Although each company insists that no commercially sensitive information is exchanged, the nature of the business is that many either share or are aware of the other's suppliers. For example, when Company A visits a Finnish supplier to discuss certification issues, it may also represent the interests of Company B when they share the same supplier. Company B would then reciprocate on a similar fact-finding visit to Malaysia. Such cooperation has also been facilitated by the strong and mutually supportive inter-personal relationships which have developed within the WWF-UK 1995 Group.

To support this process, WWF-UK and four leading DIY retailers in the 1995 Group released a joint accord signed by company managing directors "to send a clear and consistent message" to over 500 wood-product suppliers in the UK and overseas. The joint accord was released at a point when suppliers felt that they were getting mixed messages from the DIY retailers. In some cases, suppliers were using these inconsistent messages to play one retailer off against another to avoid taking action. The accord was meant to overcome such situations by making suppliers aware that the retailers were a united force. One of the DIY managers illustrates how the first joint accord had a major impact upon one of his company's suppliers:

> *I had a supplier come to see me just after the Joint Accord was published and he said: "That was the last straw, I was trying to resist it, I didn't believe you were serious and suddenly I saw this Joint Accord. I don't even supply the others but when I saw that I suddenly realised this is a major change in business culture.*

Managing the relationship

Much of the cooperation described above was facilitated by WWF-UK through its regular seminars for group members. WWF-UK has advised all the member companies on key aspects of policy development and implementation, including complex sourcing and certification issues associated with products such as plywood and chipboard. This was the environmental group's supporting role and it was also required to perform a monitoring role.

Box 4.4: New relationships with suppliers

In recent years there has been a development in supplier–buyer relations towards a more cooperative approach (see Paul, 1996). The experience of the WWF-UK 1995 Group exemplifies this emerging trend.

Whereas initially the policy was perceived as an idea that was being imposed upon suppliers either by WWF-UK or the retailers, this view changed as suppliers began to realise that the policy had the potential to provide suppliers with secured orders. Although each company has approached the supplier issue in its own way, several themes resonate. The retailers generally sold the policy to their suppliers as a means of developing long-term relationships, enabling them both to plan ahead more effectively. The retailer–supplier relationship evolved, from initial questionnaires and reluctance to systematic planning and from arm twisting to ongoing communication and education. Bill Martin of J. Sainsbury notes that "[we] have much better knowledge and understanding of procurement supply and assessment [which has] improved greatly". A total of 409 supplier action plans were agreed by group members and their suppliers by the end of 1995, each of them outlining a timeframe for progress towards source identification and source certification.[16]

While there is evidence that the policy has in many cases facilitated collaboration between the retailers and their suppliers, head-to-head, hard financial negotiating has not been eliminated. Again the role of the buyers is significant. Despite the introduction of the new policy, most product managers and buyers continue to have much more frequent contact with suppliers than environmental and/or quality managers. Buyers also continue to use the commercial clout of their relatively large companies to carry out tough negotiations with their much smaller suppliers. From the retailer point of view, an essential part of a buyer's role is to negotiate the best deal possible and this has not changed. However, it does appear that buyers are beginning to see the timber-sourcing policy as part of their day-to-day responsibility. From the suppliers point of view, they want assurances that new investments in timber sourcing and certification will result in commercial benefits. This suggests that, after initial repositioning, the move towards environmental certification may lead to more rigid and secure supply chains.

The WWF-UK 1995 Group can be understood as an informal Environmental Management System (EMS) accreditation process with set targets and objectives. However, there was no formal verification of any company policy, due in part to WWF-UK's limited staffing levels and other resources. Instead there was an informal recognition of a company's commitment and efforts – by allowing continued association with WWF-UK. This meant in technical terms that companies endorsed WWF-UK and not vice-versa. This was why the 'Panda Logo' was not awarded to member companies.[17]

The absence of a system for verifying the reported performance of member companies was not seen as a problem for two reasons. First, detailed reports were required which were taken on trust. These were accepted as WWF-UK believed companies would have run a higher risk by maintaining membership of the group under false pretences, than by leaving the group. Second, member companies were committed to a separate product monitoring and standard verification system through their commitment to the FSC. The efficacy of this informal monitoring strategy is suggested by the following story.

In 1993-94, one of the DIY retailers had its membership in the 1995 Group suspended for six months. WWF-UK felt that this company had not adequately met reporting requirements and that the company was continuing to label their own brand products with environmental messages which WWF-UK felt could not be substantiated. The DIY retailer concerned characterised the temporary split as an administrative misunderstanding. The company also felt at the time that WWF-UK had asked them to achieve the unachievable. There was also a reluctance on the company's part to publicise its participation in the initiative. The company wanted to take a more gradual, understated approach in the early stages. During its time out of the 1995 Group, discussions continued with WWF-UK to clarify disagreements. By mid-1994, the DIY retailer concerned had rejoined the group. Subsequently this company has become one of the leading advocates of the 1995 Group and wider FSC process.

The axis of credibility for the 1995 Group is that WWF-UK is a respected charity. In a recent opinion poll, it was found that more people believed what WWF-UK said than the government, the opposition, big business or other NGOs.[18] By not taking any subscriptions from member companies, WWF-UK maintained its financial independence from members of the group and therefore the public confidence in their campaigning integrity. The future credibility of such a partnership depends on an ability to continue to finance the initiative as it continues to grow, without becoming dependent on a vested interest (or even seen to be dependent).

Performance of the WWF-UK 1995 Group

One aspect of the group that marked it out from other voluntary environmental initiatives was the setting of specific targets for members. The end of 1995 came and went. What progress had been made by individual companies and the wider group and how did this compare with the initial targets?

By December 1995, of the 47 1995 Group companies, 23 had some certified timber either in their systems or on order.[19] What of the others? Fourteen companies dealt primarily in paper and pulp products, for which there was unfortunately no certified source at that time. The other companies came close to meeting the target and group manager Justin Stead argues "failure to meet the deadline reflects more on the logistics and time-frames of the certification process and product development than a lack of commitment on the part of the companies."

Group companies provided a number of firsts relating to the purchase and use of certified timber. Milland Fine Timber took the first shipment of certified timber in the UK. Woodlam Products became the first company in the UK to only trade in certified products. Laing Homes became the first housing construction company to use certified wood. B&Q plc became the first DIY store to sell certified items and J. Sainsbury plc became the first high-street grocer to do so. In total, certified timber constituted four per cent of the group's trade by the end of 1995, a trade of about £97 million per annum.

The sourcing of wood products is a necessary step towards the certification of existing supplies. First, locating the forest source is important so that a certification organisation can visit it and perform an assessment. Second, the opening of dialogue with the supply chain and forest of origin about the environmental aspects of a product's specification and the need for certification is essential. Therefore the environmental auditing of wood-product supply chains was a crucial intermediate (and immediate) tool to influence forest management and prepare the trade community for independent certification.

By December 1995, 26 1995 Group companies had ascertained the origin of all their wood products. Of the 21 remaining, 10 had reduced unknown or badly managed sources to a level of less than five per cent of their trade in wood products. A number of the remaining 11 were large companies who joined the group in the last year when it was not at all realistic that they could source all of their wood products in 12 months. The case of Sainsbury's is illustrative, as their environmental manager, George White summarised:

> *Between May and November 1995 information on all Group suppliers and their products was analysed for a timber content. As of January 1996, over 70% of all timber and paper products have been traced to 'well-managed' forests.*

Despite such rapid progress it should be noted that the target for all wood products to come from well-managed forests was not achieved. More importantly companies were not always swift to delist a supplier if they could not trace their products to a well-managed source. Therefore, in reviewing progress, some of the companies noted the insufficient buy-in to the process by product managers and product buyers. Given their traditional focus on low prices and high quality, some of the buyers found it difficult to integrate environmental issues into their negotiations with suppliers (Box 4.4). Whereas the group members delisted a total of 99 suppliers for failure, in part, to provide the required environmental information, in many cases suppliers had been told that price and quality continue to take precedence over the wood-product sourcing policy. Other companies took a more fundamental stance. For example, B&Q's Alan Knight assured that:

> *To provide an incentive for suppliers of timber based products to use independently certified timber, B&Q has stated that products which have been independently certified and carry the FSC logo will not be de-listed in favour of equivalent but non-certified products (unless there are serious quality or supply problems, and only then can the decision be made by the B&Q Board).*

Some suppliers complained about the mixed messages they received from the retailers and their buyers, which was due in part to WWF-UK failing to state what it expected companies to do in their day-to-day purchasing decisions.

Another area of only limited success relates to the use of unverified claims concerning forest management. Member companies were committed to the concept of independent verification of claims about forest management practice. This commitment required member companies to remove all unverified environmental claims from wood products designed after the company's membership of the group was confirmed (the agreement was not retrospective). In 1991 research commissioned by WWF showed that 50 per cent of the companies questioned made claims about the environmental credentials of their wood products. Of these "none could be considered to have answered fully the questions raised regarding their sources". By December 1995 WWF-UK believed members of the 1995 Group did not have products on their shelves, designed or purchased after joining the group, which carried unverified or misleading environmental claims. However, checking all stores and points-of-sale was a huge logistical task and beyond the scope of WWF. (In 1997 a number of retailers still carried some products with non-FSC claims about forest management.)

Companies were not required to report on the use of forest management claims. Instead the reporting process focused on progress towards certification. The level of reporting was extremely good if one compares it to other voluntary initiatives such as the CBI Environment Business Forum, where company reporting on environmental performance reached such low levels that the initiative had to be abandoned (ENDS, 1994). Whereas voluntary initiatives are often condemned as industry-led attempts at greenwashing (see Maltby, 1995), the 1995 Group tells a different story.

As mentioned above, WWF-UK required a report from members every six months. For the major duration of the group these reports were not required to be very detailed and a format was not prescribed. However, in the summer of 1995 WWF-UK realised it needed detailed information on the performance of the group in order to assess companies and communicate performance to their members and the public at the end of the year. To this end they brought in a consultant who proceeded to design a formal system of reporting for all companies and then compile the information on their 56,000 product lines onto a central database.

Companies were forthcoming with information on wood volumes, product lines, suppliers, countries of origin, trade species, and management status. Indeed, a 94 per cent response rate was achieved from the 52 companies, and the remainder were delisted or submitted reports at a later date.

Confidence in the integrity of WWF-UK was key to the agreement and members of the group respected the need to keep WWF-UK in a knowledgeable position: "establishing a proper reporting system is crucial to any credible voluntary initiative. It was therefore essential that member companies provided WWF with detailed information on their progress towards the 1995 target", argues B&Q timber consultant Chris Cox.

Success was not shared by all members of the 1995 Group. Eight companies resigned or were asked to leave the group in the months or years prior to 1995, in most cases because of an inability to demonstrate progress towards the group's targets.

The initiative achieved more for forest conservation than that suggested by an analysis of performance against set targets. With a trade equivalent to 11 million cubic metres of trees in 1995, if national figures were correct, the group accounted for almost a quarter of the UK consumption of wood products.[20] By incorporating a large section of the timber trade the group could educate suppliers who had not considered the forest management of their wood supply, suddenly found customers demanded this information. Well over 4,000 environment-oriented questionnaires were sent by group companies, which provided a mechanism for increasing environmental awareness and knowledge at every stage of the supply chain – from mill owner to magazine publisher.

Before the group there was no functioning mechanism whereby consumer power in western industrialised countries could be captured to promote sustainable forest management around the world. When the FSC set out to establish such a mechanism, its success depended crucially on the support of consumer markets. The 1995 Group provided this support, acting as a major pull on the process of certifying timber by buying from a majority of the currently certified forests. This substantive commitment to the FSC has helped it to become a fully-functioning organisation.

The future of the initiative

At the end of 1995, WWF and its business partners decided to continue to work together on new targets for the end of the decade. Initially, WWF 1995 Plus Group companies agreed to the new target of purchasing only certified wood and wood products by 31 December 1999. However, the requirements were changed following a challenge from the timber trade body TTF.

For many years, the TTF has been opposed to the WWF-UK and FSC visions of sustainable forest management. The TTF has criticised the FSC's disproportionate NGO representation and its lack of accountability to governments. In April 1996, the TTF informed WWF-UK it was of the opinion that "the exclusive commitment to the FSC by the members of the 1995 [Plus] Group might well be contrary to the principles of free competition and free movement of goods under both EC and UK law." The TTF wanted WWF-UK and its business partners to revise the group's requirements "to accommodate any recognised systems" of certification such as the Canadian Standards Association (CSA) or ISO approach (see Harris, 1996). Faced with free-trade regulations such as Article 85 of the Treaty of Rome, WWF-UK decided to review its membership requirements. Now companies are no longer committed exclusively to the FSC. Rather it is the only system which fulfils their criteria for recognised certification schemes. Neither are members committed to only trading in certified products by a specified date or the principle of only trading in certified products. Despite this many members have come forward with public statements that they will work to a "100 per cent FSC by 2000" target.

The TTF challenge is indicative of a growing industry backlash to the reform process, perceived by some within environmental groups. The Canadian Pulp and Paper Association (CPPA) has lent financial support to the CSA certification scheme which many NGOs have criticised for taking "dangerous short-cuts", and for its acceptance of "large-scale clearcutting" (WWF-International, 1995, p 3). The ISO was encouraged by the CSA to use this system for an international forestry standard, a move which may have led to major confrontation between FSC and CSA/ISO supporters. In the event ISO decided not to develop a forest management standard. However, concern still exists that the ISO 14001 environmental management quality assurance system may be used by forest managers as a means of communicating sustainable forest management and that confusing messages may be given to the international timber trade and consumers.

New battle lines may be drawn around the ISO 14027 specifications for ecolabels. Three sets of guidelines are being prepared which relate to manufacturer's claims, the use of logos and claims by independent bodies. At the time of writing there are disputes over whether independent claims should be differentiated from manufacturer's claims. If disputes arise over these criteria, we believe it will be indicative of the lack of democratic, stakeholder, participation in the standard-setting process employed by ISO.

Despite these problems, enthusiasm for the group remains and new companies keep joining.[21] This will pose a dilemma for WWF-UK. Whereas the NGO's conservation goals will be best served by a continually expanding group, its financial resources are limited. A rethinking of the group's funding structure may therefore be required, one option being to devolve the management of the group to a WWF-accredited consultancy which would then charge a fee of member companies for its role.

Commercial costs and benefits of working with WWF-UK

Some of the motivations for companies joining the group were described above. Many managers believed it made good commercial sense to work with WWF-UK. In Chapter three we described how many in business regard a proactive stance towards environmental challenges as sound business practice, sometimes described as the theory of competitive environmental advantage. For reasons of marketing, recruitment, employee motivation and risk management (preventing boycotts, protecting share prices) it is seen to be prudent to cultivate the public impression of a socially and environmentally responsible business. In addition, responsible companies may identify efficiencies, better understand their supply chains and anticipate environmental legislation.

Now that member companies have been in the group for sometime, the costs and benefits for participating business are becoming clearer. A survey of the attitudes of managers responsible provided some evidence that companies had already benefited. For example, 36 per cent of responding group managers believed the marketing and public relations performance of their company had been improved due to their membership, compared with 27 per cent who did not. Major retailers received the bulk of the media coverage in 1996, with numerous articles using their names as examples of group members. This was a major advantage given the context from which most companies joined the group. According to Mike Inchley of Do It All:

> It was the one area where we received the most letters from customers.... And I guess a lot of that was on the back of reports on TV and through the media on deforestation in the Amazon Basin.... All sort of emotive stuff. And we also took the view that we actually believed, do believe, that maintenance of the world's forests actually is not only ecologically vital, but also commercially extremely important.

The WWF-UK press and communications department produced regular press releases on the group. All managers interviewed felt this provided a significant advantage. Over half of respondents believed that membership of the group had increased the credibility of their company's environmental policy in the eyes of stakeholders, while other managers had not seen any evidence of this but predicted an improvement in their company's credibility because of their membership.

The exchange of information from WWF-UK to member companies was seen as a significant advantage: WWF-UK's staff were a source of conservation expertise, free of charge. As one DIY manager noted, "We needed guidance and one way of getting that guidance is to join up with people who know what they're talking about." The group thus provided a forum for companies to share their experiences and jointly target key suppliers. It also seems to have improved relations between participating businesses and the environmental movement. One environmental manager said of the timber trade, deforestation and direct action, "it is no longer an issue with them [NGOs]".

Membership of the initiative did place some burden on member companies. The draw on management time was cited by 63 per cent as one of the greatest costs of the programme. Surprisingly, over half of the respondents did not have a specific budget allocation for their membership. Although trade-offs between environmental performance and price were discussed, 82 per cent believed that prices had not been significantly affected by the partnership. However, a few suppliers reported increases of seven per cent for certified materials, with limited scope to increase their sale price.

Almost three quarters of the managers said that trade-offs between environmental performance and product quality were discussed, which was a distinct development from the situation in 1994 when less than half of those in the group entertained such discussions (Bendell, 1995). Some paper and pulp companies anticipated the opportunity costs of having to reduce buying indiscriminately on the spot market – a change in the kind of flexible 'just-in-time' procurement policy traditionally used by a number of paper and pulp companies.

Some of the commercial drawbacks of the process can be specifically attributed to the role of the organisations WWF-UK and FSC. The main non-financial drawback of the process, surprising given environmental demands for immediate action on the environment, was the slow nature of environmental group action. Setting up the FSC took a lot longer than many of the companies and WWF-UK had originally anticipated. The FSC logo and labelling system was not launched until early 1996. Part of the delay has been the FSC's commitment to involving a wide range of stakeholders which has made for a lengthy and often contentious consultation and decision-making process. Some of the 1995 Group companies have argued that the FSC's commitment to multiple stakeholders is making the certification process slow and cumbersome. This is a concern which is shared by many of the small suppliers to the DIY retailers who have invested heavily in product sourcing and certification.

Environmentalist concerns with the partnership

Despite our desire to describe clearly the significant successes of the 1995 Group, it would be inappropriate to conclude the analysis without a discussion of some of the concerns expressed by environmentalist observers of the process. The partnership raises a number of questions about the role, legitimacy and independence of environmental groups.

First, the initiative has been expensive and time consuming. WWF-UK has employed a number of people who effectively worked as free environmental consultants to members of the timber trade. If, as we argue in Chapter three, proactive work on environmental management makes sound business sense, why should a non-profit environmental group foot the bill for these services?

A second concern is that original campaigning priorities may become obscured by closer and closer collaboration with business. Some may wonder what is being lost by investing so much time and money in business collaborations and certification. WWF-UK has a number of other campaign priorities, such as the reduction of timber consumption and the increase in protected areas. Enthusiasm for business partnerships may be sidelining these objectives. It is useful to remember that the 1995 Group originally grew out of a concern for tropical rainforest deforestation. Although temperate deforestation has been wrongly overlooked in the past, the threats to the tropical forests of the world remain ecologically, socially and ethically more troublesome. The focus of the 1995 Group's work over the past year has been on trying to obtain certified products from temperate and boreal forests. The main reason is because the group is now dominated by the interests of companies selling paper and pulp products. Due to logistical and technical reasons, no paper or pulp-producing forests have been certified to date. As a result, both WWF-UK and the FSC have faced considerable pressure from 1995 Group companies to meet their need for FSC-certified paper and pulp products. Some environmentalists would argue that this demonstrates how business interests are undermining WWF-UK's agenda, and obscuring the original environmental objectives of the partnership. Rather than placing so much emphasis upon temperate and boreal forest issues, some might argue that WWF-UK could use its resources more effectively by supporting indigenous rainforest communities with local conservation projects, for example.

Another concern is that the initiative may have a deleterious effect on the organisational culture of WWF-UK. Perhaps too much of its ethos has been sacrificed in the 1995 Group's efforts to win credibility in the business community. For example, in February 1996 WWF-UK spent thousands of pounds on hosting the launch of the FSC Mark to members of the wood-product trade. This allowed the FSC to be presented in a business-like manner to the attendees. Whilst this is important for developing the impression of the FSC as a professional organisation, such a strategy might be questioned by WWF-UK staff and supporters, and other environmentalists.

Many would agree that a sustainable society cannot continue to institutionalise the profligate use of resources as the cultural norm. Perhaps, therefore, even 'professionalism' needs to be redefined in light of sustainable development – retaining the essential benefits of professionalism such as reliability, cost effectiveness and good external communications, while challenging resource-intensive trappings such as exotic buffets and glossy brochures. If WWF-UK is to retain its credibility and links with more radical greens, it must be sensitive to calls for cultural change in line with the constraints of ecology.

Campaigners who view ecological and social problems as symptoms of a defective economic, social and cultural system believe that protest needs to continue in order to bring the fundamental changes required for a more sustainable society. As more and more of those who would be doing the protesting begin working on incremental solutions (a difficult term when we do not fully understand the dynamics of the forest ecosystem), the political space for an alternative vision of society may diminish.

The role of grassroots protest has been significant in making the forest issue a business concern. Indeed the roots of the 1995 Group lie in the innovative and often confrontational campaign strategies of other environmental groups. FoE-UK's former forest campaigner, Simon Counsell, explains his organisation's role in making the world's forests a significant environmental policy issue both within the UK and internationally:

> *It was quite a distinct and major departure for the environmental movement to start campaigning through ... political and consumerist channels in 1985, and ... I think we have to take much of the credit for all of the kind of campaigning work that's happened subsequently from the development of radical activist groups like perhaps Earth First! and the Rainforest Action Groups to initiatives like the Forest Stewardship Council ... a lot of those have really flowed from the kinds of things that we started in the mid 1980s ... I think we've had an absolutely profound effect on the all of those involved in the forest industry ... particularly at the retailing end.*

The key role of protest in providing a context within which partnership may grow should not be overlooked.

Finally, there is the issue of transparency. The relationship between an environmental group and a company requires a degree of confidentiality. This inevitably conflicts with the environmental group's accountability to its membership. The reaction from environmental groups to queries from members is often along the lines of 'trust us'. With increased emphasis upon business partnerships, there is a danger that the environmental group may begin to adopt the kind of paternalism normally associated with 'establishment' institutions.

The 1995 Group does not represent a perfect model for collaboration. What it represents is the first stage in a development towards a new form of social regulation with environmental groups playing a substantial role. Whereas the spirit and commitment of the participants has managed to carry WWF-UK and a limited number of companies through a rather haphazard process up until now, a more strategic approach will be required for future collaboration if the autonomy of WWF-UK is to be maintained with an ever expanding number companies becoming partners.

Similar initiatives worldwide

The experience in the UK is not unique. Growing numbers of companies in The Netherlands, Sweden, Austria, Belgium, Switzerland, Australia and North America have also bought into the idea of independent timber certification. WWF-International, its national affiliates and other NGOs have taken leadership roles in facilitating so-called buyer groups and/or FSC working groups. Indeed the FSC is now supported by large numbers of environmental, social and human rights groups worldwide as the most appropriate mechanism for independent certification.

Hart voor Hout

The Hart voor Hout (Heart for Wood) campaign was launched in early 1992 by Milieudefensie (FoE-Netherlands) and the development NGO Novib. Although WWF-Netherlands was not a formal campaign partner, Hart voor Hout maintained close relations with the Dutch WWF's forest programmes. At the outset Hart voor Hout had one goal: to reduce Dutch consumption of tropical timber to a level supplied only from sustainable sources. At that time The Netherlands was the second largest per capita importer of tropical timber in the world and NGOs felt it was one area that they could make a major impact upon.

Similar to the UK experience, a lack of effective government action was a significant factor in making environmental groups turn to the industry itself. In 1991 the Dutch government had released a Policy Paper on Tropical Rainforests, which stated the governments wish that "from 1995 onwards ... the use of tropical timber is limited to timber from countries or regions with a forest management system geared to protection and sustainable production". At the time NGOs felt the battle had been won but it soon became clear when the policy stalled on the defining of "sustainable production" that it would not be taken forward.

Therefore, just as had happened in the UK, Mileudefensie planned direct action protests against the DIY chain Inter-Gamma for early 1992. After a second wave of protest at the end of 1992, the company signed a declaration of intent to stop selling tropical timber products by the end of 1995, with the exception of tropical timber which is sustainably produced. Another parallel with the UK case was that after the first company changed direction others soon followed. With the second most important DIY store in the country, Praxis, now alongside InterGamma, Hart voor Hout had cornered almost 70 per cent of the Dutch DIY market. The same retailer-targeted strategy used by WWF-UK had proved even more successful in The Netherlands, as Hart voor Hout campaign leader Gemma Boetekees explains:

> *In The Netherlands, tropical timber is not done, it's a bit like fur. You don't wear a fur coat ... so in the same way you don't buy tropical timber ... [M]ost of the retailers want to have an environmentally-friendly image.... Nobody knows Wijma [the timber importer and original target for direct action]. If you buy timber you don't know it comes from Wijma so it's of no use to them to have an environmentally friendly image.*

In addition to its focus on retailers, the campaign has sought to embrace the building industry and housing associations. In one instance a municipality threatened to cancel a planned contract with a company unless it signed a letter of intent to obtain well-managed supplies of wood.

One other major difference between the UK and Dutch experience has been the role of formal government lobbying by NGOs in The Netherlands. For example, in September 1995, Milieudefensie and Novib called upon a number of its Hart voor Hout partners to join them at a meeting with nine Dutch parliamentarians. The purpose was to obtain cross-party parliamentary support for a series of questions about the FSC directed at four government ministers (Environment, Development, Agriculture and Economic Affairs). Eric Jan Schipper, Inter-Gamma's policy champion, was there "to tell the parliamentarians that the market was already ahead of the government".

Another difference is Milieudefensie's continued use of the carrot and stick approach. While it continues to develop closer ties with progressive companies, the organisation does still call upon its 120 volunteer groups across the country to protest against timber users who have not yet signed the Hart voor Hout letter of intent to stop selling timber from badly-managed forests.[22]

Despite these differences of strategy there are huge parallels in the thinking of business and environmental groups in the UK and The Netherlands. The process of thinking and working together in a spirit of openness and mutual trust is clear in Eric Jan Schipper's reflections on the process:

> *The NGOs are not telling us what we shouldn't do but are discussing with us what we could do for the environment. They are not easy on us. They are telling us that there are a lot of things we do wrong in their eyes but we're on a working level with each other. They think with us and they see where our problems lie and what we can do about it and what we can't do, and what we are trying to do. I think the effect is bigger, what they do now. Because they're trying to work with the few companies who are willing to change and the environmental effect is larger.*

The fact that the Dutch experience echoes that of the UK initiative in spite of there being virtually no communication between the different groups involved, lends weight to the argument that a new social realism is gripping western societies (see Chapters two and seven) and is providing the context within which partnerships can flourish.   Today communication between different national initiatives is being undertaken on a more formal basis by WWF-International, a process which may prove helpful with the planning of new buyers groups, such as that in North America.

North American Buyers Group

In early 1997, the North American Buyers Group (NABG) was launched.   An independent not-for-profit organisation, the group coordinates the efforts of timber manufacturers, suppliers, retailers and major users that are committed to the responsible management of the world's forests.   The current mission statement of the group explains the rationale:

> By leveraging the combined knowledge and commitment of members and stakeholders, the Group aims to improve forest management world-wide by championing and promoting responsible forest product buying practices.   Specifically NABG will facilitate and increase purchases of independently certified forest products.

The launch of the group was the culmination of 18 months' consultation between business and environmental groups, administered by the environmental investment and consultancy firm Environmental Advantage (EA).   The group differs in a number of ways from the experience in the UK and The Netherlands, having been designed in close cooperation with future members rather than being predetermined by one environmental group or a coalition of NGOs.

The first meeting to discuss the establishment of the buyers group was between interested companies and potential funding bodies.   These included the MacArthur Foundation, Rockefeller Brothers Fund, Patagonia, The Gap, Home Depot, Starbucks, Habitat for Humanity and Colonial Craft.   Subsequently four environmental groups were invited to contribute to the design of the group: WWF-US, National Resources Defense Council (NDRC), Rainforest Alliance, and the Environmental Defense

Fund (EDF). EDF latterly withdrew from the process, a decision which EA explain as a result of EDF wishing to pursue more direct one-to-one contacts with companies (see Chapter six).

The possibility of group management being performed by an environmental group in the same way as in Europe was suggested during the initial discussions but "buyers firmly dismissed this option" says Rachel Crossley, Buyers Group Coordinator at EA. One of the reasons environmental group administration was rejected relates to reporting and confidentiality, as Crossley explains "the idea that they would submit reports and be 'judged' by anyone outside the company is anathema to them". However, at least one of the companies has been fully committed to social and environmental reporting and auditing for a number of years. Home Depot operate a supplier policy whereby any new supplier to the company must complete an environmental report and send it to the FSC accredited independent certification company Scientific Certification Systems (SCS) for assessment. The reasons for the unwillingness to have environmental groups 'in charge' probably relate more to a concern about the perceived fundamental stance of environmental groups.

Whereas in the UK environmental groups developed wide public recognition and respect and posed a threat to business nationwide through coordinated direct action and media work, they do not occupy a similar position in the US. Crossley explains:

> [In the US] the environmental [groups] ... have a much shallower penetration than those in the UK. Whereas nearly everyone in the UK has heard of WWF and knows the Panda logo, that isn't the case here for WWF or any others ... it seems that Jo Public has never heard of WWF or any other NGO.

The problem for timber buyers in the US is therefore a different one. It is not a strategic problem involving the mediation of potentially sales-damaging environmental protests but a problem with finding practical ways of implementing commitments to sustainable development made by the business community since 1992 (see Chapters one and three). Because of these motivations, close cooperation with environmental groups has not been necessary. With policy development overseen by a board drawn from corporate members, environmental group involvement is restricted to that of an advisory council. Targets for improvement and methods of reporting are being left to the discretion of the companies. The difference between this model and a trade association is small and independence from overdue short-term commercial considerations may be secured within the structure of the organisation.

The fact that the corporate motivations behind the development of the group have been fairly autonomous of pressure from environmental groups and consequently the values of these stakeholders, may have implications for the future policy of the group. As a tool for the practical implementation of business-defined sustainable development, the group appears to be addressing environmental specifications in a technical fashion, and does not appear to be embracing the third-stage sustainability agenda we described in Chapter three. This is expressed in two ways.

First, there is a danger that sustainability may be defined in far narrower terms than a wider range of stakeholders would agree upon. The FSC certification scheme reflects a broad view of sustainability, embracing social, cultural and ethical concerns as well as the purely ecological. Without pressure from environmental groups, it is debatable whether this broader view of sustainability will be accepted by the group in the longer term. Membership of the group does not presently incur commitment to the FSC system in the same way that the UK 1995 Group has done. Admittedly not specifying the FSC in the group documents is partly the result of concerns over anti-trust laws. However, companies themselves do express other reasons for not committing themselves to the FSC system. A member of Home Depot's environmental department, Vanessa Carter, explains:

> *The FSC did not endear itself to the North American forest products industry [as they] shut many of the worthy players out of the founding assembly, [therefore] portraying themselves as not giving fair representation to industry. At least that is how industry felt. [The] FSC also did not (and still does not) understand how ecolabelling works in the US.*

Second, there is no overt commitment to only selling products from environmentally-sound sources. This may reflect a different understanding of corporate social responsibility by participants in the US compared to participants in the UK. In the UK most companies now believe that the consumer has a right to expect that when they shop in a particular store the retailer has acted responsibly in putting products on the shelves. Responsibility is seen to lie with the company as much as it does with the customer. In the UK, Alan Knight has stated he looks forward to the day when B&Q shoppers will not have the choice to buy non-sustainable products:

> *What we need to do is to create an environment where we don't really have to do any work. [We need] people to realise that if you want to do trade with the DIY sector in the UK, you have to be independently certified and you have to know where your timber comes from, and there is no point in even approaching us unless you have that information.*

In this way it can be argued that DIY retailers in the UK have been elevated in the public psyche to a position similar to that awarded to governments: from DIY retailing to DIY politics. However, in the US there is a traditional allegiance to the virtue of personal freedom of choice. The problem therefore is not whether the company acts irresponsibly by offering products from unsustainable sources but whether it acts irresponsibly by not providing the customer with the choice of environmentally sound products. Therefore even the most ecoconscious American companies "do not believe in the advocacy route."[23]

The corporate social responsibility of US firms involved in the North American Buyers Group may be less revolutionary than that of the UK firms in the 1995 Group. Perhaps the managers who champion consumer choice should ask themselves when was the last time a customer specifically requested a product that was guaranteed to be from a destroyed rainforest? Business can decide to be a more responsible corporate citizen.

Whether the North American group will be able to promote the kind of dialogue and understanding that has developed in the UK and The Netherlands is uncertain. It is anticipated that environmental group involvement will be restricted to the giving of advice, the promotion of certification and close collaboration on specific projects with individual companies. It appears that this is a practical response to the business–environmental group climate in 1990s America. Rachel Crossley explains:

> *There hasn't been a very positive experience here to date with respect to NGO/corporate relations. The atmosphere and relationship has been adversarial, so business is wary of environmental groups. They don't know them well and don't trust them. Until the EDF/McDonald's partnership I don't think there was much working together ... which is what we are trying to do. We're going into uncharted territory and neither side trusts the other very much.*

Here we see how trust is the key for successful partnerships. In Chapter six we describe the trust that grew between individuals in McDonald's and the EDF. This trust between individuals in traditionally warring organisations allows space to be opened for constructive dialogue and the development of a new consensus on which to act. It is not only changing systems and structures that produce partnerships but equally individuals. First, a comment from Francis Sullivan of WWF-International:

> *Success has boiled down to the commitment of individuals and the support that senior management has given to those individuals.... You have some companies that are not particularly committed themselves, but you have got an individual in there who is unbelievably committed to actually getting the thing sorted out.*

Second, a similar perspective from Saskia Ozinga, original campaign leader of Hart voor Hout:

> *A lot has depended on persons within the companies ... they are just very, very committed people to all environmental issues. They really are and that has made all the difference.*

The support that these individuals have received in different companies, organisations and countries illustrates how the boundaries of corporate social and environmental responsibility have been shifting dramatically, alongside rapid developments in the thinking and action of environmental groups in northern industrialised countries. We have observed the role of environmental groups in raising public and consumer awareness about global environmental issues such as the adverse effects of deforestation and it is certain that protest has been a major catalyst for subsequent partnerships in many cases. At the same time, market leaders have responded to this pressure as an opportunity to maintain leadership in a changing marketplace. This in turn has cleared the way for more cautious competitors to follow, thereby setting in motion a revolution in the timber trade.

But much more in the way of radical change is still needed. The partnerships described above have not yet stopped forest loss nor have they prevented the associated adverse social and ecological impacts. We now know that Brazil, the host nation of the 1992 Earth Summit, has experienced an increase in deforestation in the intervening years. Whereas just before the Rio conference Brazil's deforestation was just over 11,000 sq kms per annum, it has now reached almost 15,000 and is likely still to be on the increase. For all the talk of politicians, business people and environmentalists post-Rio, the trees keep falling and the forests continue to burn (see Box 4.5). As Amazonian Chief Tamakurale of the Parakana Indians said in 1997:

> We do not want the loggers on our land. They give us diseases. They kill the forest animals and take turtles from the river so we have nothing to eat. They cut down the trees. If the trees go, some of our children may survive but they will not be Parakana.[24]

In fact nothing less than a global partnership revolution is still required, one which fully embraces sustainability, responsibility and, yes, constraint.

Box 4.5: Global forest policy debates post-Rio

Global forest policy debates since Rio have continued to be contentious with ongoing disagreements about appropriate levels of overseas development assistance and about the need for a legally binding international forest convention, among other issues. Whereas at Rio most divisions were either along North–South or business–NGO lines, current divisions tend to be more complex and multi-faceted. The Intergovernmental Panel on Forests (IPF), which met four times between September 1995 and February 1997, revealed ongoing North–South tensions about finance and the meaning of sustainable development. However, on the possible need for a forest convention there was much more controversy and division. Key convention supporters included Canada, the European Union, Malaysia, Indonesia, Russia, as well as one major NGO, the Environmental Investigation Agency, and a number of industry associations, most notably the Canadian Pulp and Paper Association. Major opponents were the USA, Australia, New Zealand and India, along with most NGOs (including WWF-International and Greenpeace-International) and one major industry group, the American Forest and Paper Association. A large number of countries, particularly Japan, China and Brazil, were unwilling to make a commitment either way and instead argued that more time was needed to reach consensus on a potential convention. Although the rationale behind the various government, NGO and industry positions varied widely, the end result of the two-year IPF process was a list of three options for different forms of ongoing policy dialogue which may or may not lead to an international convention early in the next century. Call it new global political reality or post-modern 'glocalism', the IPF reaffirmed the image of a formal international policy process which remains slow, cumbersome and inconclusive.

Notes

[1] The chapter is based upon three previously published papers (Murphy, 1996a, 1996d; and Bendell and Sullivan, 1996).

[2] The UK's DIY home improvement retail sector has experienced a boom over the past three decades, with total sales reaching almost £9 billion by the end of 1996. In the 1990s the six leading retailers are B&Q (13.8%), Texas Homecare (8.1%), Do It All (4.6%), Homebase (3.1%), Wickes (2.8%) and Great Mills (2.5%) (Verdict/ Economist Intelligence Unit, 1993). Others, independents and specialists comprise the remaining 65.1%. In early 1995 Texas was taken over by Sainsbury's Homebase. The rise of the DIY sector can be attributed to three inter-related factors. First, home ownership has increased dramatically – from 43% in 1960, to 59% in 1980, to almost 70% by 1990. The introduction of the 'right to buy' by the first Thatcher Government in 1980 gave many public sector tenants the opportunity to purchase the freehold on their homes. Subsequently from 1981-91 almost 1.4 million former public-rented dwellings were converted to owner-occupation. The second major factor contributing to the growth of the DIY sector has been the increased costs of employing professional carpenters, plumbers, electricians and other home-construction specialists. Third, market research indicates that many home owners have had more leisure time available to undertake home improvements. In parallel with this increase in consumer demand, the supply side of DIY has also changed radically. The traditional high street DIY stores of the 1960s were superseded by aircraft-hanger sized, out-of-town superstores in the late 1970s. In some cases, prior secondary sites such as factories, cinemas, garages and bus garages were acquired for the emerging DIY superstores. In other cases, new stores were built at relatively low costs. The larger shed-like, one-stop shops were able to beat their high street competitors on quantity and variety of goods, advertising expenditure and most importantly, price.

[3] Vanclay's figures are also misleading for aggregating rainforests with non-moist tropical forests – areas more likely to be exposed to fuelwood demands from towns and also to be converted to agriculture.

[4] It has been calculated that for every cubic metre of timber harvested one fifth of a hectare of forest is destroyed by farmers who press in close behind the loggers. See Myers, 1992.

[5] Officially Friends of the Earth has two national divisions operating in the UK, FoE-England and Wales and FoE-Scotland. FoE-UK is used here to refer to the former.

[6] ITTO grew out of the 1983 UN Conference on Tropical Timber which was organised by the UN Conference on Trade and Development (UNCTAD). It administers the 1983 International Tropical Timber

Agreement (ITTA), the first international instrument for forests, which provides a framework for cooperation and consultation between tropical timber producers and consumers on a range of issues.

[7] FoE-UK has been frustrated by what it sees as the failure of international agreements such as the ITTA and the World Bank's Tropical Forestry Action Plan (TFAP) to tackle the underlying causes of deforestation and put in place sensible international and regional policies.

[8] WWF-International's first forest-related programme was a spin-off of its Operation Tiger campaign in India in the mid-1970s. See Pearce, 1991, p 182.

[9] According to B&Q, the RAG campaign consisted of only a two-hour leaflet campaign outside six of its stores. However, a review of RAG files indicates that no fewer than eight groups were active, organising a larger number of protests against B&Q in the April-July period.

[10] The RAG activists were frustrated by FoE-UK's unwillingness to cooperate. They suspected that FoE was primarily concerned about the impact of the RAG protests on FoE's fundraising. Were the RAG activists stealing media attention which otherwise would have gone to FoE? Simon Counsell of FoE offers a different interpretation of the FoE-RAG impasse: "There was a dialogue ... between us and some of these semi-autonomous groups ... loosely under the banner of Rainforest Action Network or Earth First! or whatever. Groups such as those have had on occasion quite high expectations from FoE who they see as being extremely well resourced. We've got a very well established network of local groups, [which] they see as potentially adding a massive weight of protest ... to their own protests. It has on occasion been frustrating for those groups that we can't sort of turn our network on and off at will, like mobilise these 300 activist groups around issues that they see as being important at any given time. It's unfortunate that we can't do that but we simply can't because we have ... four other campaign areas in this organisation all of which have their own demands on the local activist networks.... That often precludes the option of simply being able to click our fingers and get them all out on the streets doing whatever it is that other non-affiliated groups ... might like them to do. That can be a source of frustration because those groups sometimes don't understand that."

[11] The tension between B&Q and FoE-UK had its roots in Alan Knight's initial research on timber sourcing back in 1990. At that time, Knight had disagreed with FoE's support for a tropical timber boycott and its lack of action on temperate forest issues.

[12] Defined by ITTO as: "the process of managing permanent forest land to achieve one or more clearly specified objectives of management with regard to the production of a continuous flow of desired forest products

and services without undue reduction in its inherent values and future productivity and without undue undesirable effects on the physical and social environment." (International Tropical Timber Council Decision 6(XI), Quito, 8th Session, May 1991.)

[13] Early in the process, WWF-UK had to identify appropriate language to communicate its message about sustainable forest management to the companies. The term 'sustainable' was widely used at international policy meetings in the late 1980s and early 1990s. Many countries were claiming that their forests were sustainably managed. Such claims became a major point of contention which led to breakdowns in communication between NGOs; between NGOs and industry; and NGOs, industry and governments. WWF-UK decided it would not be a good idea to use if for the 1995 Group. In its discussions with the companies, the term 'well managed' offered a clearer context. For companies who are managing people and things, 'well managed' had an appealing resonance. WWF-UK based 'well managed' upon the FSC principles and criteria (Box 4.3).

[14] In 1991, Greenpeace-International launched its North American temperate forests campaign which promoted this image.

[15] International inaction on forestry policy contrasted with considerable local-level action. Before the 1992 Earth Summit, 450 city councils in Germany and a majority of Dutch local authorities had banned the use of tropical timber. Although less extensive than in Germany and The Netherlands, a number of UK local authorities also introduced wood purchasing policies. In the USA, the states of Arizona and New York prohibited the use of tropical timber in public construction projects.

[16] A supplier action plan was defined as a direct and specific contact with a supplier over forestry management issues where a time frame for improvement was agreed.

[17] WWF-UK claims that where the panda logo is used by companies it is not meant as an eco-label or endorsement, either of a product or a company's environmental status. WWF is very careful about who is allowed to use the logo and how it is used. Copyright laws protect the logo and stipulate how and when it may be reproduced (see King, 1995).

[18] A 1995 confidential summary of a research report into public confidence by MORI, commissioned by a major UK company.

[19] All statistics relating to the performance of the WWF-UK 1995 Group are the product of research by Jem Bendell when working at WWF-UK. They will not be referenced from this point on.

[20] The Forestry Commission of Great Britain estimated UK apparent consumption of wood and wood products at 50 million cubic metres in 1993 (Williams, 1994). Using the same standard and conversion factors

for measuring wood products group, companies calculated their own wood-product consumption.

[21] As of April 1997, there were 78 members in the group.

[22] As of January 1997, Hart voor Hout had attracted the following buyers group partners: 252 municipalities, 10 state departments, 72 real estate developers, 139 housing associations and the three largest DIY retailers. Together these organisations represent one third of the Dutch timber market. All have pledged to purchase timber which comes from well-managed forests whenever possible. Given Hart voor Hout's explicit support for the FSC goals and mission, this essentially means that buyers group members are committed to purchasing timber from FSC-certified forests. In June 1996, WWF-NL joined Milieudefensie and NOVIB as a full Hart voor Hout partner (source, Hart voor Hout, 1997).

[23] Vanessa Carter, 1996 pers comm.

[24] Quoted in Drummond, 1997, p 13.

five

Keeping good company: an overview of business–environmental group partnerships worldwide

In this chapter, we provide an overview of partnerships between business and environmental groups worldwide. Our overview includes a closer look at three partnerships which we consider to be of key significance: Dow Europe's alliance with various environmental groups through the European Partners for the Environment, Unilever's work with the World Wide Fund for Nature International to establish the Marine Stewardship Council and Loblaws' collaboration with Pollution Probe in Canada. We end the chapter by turning to the wider green movement to describe emerging social and ethical partnerships which bring together development NGOs and progressive retailers to address issues such as social auditing and development projects in the South.

As the cases presented cover a variety of environmental issues, product sectors and business processes, we begin with a review of existing partnership typologies and then propose our own matrix for business–NGO partnerships (encompassing collaboration with environmental groups, human rights groups and development NGOs). This new matrix enables us to describe and analyse three broadly different types of partnership concerned with internal company matters – processes, projects and products. Other matrix variables include the NGO role and the number of issues addressed.

The business–NGO partnership matrix

Many participants in business–environmental group partnerships describe them according to the environmental issues they address, such as natural resource utilisation or pollution abatement. This method of describing partnerships can mask insights into their successful management, by ignoring cross-sectoral similarities such as the processes employed in an initiative or the relationship of the initiative to legislation. In order to better explain such issues, a number of typologies have been used in the management literature to describe partnership relationships between environmental groups, business and government.

In its work for the US President's Commission on Environmental Quality, McKinsey and Co (1992) proposed a way of analysing partnerships by their intended impact on regulation. They attempted to determine whether partnerships preempt, inform or respond to environmental legislation. Despite its legislative focus, this framework does not consider how partnerships may result from disenchantment with the legislative or regulatory process, an important dimension of the partnerships described in this book.

Another set of typologies are based on the degree of commonality in goals between the environmental group and business partners. SustainAbility (1996) describes relationships that range from those where there is no commonality ('challenge') to those characterised by high commonality ('strategic joint venture'). This approach provides business leaders with analytical tools to better understand potential and existing relations with environmental groups.

The Management Institute for Environment and Business (MEB, 1995) describes pre-emptive, coalescing, exploration and leverage forms of partnership:

- **Pre-emptive partnerships** attempt to defuse an already or potentially confrontational situation.

- **Coalescing partnerships** bring together traditional rivals with different motivations but shared goals which can be achieved together.

- **Exploration partnerships** attempt to research issues of joint concern.

- **Leverage partnerships** are initiatives which aim to pool resources to allow partners to reap higher returns than would be gained alone after modest investments of time and money (the partnering approach).

These frameworks and typologies are useful for describing the range of business–environmental group relations that exist, including those which involve government agencies. However, they do not fully address partnerships which involve NGOs in internal operational issues of participating businesses, the focus of this book.

There is a body of literature on negotiation and game theory that can be employed to describe types of business–environmental group partnership (Warty, 1997). Social science academics and negotiation practitioners have for a number of years attempted to explain how interest groups interact with each other and how they arrive at solutions to problems and conflicts. Techniques for processes such as agenda setting, information sharing and dispute resolution are well described in management texts and are employed by a number of organisations who facilitate dialogue between business and environmental groups. The partnerships we describe in this book are, however, not primarily about resolving disputes, even if many grew out of initial conflict. Instead they are about working together in order to achieve goals which the partners would otherwise be unable to achieve individually. We believe that a dispute resolution model does not enable us to consider the broader range of issues emanating from our partnership case studies.

In order to illustrate the complex inter-play of issues involved in the partnerships described in this book, we offer a business–NGO partnership matrix which is outlined in Box 5.1.

How a partnership affects core business practice is our first variable. Partnerships can deal with company management processes, strategic projects and specific products. Management processes could include environmental management systems or supply chain auditing. Strategic projects could include developing new mechanisms to assist the business concerned in moving towards sustainability. Product performance issues could involve partnerships to develop new products or environmental group endorsement for existing company products.

Box 5.1: The business–NGO partnership matrix

The part of the business operation that is affected:
- management processes;
- strategic projects;
- product performance.

The primary role played by participating NGOs:
- endorsement;
- development and implementation.

The number of environmental, ethical and social issues addressed:
- single issue;
- multiple issues;
- total quality analysis.

Accordingly the role of participating NGOs is also a key dimension to any partnership initiative and is our second variable. This divides the role of NGOs into the endorsement or development and implementation of the processes, projects or products concerned. In some cases, NGOs may begin by endorsing a project idea, for example, and then later collaborate with the business partner on project development and implementation. In others, the NGO involvement in the partnership may stop at the endorsement stage.

The significance of a partnership for participating businesses and NGOs, as well as wider society, is suggested by the number of issues addressed, our third variable. This means that partnerships can focus on a single issue such as fisheries management, a multiple number of issues related to deforestation, pollution prevention or eco-efficiency, for example; or perhaps on total quality issues of a particular business

Our categories are not exclusive and some initiatives involve different types of partnership. For example, in the previous chapter we described how the 1995 Group acted primarily as an endorsement of a single management process – timber supply chain assessment and the creation of incentives for certification. However, we also described how the partnership involved an exchange of skills and knowledge with, to a limited degree, WWF-UK helping develop and implement the supplier assessment process. The partnership was also closely linked with product endorsement partnerships through its promotion of the Forest Stewardship Council (FSC) system and logo.

Although we do not explore operational issues in detail, we do hope our matrix and variables will help to deepen organisational and individual learning about the partnership process and provide a useful framework for the analysis of partnership management (see Annex).

Process-oriented partnerships

Process-oriented partnerships are those collaborations between businesses and environmental groups that involve environmental groups with internal management processes in some way. They need not involve the endorsement or development of new product lines. Instead they may focus on broad issues such as environmental policies, eco-efficiency strategies or improving the performance of suppliers. Examples of these forms of partnership include the WWF-UK 1995 Plus Group and Hart voor Hout (see Chapter four); the Groundwork and Hoover suppliers initiative in the UK; and the Oregon Growth Management Initiative in the USA (see Box 5.4). The following case study is of a management process partnership that focuses on multiple and complex sustainability issues. The case focuses on collaboration between various environmental groups and the chemical company Dow Europe.

Dow Europe and the European Partners for the Environment[1]

In 1996, Dow Europe agreed to work with a number of community and environmental groups on a project entitled 'Building trust through EMAS: what can we learn from Responsible Care?' The project enabled local, national and European environmental groups to discuss environmental management and stakeholder engagement issues related to one of Dow's manufacturing sites in the European Union. In particular, the project assessed how stakeholders could become involved in implementing the Eco-Management and Auditing Scheme (EMAS) within the chemical industry, and whether additional lessons could be learned from the industry's Responsible Care programme (Box 5.2).

This initiative was the result of a number of years of building trust between Dow, other large companies, environmental consultants and campaigning organisations. This trust was largely built through the European Partners for the Environment (EPE): a multi-stakeholder group committed to the implementation of the EU's Fifth Action Programme on the Environment, set up with the help of Dow Europe. Given the importance of the chemical industry to modern lifestyles and many years of antagonism between environmental groups and the chemical industry this initiative is a remarkable example of third-wave environmentalism and third-stage business response in action. Below we provide important historical background to Dow's recent partnership efforts. Similar to the experience of the DIY sector in Chapter four, Dow experienced many years of protest before adopting a more proactive stance on environmental issues.

Chemicals and modern life

On the inside cover of the Dow Chemical Company's 1995 annual report, we are reminded of the pervasive influence of today's chemical industry: "From the food we eat to the homes we live in and cars we drive, chemistry touches every aspect of our modern life." Chemical companies such as Dow regularly tell us that they manufacture products which "bring comfort, safety and convenience to our daily lives".[2] The popular trademarks of chemical products are almost synonymous with ideas of progress and modernity: Styrofoam, Nylon, Lycra, Dacron, Teflon, Quallofil, Kelvar, Styron and Saran Wrap to mention but a few. It is not surprising that some analysts have described the chemical industry as "the point of application of one of the great positive sciences to human affairs" (Hardie and Pratt, 1966, p xi).

Box 5.2: Responsible Care

Responsible Care was launched by the Canadian Chemical Producers Association (CCPA) in 1984 as a voluntary programme of continuous improvement in environmental performance following the Union Carbide disaster in Bhopal, India. The CCPA revised its programme in 1988 following four years of consultation with its members. It also sought the advice of public opinion specialists and found that the general public wanted to be able to monitor the environmental performance of chemical companies. The message was that companies had to make information available to the public, to respond to questions and to maintain a consistent, continuous dialogue. Responsible Care is based upon a wide-ranging set of principles and codes of practice regarding the management of chemicals and chemical products. In 1988, the American chemical industry's Care Code initiative adopted the responsible care name and programme. In the UK, the Chemical Industries Association developed its own version of Responsible Care in 1989.

Despite numerous attempts to project a positive public image, the chemical industry has been the target of sustained environmental and consumer group pressure at least since the 1962 publication of *Silent spring*. Following its publication, Dow, Monsanto and other chemical companies responded by establishing 'front groups', running media campaigns, conducting 'hostile mailings' and organising public forums of so-called third-party experts. The chemical industry and its expert allies attacked Rachel Carson's "personal and professional credibility while defending the use of DDT and other toxic compounds". The industry campaign achieved some degree of success when even *The New York Times* challenged Carson's credibility (see Helvarg, 1996, p 20). No amount of public relations activity, however, could stop the growing public concern about pesticides in the early–mid 1960s. Andrew Hoffman captures the dynamic between the industry and its opposition at the time:

> In 1964 ... one million dead fish wash up on the shores of the Mississippi River, causing a severe controversy. This spurs talk of pesticide bans, and once again industry defends the position it took against *Silent spring* – primarily one of denial. (1996b, p 54)

Twenty years later, the chemical industry came under worldwide attack following the Union Carbide disaster in Bhopal, India which killed up to 8,000 people and which injured as many as 600,000 more. Bhopal was a rude wake-up call for both the industry and regulators everywhere. In addition to concerns about lower environmental and safety standards in southern countries, there was the inescapable fact that some pesticides, long since banned in the North, were (and still are) being marketed in various parts of the South (see Lamb, 1996, p 120).

The need for enhanced regulation

Environmentalists have continued to call for more effective national and international regulation on the use and trade of toxic chemicals. In the UK, FoE has campaigned for many years for the public's right to information about government and industry research about pesticides and toxicity. More generally, environmental campaigners have identified the following criticisms of existing regulation governing chemicals:

- lack of comprehensive international treaties to stop the use and harmful effects of biologically active persistent compounds (eg, PCBs, DDT);

- disregard for the additive, interactive or cumulative effects of different chemicals;

- over-reliance on voluntary agreements with industry;

- lack of reporting requirements concerning quantities of endocrine-disrupting compounds contained in products sold or transported (see Colborn et al, 1996 and FoE-UK, 1995).

At the international policy level, Chapter 19 of Agenda 21 is devoted to the environmentally sound management and trade of toxic chemicals. Although Agenda 21 contains specific recommendations about waste reduction, materials recycling and safer waste disposal, Greenpeace-International responded with a detailed critique of the way in which the chemicals' issue was handled. One of the major gaps identified was Agenda 21's failure to challenge the export of hazardous waste from industrialised countries (see Chaterjee and Finger, 1994; Greenpeace-International, 1992).

Implementation of Agenda 21's recommendations related to chemicals has been allocated to a variety of intergovernmental bodies. While there has been much talk since Rio, governments and UN agencies have yet to address many of the concerns outlined above. For example, UNEP's governing council has taken two decisions with regard to Persistent Organic Pollutants (POPs) – dangerous, bioaccumlative chemical substances. One of the UNEP decisions agreed upon "the need for international actions to reduce or eliminate releases and emissions of POPs" and "put in place a process to determine ... the adequacy of existing information" (Whitelaw, 1996, p 5). Although it is expected that UNEP will call for immediate international action in early 1997, the next step will be to begin the long and cumbersome process of negotiating an international legally binding instrument. On a related matter, governments have decided that it is too early to develop an overarching legal instrument to promote more effective global regulation of all chemical-related matters.[3]

Alarm bells still ringing

While governments continue to talk in the late 1990s, we find the chemical industry still being challenged worldwide by a range of environmental and consumer groups about the health and environmental consequences of chemical-based production processes and products. Media headlines continue to ring alarm bells:

"Green onslaught may sink chlorine"

"Peril of the pesticides"

"Sex-change chemicals in baby milk"

"Why today's man is losing his virility"

SustainAbility reminds us that "most of the major environmental problems and issues of the past few decades have had their roots in industrial – and particularly organic – chemistry" (1995b, p 36). The industry response to environmental group concerns has ranged from denial and defensiveness typified by the onslaught against *Silent spring* to frank dialogue with its critics. Over the past decade, the industry has endeavoured to enhance its environmental record and image with self-regulating schemes such as Responsible Care (see Chapter three and Box 5.2). Some companies have gone further and entered into partnership agreements with environmental groups. However, when faced with criticism, the industry response still tends to be defensive, particularly in North America. Following the 1996 publication of *Our stolen future* (Colborn et al, 1996), a book which links synthetic chemicals to hormonal disruptions in humans and wildlife, the American chemical industry launched a damage-limitation exercise by attacking the credibility of the book's authors and their claims (see Helvarg, 1996).

Dow, protest and response

Dow Chemical Company is a transnational corporation based in Michigan, USA, and is currently the fifth largest chemical company in the world with an annual global turnover of more than $20 billion and 40,000 employees. Its subsidiary, Dow Europe, currently oversees 8,600 employees in Europe, the Middle East and Africa. Dow Europe has annual sales of $6.4 billion from 2,000 products in plastics and a variety of basic and specialty chemicals.

Following more than two decades of sustained public pressure about the environmental impacts of Dow's products and production processes (see Box 5.3) the company began to adopt a more proactive stance on Environment, Health and Safety (EHS) issues toward the end of the 1980s. Dow's 1989 annual report included for the first time a special shareholder's report on the environment. Environmental impact also became more than a matter of production as life-cycle analysis issues took on greater importance. In the early 1990s, Dow established its first internal Global EHS Council and a Corporate Environmental Advisory Council made up of global policy and opinion leaders to advise the company. Dow Europe subsequently formed its own regional administrative EHS Council in 1991, the same year it published the first annual environmental report within Dow worldwide. Public dialogue of different forms intensified and the company facilitated the formation of community advisory panels adjacent to many of its sites. Also in 1991, Dow Europe set a target to reduce releases of 58 hazardous chemicals to air and water by 50 per cent between 1988 and 1995, with a similar target for landfill disposal. The targets were met in 1994 a year ahead of schedule. While Dow has for many years seen EHS matters as site-level priorities, recent corporate restructuring has meant that environmental management will be increasingly integrated into core areas of business activity.

Since its formation, Dow Europe's EHS Council has been headed by Claude Fussler, vice president of EHS, Public Affairs, and New Businesses. Under Fussler's leadership, Dow Europe has placed greater emphasis upon issues such as public dialogue, eco-efficiency and the company's overall response to the Rio Conference and Agenda 21. For example, Fussler was instrumental in the formation of EPE which is described below.

Dow and the formation of EPE

In late 1992, the Director of the United Nations Environment Programme (UNEP) invited people from various sectors to discuss follow-up to the Rio Conference. UNEP wanted to find ways of making the spirit of partnership work. Dow's Claude Fussler attended this meeting and met Raymond van Ermen from the European Environmental Bureau (EEB), an umbrella organisation of 150 environmental groups. Over lunch they discussed ways in which the two sectors of business and the environmental movement could collaborate. Fussler and van Ermen agreed that there was a need to change the prevailing adversarial pattern of business–environmental group relations. Before embarking upon any joint action, both saw a need to build awareness about the benefits of partnership.

Van Ermen and Fussler of Dow Europe began to explore the potential for developing a multi-stakeholder forum to discuss sustainable development issues and to operationalise the European Commission's concept of shared responsibility in the Fifth Action Programme. According to Fussler, various groups were "working in their own little sectors and were not getting together to pool their expertise." Fussler and van Ermen saw a need for a forum to promote the exchange of views between sectors. Following a series of round table discussions organised by EEB, van Ermen invited representatives from business, public authorities, research institutes and environmental groups "to discuss the launching of a European initiative to foster economic recovery based on green economics and green industries" (EPE, 1994c).

Box 5.3: Dow and environmental pressure 1960-88

1960-70: Environmental issues were primarily handled at the local level as site specific processes. In 1966, Chairman Carl Gerstacker acknowledged that most Chief Executive Officers (CEOs) did not really know how much pollution their companies were producing. In 1969, Dow's board formed an ecology council to accelerate and expand environmental efforts world-wide. Nevertheless, during this period public concern and hostility grew with Dow targeted as the producer of napalm used in the Vietnam war.

1970-82: This period saw Dow's frustration with regulations and ongoing attacks concerning the health effects of napalm on Vietnam veterans. The company was also publicly antagonistic about new environmental regulations. Later in the 1970s, the company tried to show that it was taking greater responsibility for its products. An example of the more responsive Dow was a press conference and open house in 1978 which invited the public and shared and explained scientific data concerning dioxin pollutants and cancer rates. Although Dow was confident that its dioxin emissions "were too small to be dangerous", critics continued to raise questions about "the degree of carcinogenicity and the triggers of health effects" (see Kleiner, 1992, p 32).

1982-88: Dow's environmental policy became more formalised in the mid-eighties. Greenpeace stepped up its campaigns against Dow, plugging its Midland (Michigan) discharge pipes in the spring of 1985. Dow realised that it had to listen to its critics and communicate scientific information more effectively to the public. Dow had to demonstrate that it cared (see Smart, 1992). In 1988, the company embarked upon the first phase of its new environmental agenda when it formalised its Waste Reduction Always Pays (WRAP) programme in the USA, a scheme which shortly thereafter became operational in Europe.

In February 1994, the EPE was formed at a meeting in Brussels. EPE sees itself as an awareness-building organisation which aims "to get real partnerships in action initiated." EPE started as a pilot initiative to enable the participants to analyse the success factors for partnerships by reviewing various models. The outcomes of these activities are recorded in the EPE workbook *Towards shared responsibility* (1994c).

In its second year, EPE was in transition and started to look at specific policy issues such as mobility, transportation, communication, agriculture, food production and sale, packaging and waste, and sustainability measurements. By bringing together representatives of various sectors in workshop settings, EPE participants hoped to identify more precise follow-up actions. One of the more prominent EPE members is the London-based environmental consultancy SustainAbility. Andrea Spencer-Cooke, an associate of SustainAbility, agrees that current business–environmental group relations pose a hurdle to future functional partnerships:

> *You sit around the table with a bunch of business people as an environmental group and you're accused of complicity or ... you're in danger of capture. It's a very difficult issue for environmental groups in particular I think, being seen to be friendly with the enemy.*

In her assessment, EPE's greatest achievement is simply being a forum where environmental groups, businesses, public authorities and other sectors can sit around the table and discuss issues. Spencer-Cooke believes that the personal learning experience is what participants take back to their organisations. The hope is that EPE participants will think much more readily about involving stakeholders in their own organisations by learning from the EPE process. Spencer-Cooke explains:

> *There are very few such fora for that to occur. I think all the individuals that have been involved so far have found their universe enriched through the process.... I think there's a personal and organisational learning experience going on that's very important.*

From EPE to EMAS-Plus

Dow describes its involvement in EPE as a means of building bridges with the environmental movement. In theory, Dow is quite capable of developing new and innovative environmental technology. The anxiety for Dow is always: Will somebody buy it? Will there be a market? By being able to speak at an early stage with environmental groups, Dow has a "much better capacity to assess market risk and even to create some allies" for its new technologies.

Through EPE the company has the potential to develop contacts with environmental groups working on related issues. By learning from each other, Dow and the environmental groups hope to discuss potential technologies, the bottlenecks and dynamics of the market, and the need for product redesign in order to obtain an eco-label, for example. Such a process would enable Dow to minimise some of the risks. Dow hopes that such partnerships can materialise through its involvement in EPE, yet realises that it will be some time before specific business–environmental group partnerships on environmental technology develop.

SustainAbility's Spencer-Cook views Dow's commitment to EPE as Fussler's personal crusade for partnership which is strongly supported by people at the top of his organisation:

> *I think his motivation is linked to really believing that partnerships are necessary, particularly when you start to deal with the more complex kind of trade-offs that the environmental and sustainability agendas bring. Claude's particular interest is to try and find ways of getting win–win solutions across various areas, and he certainly sees partnerships as rather more promising ways of trying to achieve those ... Dow's prime involvement has been in providing resources and providing an institutional support for what Claude himself is pioneering.*

Although, specific Dow–environmental group partnerships related to environmental technology have yet to emerge, Dow's participation in EPE has brought new ideas into the company as illustrated by the groundbreaking EMAS project which involved "Stichting Natuur en Milieu" (SNM: Netherlands Society for Nature and Environment).

The project offered EPE members an opportunity to investigate potential links between stakeholder relations in Responsible Care and proposals for extended stakeholder participation in EMAS or EMAS Plus. EPE describes EMAS Plus as "a first step in the development of sustainability management practices" (EPE, 1996).

An EPE research group of 16 people was formed and a one-day, participatory workshop took place on 1 November 1996 at the Dow site concerned. SustainAbility provided two facilitators. Research group members included representatives of EPE, Dow

Europe, other businesses, SNM, regulators, Dow's local community advisory panel (CAP) and the company's local site staff.

Workshop participants addressed the following questions based upon Dow's local experience:

- [How] does Responsible Care involve stakeholders, and what is the nature of the dialogue?

- What have been the results of stakeholder dialogue under Responsible Care?

- What synergies might exist between stakeholder dialogue in Responsible Care and EMAS?

- Is it possible to identify commonly applicable 'good stakeholder practices'?

- What are the benefits and limitations to stakeholders of verification? (EPE, 1996)

Workshop conclusions and recommendations included relevant information for both Dow and its various stakeholders (see EPE, 1997).

Key conclusions:

- Responsible Care provides opportunity for dialogue through CAPs, local authority programmes, open site days and schools programmes;

- issues addressed by CAPs range from socio-economic to environmental;

- effective dialogue requires time, commitment and a diverse mix of participants;

- both formal and informal mechanisms for dialogue are needed;

- interests of other stakeholders need to be addressed, such as regulators or national NGOs;

- both Responsible Care and EMAS see stakeholder processes as a key component of transition to sustainability;

- stakeholder participation in EMAS verification would build trust;

- EMAS is not in itself a sustainable management tool;

- other instruments are needed for sustainable development.

Recommendations:

- Dow to involve stakeholders at all levels;

- EPE to play a key role in developing EMAS Plus;

- EPE to identify interested stakeholder groups, identify their needs and prepare case studies;

- EPE to suggest how, where and when different stakeholders should participate in the process;

- EPE to seek examples of business-stakeholder relations beyond site level;

- EMAS should have a requirement for a stakeholder management system;

- EMAS 1998 review should recommend that sites demonstrate evidence of stakeholder engagement.

Dow's participation in this EPE pilot project and its general support for EPE represents significant and strategic moves by a global chemical company to identify and establish partnerships outside of industry in order to exchange viewpoints, to develop joint activities, to influence legislation and to prepare Dow for the challenges of the next century.

Dow and the future

Looking back at the past three and a half decades, Dow has faced major criticisms about napalm, dioxins, emissions levels, among many other issues. Dow learned it could not dismiss environmental group protest nor public concerns about the health, safety and environmental impact of its products and production processes. From the above discussion it is apparent that the company has gone a long way to enhance its relations with environmental groups and other stakeholders. There is also some evidence to suggest that key people in the organisation recognise that Dow will need to develop alternative processes and products for future markets and customers.

As mentioned earlier, Dow and other chemical companies still find themselves under attack. With the recent publication of *Our stolen future*, the chemical industry may be in for another *Silent spring*. Extensive media coverage and Greenpeace's related consumer and retailer campaign in the UK – *Taking back our stolen future*[4] – which targets the use of PVC in packaging and building materials, are evidence of a gathering storm of public concern.

Dow has not yet prepared a formal public response to *Our stolen future* or the related Greenpeace campaign and publications. Mike Kolleth, Dow Europe's Environment and New Business Communications Manager, offers the following comments:

> *[With] regard to Our stolen future: Dow shares the view of many in the academic and scientific communities who believe that the book is based on a yet unproven hypothesis. We are, however, aware of the concern about endocrine-related issues. We are working with the European chemical industry's trade association CEFIC and other interested parties to study the issue more closely.*
>
> *[Concerning] the Greenpeace PVC campaign, Dow believes that when produced, used and disposed of in a safe and appropriate manner, PVC is, and will remain, a viable product in packaging and many other consumer applications.*

While Kolleth's comments echo in some respects the chemical industry's initial dismissal of *Silent spring* in the early 1960s, the fact that Dow and other members of CEFIC are working on the issue indicates that there is growing concern within the industry. *The Economist* notes that "chemical firms throughout the rich world are pouring millions into research on the science of gender-bending – partly out of fear that governments will react to the scare by banning a much wider range of chemicals" (1996b, p 77).

Dow's pro-active stance on the environment since the late 1980s should mean that it is prepared for this latest onslaught of criticism. The company has cultivated allies from the local to the global levels and has clearly set itself apart from many other chemical companies as an industry leader on environmental issues. As mentioned above, Dow has relied heavily upon charismatic individuals within the company, such as Fussler, to lead the change both externally and internally. Given the added pressure of *Our stolen future* and related Greenpeace campaigning, there will be considerable pressure upon Fussler and his colleagues within Dow Europe to find an appropriate way to respond. While Dow has always insisted upon the need to balance environmental concerns with commercial realities, the company may have to move more quickly than planned to develop new products in the face of renewed and widespread criticism, and the threat of future legislation on PVC and dioxins. Developing closed-loop systems and introducing full cost accounting for existing products may not be enough.

Dow's experience with partnerships to date indicates that it is still not clear what Dow considers to be purely internal policy matters or what the company now accepts as public domain. The growing influence of social responsibility and sustainable development within Dow is making internal–external and private–public divisions harder to maintain. While Dow has established itself as an industry leader on the environment, Dow's long-term response to the challenges from environmental groups and other stakeholders depends upon complementary changes in consumer demands, supported by government policy and the assistance of the chemical industry. A genuine partnership approach will be needed to transform both the current economics and unsustainable nature of chemical production, products and use.

Box 5.4: Other process-oriented partnerships

The timber partnerships in Chapter four are management process-oriented partnerships, although also concerned with product endorsement. They are all single issue initiatives, dealing only with deforestation. The WWF 1995 Plus Group is a one NGO to many businesses partnership, with WWF-UK maintaining a hold on the partnership's agenda. Hart voor Hout constitutes a many-to-many partnership with a number of NGOs and businesses developing the future of the partnership together.

In Oregon, USA, the environmental group 1000 Friends of Oregon (1000F) and the industry group Home Builders Association of Metropolitan Portland formed a "coalition to promote denser single-family and apartment development within cities" (Law, 1992, p 12). 1000F wanted to protect rural lands from encroaching urban sprawl, while the association wanted clearer guidelines to avoid costly legal actions. In 1981, the partnership developed project planning guidelines for building companies to follow, which were subsequently adopted by the State's Land Development and Conservation Commission as the Metropolitan Housing Rule. In helping to develop this rule, builders were effectively committing to restrict the area of individual developments in the future.

In subsequent years the partners went their separate ways but in 1991 they collaborated on follow up research to test the effectiveness of the Rule. Their study concluded that without the housing rule, development "would have consumed and additional 1,500 acres of land" (MEB, 1995, p 235).

From 1995, Hoover plc and the UK charity Groundwork initiated a one-to-one partnership by working together to encourage Hoover's suppliers to improve their environmental performance. Hoover sent letters out to each of the suppliers, encouraging them to contact Groundwork for information and to get involved in a sustainability training programme. This partnership differs from most of those described in the book as finance did change hands.

Project-oriented partnerships

Project-oriented partnerships are those collaborations between businesses and environmental groups that focus on discrete projects to achieve objectives with significant implications for core business practice. They differ from management process partnerships as the relationship does not necessarily involve environmental groups with internal management decisions. Examples of these forms of partnership include the McDonald's–Environmental Defense Fund collaboration (Chapter six) and the Washington State Timber/Fish/Wildlife Agreement between Native American groups and logging companies in the USA (see Box 5.5).

The following case study is a project development and implementation partnership, which deals with one environmental issue and at the outset involves one environmental group and one company.

Unilever and WWF-International

In February 1996, the World Wide Fund for Nature (WWF) International and Unilever plc announced that they were to work in partnership to help establish an organisation which would utilise market mechanisms to alleviate the worldwide fisheries crisis. The two organisations have different motivations but a shared objective: "to ensure the long term viability of global fish populations and the health of the marine ecosystems on which they depend" (WWF-International, 1996a, p 1).

> The Marine Stewardship Council [MSC] will be an independent, non-profit, non governmental body. Following extensive consultations the organisation will establish a broad set of principles for sustainable fishing and set standards for individual fisheries. (WWF-International, 1996a)

Unilever has pledged to source their fishery products only from well-managed fisheries certified to MSC standards by the year 2005 and with WWF-International is encouraging other seafood companies to make similar commitments.

The similarities with the WWF-UK 1995 Group and the FSC (Chapter four) are not just coincidence: the MSC initiative is using the FSC as its inspiration. Although it is too early to assess the success of the initiative the very fact that something so similar is occurring in a completely different trade sector faced with different issues and involving different personalities, does suggest some common factors are at play. The lack of political commitment and capacity to agree and enforce the necessary legislation, the role of business in contributing to the problem and the growing levels of public protest provide a context for both initiatives.

WWF-International and Unilever have set themselves a difficult task. The Food and Agriculture Organisation (FAO) reports that 70 per cent of the world's commercial fisheries are either fully utilised, over-exploited, depleted or slowly recovering (FAO, 1995b). In many fisheries, staple species such as halibut and cod have become "commercially extinct". For years fishers in Newfoundland landed an annual catch of around 350,000 metric tonnes. Since 1968 when a record catch of 800,000 metric tonnes was recorded, annual catches fell drastically and in 1992 a moratorium on the fishing of northern cod was declared (NLRTEE, 1995). Cod stocks in the North Sea look set to experience similar declines, and by 1993 they had fallen to about a third of the levels seen in the early 1970s (see HMSO, 1996; Cook, Sinclair and Stefßusson, 1997).

The reasons for the collapse of fisheries worldwide are still disputed. The reason heard most often is that there are simply too many fishers chasing too few fish. Although this assertion is basically correct, it does not help in determining remedial policy responses. For example, modern industrial fishing practices kill and waste 18-40 million metric tonnes of unwanted fish, birds, turtles, dolphins and other marine wildlife each year; roughly a third of the total world catch (Alverson et al, 1994). Modern types of fishing gear are known to physically damage the sea bed and adversely affect the food chain upon which commercially-valuable fish depend. A fisher from Labrador graphically explains: "If we had a piece of land and run a tractor over it 365 days a year, you just see how much would grow on it. But you can't see the damage being done on the ocean floor" (NLRTEE, 1995, p 11).

The huge growth in fishing effort worldwide and the use of destructive fishing methods are symptoms of more complex and fundamental causal factors. Figure 4 identifies the causes of the fisheries crisis as five-fold. First is the lack of awareness, understanding and communication of the issues by and between all stakeholders in the fishing industry. Second, there are the restricted options of fish workers worldwide and the difficulties with diversifying their source of income. The third causal factor is the growing dominance of overcapitalised and highly invested fishing operations, where boat owners and fishing companies must increase their catch to pay the interest on investment capital. Fourth, there is the problem with fixed capital and rigid institutional regimes which are slow to react to a changing natural resource base. The final and most fundamental problem is the profligate consumption of northern industrial countries. For example, 30 per cent of the world's catch is used for fishmeal, to feed livestock or to supply the manufacturing industry.

Fishing is one of the world's most important activities. At the time of writing, the total world catch is 102 million tonnes a year. Fish provides 20 per cent of the world's animal protein supply, with the consumption of industrialized countries being about three times that of southern countries. There are an estimated 12.5 million fish workers in the world today. With their families this brings the number of people directly dependent on fishing for their livelihood to 50 million (FAO, 1995b). These figures illustrate just how saving the world's fisheries is a matter of life or death for millions of the world's people.

The political response to the fisheries crisis

At Rio and the subsequent UN Conference on Highly Migratory and Straddling Fish Stocks in 1993, the precautionary approach to fisheries management was emphasised. However, many governments have not embraced this principle and still appear to be contributing to the problem. Worldwide, governments pay an estimated $54 billion per year in fisheries subsidies to an industry that catches only $70 billion worth of fish (FAO, 1993). Many subsidies are given as "investment for development" but can have catastrophic effects by increasing the fishing effort and upsetting the ecological balance between coastal communities and their fishery resource.

Figure 4: Problems, mechanisms and causes of the fisheries crisis

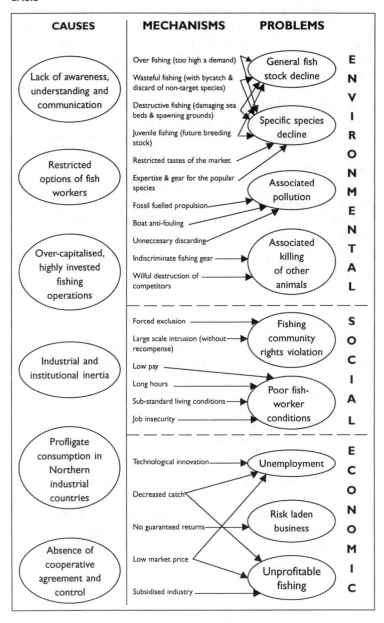

CAUSES	MECHANISMS	PROBLEMS	
Lack of awareness, understanding and communication	Over fishing (too high a demand)	General fish stock decline	E N V I R O N M E N T A L
	Wasteful fishing (with bycatch & discard of non-target species)		
	Destructive fishing (damaging sea beds & spawning grounds)		
Restricted options of fish workers	Juvenile fishing (future breeding stock)	Specific species decline	
	Restricted tastes of the market		
	Expertise & gear for the popular species	Associated pollution	
	Fossil fuelled propulsion		
Over-capitalised, highly invested fishing operations	Boat anti-fouling		
	Unneccesary discarding	Associated killing of other animals	
	Indiscriminate fishing gear		
	Wilful destruction of competitors		
Industrial and institutional inertia	Forced exclusion	Fishing community rights violation	S O C I A L
	Large scale intrusion (without recompense)		
	Low pay		
	Long hours	Poor fish-worker conditions	
	Sub-standard living conditions		
	Job insecurity		
Profligate consumption in Northern industrial countries	Technological innovation	Unemployment	E C O N O M I C
	Decreased catch	Risk laden business	
	No guaranteed returns		
Absence of cooperative agreement and control	Low market price	Unprofitable fishing	
	Subsidised industry		

When governments have acted to restrict the fishing effort it has often been too little too late. The moratorium on cod fishing in Newfoundland after the fishery had collapsed is an example of just such a response. In Europe a similar scenario is unfolding. Since 1982, the Common Fisheries Policy's conservation policy has intended to foster healthy fish stocks and secure the future of the industry. The main management tool used to achieve these aims is the system of Total Allowable Catches (TACs) or quotas. Fifteen years later it appears that the policy has been ineffective (Gray, 1997). There have been several problems with quotas. First they have stimulated a race to catch the maximum number of fish in the shortest time. Quotas have also lead to the mis-reporting of catches and have proven very difficult to enforce.[5]

Regional regulatory initiatives may have failed to deliver sustainable fishery management but at least they have been attempted, which contrasts with the situation on the high seas. "There is no recognised overall mechanism for international control of fishing for stocks which lie only in international waters" concluded a study by the UK House of Lords (HMSO, 1996). Chairman of the committee, Lord Selborne believes that "until we have something truly global that can relate to existing organisations we will not take away the politics of the issues" (Patey, 1996).

A global industry requires global regulatory mechanisms but our state-based political system seems to be unable to deliver. WWF-International's Michael Sutton concludes that "society has simply lacked the political will to forestall the fishing industry's tendency to use up its living capital and thereby destroy itself." However, the intention is not to replace the need for legislation or ignore the legislative process as a viable tool for conservation and environmental justice, as Sutton explains:

> ... to reverse the fisheries crisis we must develop long term solutions that are environmentally necessary and then, through economic incentives, make them politically feasible. We believe that through the MSC we will be able to make it easier for governments to act.

The rising tide of conflict

The lack of action to protect fisheries worldwide has led to growing conflict: between artisinal fishing communities and commercial trawling companies over the intrusion of traditional fishing grounds, between national governments over fishing rights and between environmental groups and business over destructive fishing practices.

The confrontation between the Canadian and Spanish governments over the presence of Spanish trawlers outside Canada's Exclusive Economic Zone (EEZ) is indicative of international resource conflicts now commonly known as 'fish wars'. Although not as internationally visible, regional fish wars have been waged by indigenous coastal communities threatened by the invasive activities of industrial fishing vessels for years (*The Ecologist*, 1995).

Northern environmental groups have long protested over the activities of the modern fishing industry. In 1996, the International Fund for Animal Welfare (IFAW) released a video tape of the Canadian seal hunt. IFAW claimed the video portrayed gross cruelty to animals and called on UK supermarkets to boycott Canadian salmon in order to persuade the Canadian government to ban the hunt. The fishermen cull seals each year as a means of reducing their major competitors for fish stocks and some were angered by this 'economic terrorism'. The same year Greenpeace-UK launched a direct action protest against McVities for their use of fishoil to make biscuits.[6] The fishoil was manufactured from sandeels trawled from the North Sea, where they constitute the basis of a foodchain which supports marine mammals, other fish species (eg cod and haddock), puffins and other seabirds. Dressing up as puffins, the Greenpeace-UK protesters claimed that McVities were responsible for the decline in the population of the seabird.

The response to calls for changing fishing practices and related activities has been varied. In the first case, fishing communities in Canada rejected criticism from IFAW: "These people are into fiction, not fact. They're into emotion, not education", said former Canadian Federal Fisheries minister and current Newfoundland Premier Brian Tobin (in Bailey, 1996). In the second case, after the Greenpeace protests, UK companies McVities, J. Sainsbury, Safeway and Tesco announced they would stop buying fishoil from the North Sea.[7]

In general though the fishing industry has not been proactive in trying to moderate the fishing effort. Michael Earle of Greenpeace explains:

> The precautionary approach is relatively new in fisheries, and there is enormous resistance on the part of the industry and managers to the changes that its adoption would imply. This is particularly true of the intensive, industrial scale fisheries responsible for much of the environmental and social destruction to date. (1995, p 16)

The resistance to change is understandable. In order to safeguard fish stocks companies involved in the harvesting of fish would be required to reduce their production levels and, by extension, their financial turnover. Therefore conservation measures are viewed as a threat to immediate profitability by many in the fishing industry. Reconciling the contradiction of a company's desire to grow with society's need for reduced consumption levels is essential in securing business support for market-led initiatives. A possible reconciliation is provided by focusing on fish demand, not fish supply. Buyers of fish such as processing and retailing companies can choose to buy from sustainable sources without the need to reduce their own consumption. In this way the market can transmit a message to begin to reduce catch-levels without arbitrarily putting fishing companies out of business.

In 1996, environmental groups were beginning to suggest ways in which progressive seafood companies might constructively engage the fisheries problem. A report from Greenpeace-International (1996a) on responsible fisheries ended with this statement:

> As consumers can only exercise their choice on the basis of adequate information regarding the impact of their consumption, the fish buying, processing and retailing industry must provide the public with direct access to information. This can be done, for example through detailed product labeling, or where appropriate, point of purchase and other forms of information directly accessible by consumers.

WWF's Endangered Seas Campaign

Against this background of ecological crisis and political friction, WWF-International identified fisheries as one of its key campaign areas along with forests (Chapter four) and global climate change. In 1995, the organisation established conservation targets for these areas and allocated three years of international finance for the campaigns. WWF-International shared Greenpeace's thinking on the role that seafood companies could play in helping to reverse fishery depletion and with the new finance of the Endangered Seas Campaign (ESC) they were able to act quickly.

The birth of the Marine Stewardship Council (MSC) initiative owes something to the open plan office at WWF's UK headquarters, Panda House. Located next to the Forest Unit, the ESC staff were able to learn informally about the 1995 Group and FSC initiatives. Attracted by the apparent success of these business partnerships, the ESC director brought in a member of the Forest Unit to work with a fisheries expert and analyse the transferability of WWF-UK's forest campaign to the fisheries sector. They concluded with the recommendation that WWF-International work in partnership with a major seafood processing company to establish a new organisation to create economic incentives for responsible fishing – the Marine Stewardship Council.[8]

Enter Unilever

Unilever is one of the world's largest consumer goods companies, with a turnover of around $52 billion in 1996 (Unilever, 1997). The company was established in 1930 through an amalgamation of the Dutch-based Margarine Unie and British-based Lever Brothers, two large businesses, each using fats and vegetable oils as raw materials. By the beginning of World War I, Unilever's constituent companies were already operating in 41 countries. Today it is truly a Transnational Corporation (TNC) with 500 operating companies in over 80 countries, employing some 300,000 people. Most of the company's business is in branded foods (52 per cent), detergents and personal products. Unilever's other major activity is in specialty chemicals. Fish are a major business concern for Unilever who, through subsidiaries such as Birds Eye Walls Ltd and Iglo, control 25 per cent of the frozen fish market in Europe and North America (Unilever, 1996).

For a company as large as Unilever there are a number of ethical issues to consider, including: pollution from the manufacture and use of agrochemicals; habitat destruction from the conversion of land to agriculture; payment of fair wages for southern farm labourers; and concerns with animal welfare in the meat and cosmetics industries. By 1996, Unilever had begun to address many of these issues and was able to publish its first environmental report. Introducing this report Sir Michael Perry and Morris Tabaksblat state that the company's:

> ... success and reputation are founded on the quality, efficiency and safety of our products and services, features which have won the confidence of consumers and customers across the world. This confidence must be supported by the environmental dimension of product and operational performance. (Unilever, 1996, p 1)

In keeping with this policy Unilever had been looking into the future of world fish stocks for a while and were in dialogue with the scientific community. In early 1995, a researcher from the University of Warwick, UK, recognised that WWF-International was looking into the same issues and let each organisation know of the other's interest. Dialogue was further stimulated in January 1996 by a Cambridge University conference which was convened to analyse the progress made by the 1995 Group of companies, at which Catherine Whitfield of Unilever and Michael Sutton attended, along with Simon Bryceson of the PR firm Burson-Marsteller. Burson-Marsteller was then employed to facilitate constructive dialogue between Unilever and WWF-International.

In February 1996, the directors of WWF-UK (acting on behalf of WWF-International) and Unilever met in The Hague and signed a statement of intent to establish the MSC. Each organisation committed to finance the initial set-up costs and began to advertise the initiative to the world's media so that wide participation might be encouraged. In September 1996, the MSC held the first in a series of workshops. Fourteen specialists on various aspects of fisheries and fisheries regulation developed a draft set of principles and criteria for sustainable fishing to serve as the basis for further discussion at future workshops. The draft, a work in progress rather than a final product, is inclusive of current international standards and agreements. NGO, fishing industry, fisheries regulation and retail representatives are being invited to attend regional workshops and provide their input to the draft principles and criteria and the process in general.

Lessons from the forest

The process of international consultation with a focus on the development of principles and criteria for certification and ecolabelling closely mirrors the early years of the FSC.

Although both industries are based on natural resources, the structure of the forestry and fisheries trades obviously differ. The difference particularly relevant to certification is the ownership of the resource. If a forest is certified it is protected from the operations of other foresters. The protection of discrete areas of certified forest has meant that the FSC, other environmental groups and the timber trade could argue that if a forest was certified it was being protected from competing land uses such as mining and agriculture. In the marine environment the situation is different. Ownership of the high seas is less well defined and far less easy to police. This is complicated by the fact that whereas trees are stationary, fish can move.

At the workshops participants have identified up to 14 potential units of certification, ranging from individual fish to regional fisheries. If the MSC ultimately decides to attempt certification of geographically specific fishery areas it will need to resolve the problems of defining ownership of areas, allocating quotas and protecting them from unauthorised fishing. Therefore *Fishing News International* has expressed a concern that the MSC maybe trying to reinvent the wheel:

> What should be remembered is that mechanisms aimed at achieving much of what the MSC is setting out to do already exist in many fisheries ... surely, it is better to strengthen what we have got rather than set off down a whole new route. (1997a, p 2)

Alternatively if the MSC opts for certification of individual vessels or vessel-owning companies these issues could be hurdled, the only drawback being that products would not be able to be represented to the consumer as coming from a sustainable resource. Boat certification would only secure the protection of fish stocks if all consumer markets demanded fish products from MSC-certified fisheries.

Another difficult issue the MSC will need to deal with is employment. Although research by the FAO has suggested otherwise, the conservation of fisheries is commonly thought of as anti-jobs (FAO, 1995b). The success of the MSC will depend on bringing in the fish-worker trade unions to discuss the potential costs and benefits. There is no doubt the MSC can be portrayed as an opportunity for traditional fish workers the world over. The growth of capitalised, industrial and large-scale fishing has been identified as a major cause of fishery decline. In many fisheries 10 per cent of the boats take 90 per cent of the catch. If certification is structured in such a fashion to discriminate against these larger fishing vessels, the reduction of catch and the stimulation of employment can be mutually achievable objectives. Thus the MSC could be presented as a win–win scenario for the world's fishing communities, by switching market demand to less technologically advanced fishing practices.

However, this approach may alienate the operators of and investors in large factory ships. If the industrial fishing industry anticipates a loss of business through the MSC initiative then they too may try to stall the process. To illustrate, the presence of a major industrial block rallied against the development of organic farming certification – the agrochemical industry – has been suggested as a main reason for the poor market penetration of organic produce (Dudley, 1995).

Another reason for the limited market penetration of certified organic produce (and potentially, certified timber products) may relate to finance. Unilever's Whitfield believes that "[fish certification] will not put prices up a penny. If it works, we will see more fish on the market and a decline in price." However, up until now timber traders have found FSC certified timbers to be about seven per cent more expensive than non-certified timbers. All forms of environmental certification entails two costs – the internal costs associated with changing the enterprise to comply with certification criteria (for example new fishing gear or a reduction in permissible catch) and the external costs of assessment and monitoring (the certifier's fees). Certification is regulation paid for by the market and so somewhere in the supply chain it must be paid for. A reluctance to invest in certification may therefore hinder the rapid uptake of the scheme.

These are just a few of the challenging issues for the MSC consultative process to resolve. Perhaps the most important lessons from the forest experience may prove to be the way participants in the FSC initiative managed to overcome seemingly unresolvable problems and disputes. In the establishment of the FSC the participants retained several key principles or organisational concepts. The FSC is a participatory, voluntary, independent, transnational, progressive, non-profit organisation. The organisation did not decide what constituted sustainable forestry and then defend this against wide consultation. Instead it embraced as many people and organisations as possible to make them feel that they had a stake in the organisation. It could be said that the FSC is working because of this spirit of cooperation, not because it has all the answers. This may prove a difficult task, as already some fish workers have shown deep suspicion of a process initiated by their major customers and their traditional opponents in the environmental movement – one fishing industry representative commented on the Vancouver workshop, "I'm not sure if we are really being invited to get on the train, or are we just getting to wave at it as it goes by?" (*Fishing News International*, 1997b, p 4). For the MSC to succeed will require these concerns to be assuaged so that all stakeholders in fishing feel they have a stake in the success of the MSC initiative.

Already the benefits of the transparent and cooperative approach being adopted by WWF-International and Unilever in the MSC initiative are being seen. The World Bank and the UNDP have both expressed interest in the development of the MSC, with the bank currently looking into supporting the initiative through a Fisheries Market Transformation Initiative. At the Boston workshop in November the Fisheries Council of Canada invited the MSC to run a test certification of appropriate Canadian fisheries. The WBCSD (of which Unilever is a member) features the MSC initiative as a "signal for change" in its assessment of post-Rio activities (WBCSD, 1997). These relations will be further supported by the appointment of the former OECD administrator Carl-Christian Schmidt as project director for the MSC.

If the MSC is successful we may be seeing the emergence of a new model for regulating human economic activity. However, WWF-International and Unilever are taking a leap of faith in deciding that ethical certification can deliver sustainability. The debate about whether it can do so for the world's forests still continues (Chapter four), yet given the nature of the fisheries crisis there is little time to wait for the efficacy of the FSC to be fully assessed.

Wider concerns

Quite apart from issues surrounding the efficacy of market-led initiatives for marine conservation, there are a number of issues raised by the partnership between WWF-International and Unilever. Through the MSC initiative Unilever has attained the PR benefits of an association with WWF-International, with Unilever's logo appearing alongside the environmental group's Panda in a number of publications. However, the joint venture is only dealing with one of Unilever's environmental impacts – fisheries. Different WWF-International and Unilever divisions may be in conflict over other issues such as agrochemicals and pollution, or cattle ranching and deforestation. How will WWF-International's single-issue project development partnership with Unilever affect its ability to act as a watchdog on other issues? Alternatively, by working with Unilever on one aspect of its business (fisheries) WWF-International is opening the door to the board of directors that may ultimately lead to collaboration on other issues.

Unilever believes that "in many areas, effective environmental progress can be made only in partnership with others" and the company continues to seek additional stakeholders to engage with. If Unilever takes a similarly enlightened approach to other issues then this must be applauded. However, the company's stakeholders include groups working on issues more fundamentally opposed to their operations than WWF-International's Endangered Seas Campaign and protest remains a feature of Unilever's stakeholder relations.

To illustrate this point, Lever Brothers features on Greenpeace's 'Murder on the Mersey' list of companies polluting the UK river and in 1995 the subsidiary UML was fined £35,000 ($22,000) because it had failed to report almost 1,000 breaches of its "integrated pollution control" authorisation. In 1991, the Chairman of Birds Eye Wall's Ltd revealed that the company annually imported 30,000 tonnes of beef from Brazil for burgers and other meat products (McSpotlight, 1996). Unilever's environmental report makes no mention of the issues of converting forests to pasture.

Meanwhile, Unilever remains on the People for the Ethical Treatment of Animals (PETA) list of companies that test on animals (PETA, 1994). Products tested include cosmetics, toiletries, household cleaners, foods, food additives and chemicals. Unilever claims it is "committed to the complete eradication of animal testing as soon as we are satisfied that this is scientifically possible without prejudicing human safety" (Unilever, 1996, p 45). Accordingly they state they have invested over £6 million in seeking alternatives to animal testing and have contributed to the Fund for the Replacement of Animals in Medical Experiments.

In another incident, in 1989 workers occupied the Gessy Lever plant in Sao Paulo, Brazil, seeking better pay and conditions. Although the company did eventually agree to a pay rise, 87 workers were sacked for taking action, and company management failed to recognise an elected factory committee (ECRA, 1996). This contrasts with their work in the Etah district of Uttar Pradesh in India where the subsidiary Hindustan Lever invested in a rural development programme to increase standards of living and resurrect a failing dairy economy (Wells, 1995). It appears there are two sides to Unilever: one side moving into the third stage of business response to environmental challenges and beginning to embrace the sustainability agenda; the other side remaining in the first stage and maintaining a defensive stance towards social and environmental issues. These two sides suggest that there is a management issue to be resolved, with the company's new strategic policy requiring greater dissemination to the subsidiaries working at the sharp end of Unilever's impacts on communities and the environment.

Whether this management issue can be resolved or not, ultimately many in the environmental movement would have a fundamental problem with Unilever's own vision of sustainable development:

> Unilever wishes to be part of a sustainable future,
> in which economic growth combines with sound
> environmental management to meet the needs
> and aspirations of people throughout the world.
> (Unilever, 1996, p 4)

Its environmental report makes no mention of problems associated with quantitative economic growth. Thorny issues associated with sustainability are avoided. The ethos of Unilever's management –

namely allegiance to profit maximisation, ever increasing economic growth and global expansion is anathema to many critics. Despite significant initiatives such as the MSC, it appears that Unilever is undertaking business-as-usual with ever greater effort. "The final thrust of Unilever's grand design to take it into the next century is its expansion into developing markets" (Phillips, 1996). They have re-entered China and in 1994 sales tripled. Turnover in China is expected to reach $1 billion (£660m) a year by 2000.

This global expansion is an imperative for Unilever's new management. The new chairman Niall Fitzgerald has promised a shake-up so as to reward shareholders (a stated aim of minimum 10 per cent per share growth a year). It is expected that Unilever will shelve some of its businesses and focus efforts on the most profitable areas. The fish processing industry is not a secure business, with fish stocks declining and prices of the raw material increasing. Unilever is the largest buyer of frozen fish. This translates into a lot of fixed capital in terms of factories, knowledge, skills and networks. Whether this is enough to keep Unilever in the fish business will depend on the relative profitability of the fish industry when compared to other sectors.

It is strange that big might prove to be beautiful, as the fragmentation of the fish market would restrict the potential for market-led conservation measures. Whether large companies take the longer view and invest in the future of the fish industry or the shorter view and switch capital into more profitable industries to provide higher shareholder dividends may determine the future of our oceans. That is the power of today's corporations.

Box 5.5: Other project-oriented partnerships

A well-known project-oriented partnership was between McDonald's and the Environmental Defense Fund. From 1990-91, they worked together to develop a waste reduction policy and programme for McDonald's (Chapter six).

In 1986 the Timber/Fish/Wildlife Agreement (TFW) for Washington State was an early example of a business–environmental group partnership. It was a collaboration between natural resource management agencies, American Indian groups, timber companies and environmentalists – groups that had conflicted for years over logging and its affect on the local environment, especially salmon fisheries. For years they fought to change legislation in their favour. Then, leaders from the timber industry and an Indian tribe broke the legal deadlock and brought together the relevant stakeholders to discuss solutions. Assisted by a mediation firm, 24 organisations held 60 meetings over a four-month period. The TFW outlined specific recommendations for:

- improved riparian zone (river bank) management;
- coordinated road building;
- collaborative research.

It also provided for increased stakeholder participation in the review of logging company harvesting permits and systems of monitoring.

The MEB (1995) analysis of the partnership shows how adversarial groups identify mutual interest and facilitate practical joint actions. Prior to the TFW "you only saw the opposing party in the courtroom. You weren't there to agree with them. You were there to kill them, they were the enemy" noted Steve Robinson of the Northwest Indian Commission (p 206). A bonus gained by working outside the legal system is 'adaptive management'. This is "an approach to natural resource policy that embodies a simple imperative: policies are experiments, *learn from them.*" (Lee, 1993, p 9).

Product-oriented partnerships

Product-oriented partnerships are those collaborations between businesses and environmental groups that involve environmental groups with specific product developments or endorsement. The difference between these partnerships and process-oriented initiatives are that they do not involve the environmental group with company management decisions. They are differentiated from project-oriented partnerships here due to their focus on delivering improvements in products or product sales. Examples of product-oriented partnership include the Forest Stewardship Council, Greenpeace's work with Renault and BP and the RSPCA Freedom Food initiative (see Box 5.6).

The following case study is of a product endorsement partnership that focused on a single/multiple pollution issue and involved the Canadian food retailer Loblaws and the environmental group Pollution Probe.

Loblaws and Pollution Probe

In 1989, the supermarket chain Loblaws launched its first range of environmentally sound products for their consumers. The product lines were given the endorsement of the well-known, Toronto-based environmental group Pollution Probe. The executive director of Pollution Probe at the time was Colin Isaacs. As one of the first third-wave environmentalists he advocated business–environmental group partnerships:

> Industry has been a formidable road-block to change. More stone-throwing by environmental groups from the street is not going to change that.... It is time to broaden environmental group efforts beyond just fighting pollution, to working on solutions with industry. (Gallon, 1991, p 19)

One solution for Isaacs was to provide consumers with information to enable them to consider buying environmentally preferable products. In retrospect, Pollution Probe's product endorsement partnership with Loblaws ran into a number of problems and many lessons can be learned by any business or environmental group considering a similar relationship.

Problems of pollution, problems of choice

There are a variety of pollution issues associated with household consumables. Many of the pollution issues facing chemical companies are also a concern for retailers. By selling products linked to pollution, retailers are also culpable for any associated adverse environmental effects. In 1989, consumers were becoming more aware of the issues and retailers were responding with numerous claims about how environmentally friendly their products were. Misleading or incorrect claims about the environmental impacts of products was serving to fool, confuse or dishearten the ecoconscious consumer. Regulators of advertising standards in Canada had largely ignored the abuse of environmental marketing while the government-sponsored independent labeling scheme, Environmental Choice, was still on the drawing board.

The motivations

Isaacs felt that in the absence of effective governmental standards there was a need for environmental groups to help communicate green credentials effectively to the consumer and that the use of the Pollution Probe name would be one way of achieving this. Loblaws' president, Dave Nichol, also saw the value of using endorsements from an environmental organisation to market greener product lines. Friends of the Earth Canada had briefly endorsed certain Loblaw product lines, such as organic fertilizers but when they decided not to continue, Loblaws began looking for another group to help launch new green product lines. When Isaacs contacted Loblaws' president to discuss the possibility of endorsing certain product lines, Nichol jumped at the chance.

In addition to a belief in finding practical solutions and a will to harness consumer concern in a constructive manner, Isaacs was faced with the need to keep Pollution Probe financially solvent. Loblaws offered a deal which could amount to almost $150,000 depending on the volume of sales. Loblaws motivations were clear. Whereas many of the business–environmental group partnerships featured in this book are the result of businesses primarily making a strategic response to protest and conflict, Loblaws was acting to seize a new market opportunity – the growing green consumer market.

Box 5.6: Other product-oriented partnerships

In Britain, the Royal Society for Prevention of Cruelty to Animals (RSPCA) is operating a welfare-friendly certification scheme called 'Freedom Food'. The RSPCA has established five freedoms, or principles, for livestock welfare and develops certification criteria for different types of animals based on these freedoms. Uptake of this scheme has been rapid and retailers are beginning to seek ways of increasing the number of certified products on their shelves.

In its favour, the standards and process of certification are transparent. One issue is that Freedom Food Limited will increasingly rely on income from licensing its logo (which uses the phrase 'RSPCA endorsed') to certified companies. However, as the company's only shareholder is the RSPCA and the organisation does not intend to generate additional revenue from the scheme there should not be potential for a conflict of interest.

This form of product endorsement has worked well for the Soil Association for over 50 years. Founded in 1946, the Soil Association exists to research, develop and promote sustainable relationships between soil, plants, animals, people and the biosphere in order to produce safe, healthy food and other related products, while protecting and enhancing the environment. The organic farming Symbol Scheme is administered by a wholly-owned subsidiary company of the Soil Association. Its roles include the setting of standards for organic agriculture, food processing and manufacturing. It is also responsible for inspecting and certifying, promoting the organic market using its symbol brand and offering information and advice. The scheme represents 70 per cent of the UK organic market.

However, given the potential for controversy with direct endorsements of products perhaps the safest way for business and environmental groups to collaborate on product endorsements is by using the accreditation council model, such as the FSC. Using this model the payment for certification assessments goes from the assessed company to a certification body which itself operates to standards clearly defined by the independent council or environmental group.

Not all product-oriented partnerships focus exclusively on endorsement. Greenpeace has been working with a variety of companies to develop new products with less impact on the environment. For example they have worked with British Petroleum Solar on ways of developing solar energy technology and with Renault on the Twingo Smiley Project.

Box 5.6 continued

In the latter of these projects Greenpeace Germany invested 2 million DM to develop a fuel-efficient version of the Renault Twingo. Developing the Twingo Smiley required close collaboration between Renault and Greenpeace. According to Greenpeace's Stefan Krug "The big car companies are always accusing us of being idealistic, of advocating the impossible. The Smiley is our way of proving them wrong." This kind of project suits itself to one-to-one partnership. Indeed, working with specific companies to produce leading examples rather than many companies to encourage more general progress appears to be a strategy of Greenpeace. Campaigner Corin Millais argues "Our approach is to enforce solutions by stealing the market. We're going to get into their territory and take their customers."

True to Greenpeace's history, we are seeing the emergence of confrontational collaborations: direct action through product innovation rather than protest. Whether Greenpeace can afford to divert funds away from media-friendly protests and towards providing a free research and development service for forward-looking industry is open to question. With a funding base that responds to the emotion of the moment rather than the pragmatism of the solution, this may already concern fund-raisers.

Lessons learned

The partnership proved to be successful for Loblaws, with the grocery chain generating millions of dollars in new sales of its green products (Jacobs, 1990). For Pollution Probe, the partnership proved to be controversial. A number of staff members were uncomfortable with the idea of taking money for endorsing products and were upset that products were being endorsed on the basis of narrow environmental criteria. The case of the 'green' disposable diaper is illustrative.

Every year an estimated 37,000 tonnes of waste go into landfill dumps in Ontario alone (Gallon, 1991). Apart from a lack of landfill capacity and growing groundwater pollution from landfills, many environmentalists felt that the natural resources in disposable diapers from trees (pulp) and oil (plastic) should be used again and again, and not thrown into a landfill. Pollution Probe endorsed the disposable diaper because it was dioxin-free.

Suspicion about the partnership was rife, particularly because the partners did not share information about their relationship. At the outset Loblaws did not want the partnership to be leaked before they were ready to launch the products in case its competitors tried the same approach. During the partnership Loblaws did not release information about the environmental credentials of the products being endorsed by Pollution Probe. This lack of transparency, a contrast with the other partnerships in this book, led Greenpeace-Canada to investigate the products themselves and accuse the partners of misleading the public. Coupled with the resignation of two senior members of Pollution Probe over the endorsement issue, this sparked a wave of negative media attention and has arguably damaged Pollution Probe's public image.

Although some environmental objectives were served this was not a model partnership. In an article reviewing the lessons of the green product endorsement controversy, Gary Gallon concludes:

- criteria must be established – transparent, standardised evaluation mechanisms must be used to determine which products meet the criteria for green products;

- independent testing is crucial – any consumer product that is touted as being better for the environment must have evidence to back the claim which should be made available to the public;

- endorsement for money is unacceptable – payment per endorsement can compromise the independence of the endorsing body.

- corporations must be accountable for green claims – there need to be sound guidelines for manufacturers' use of environmental claims and funding for a professional ecolabelling body (1991, p 21–24).

To these we add:

- endorsements should not be restricted to particular companies – an environmental group should not commit itself to endorsing the products of only one company: instead the endorsement process should be open to all companies that wish to be assessed.

By moving the green-product debate forward and helping to identify these issues, even in failure, the collaboration has contributed to the sustainable development agenda.

Riding the third wave: the emergence of social and ethical partnerships

Our overview of partnerships is by no means exhaustive. As we write, many new initiatives are no doubt under discussion or on the horizon. We conclude this chapter with a brief review of social and ethical partnerships between business and other parts of the wider green movement. A full examination of the emergence of these partnerships is beyond the scope of this book. Our focus here is upon partnerships which address social development issues in southern countries.[9]

The advent of partnerships between business and the wider green movement is not limited to collaboration on ecological issues. As we noted in Chapters one and three, the concept of sustainability is now interpreted in a more holistic sense and business is beginning to realise that ethical and social issues also require both a strategic and operational response similar to environmental management. In parallel with these trends, NGOs who have traditionally seen themselves as providers of international development assistance appear to be learning from the experience of environmental groups and have begun to adopt more strategic and policy-oriented campaigns which often include dialogue with business.

As we described in Chapters one and two, the resurgence of environmentalism in the late 1980s was linked to a litany of major industrial and resource extraction disasters. Business was forced to respond to consumer demands and activist protest. One of the major catalysts for the new corporate ethical agenda was a 1993 fire at the Kader toy factory in Thailand which killed 188 people and injured 469. For development NGOs such as the World Development Movement (WDM), the Thai fire has become the equivalent of the burning and pillaging of the Amazon, a key campaigning issue for environmental groups since the mid-1980s WDM describes the link between the factory fire, corporate irresponsibility and the culpability of retailers and consumers in northern industrialised countries:

> [The workers] died because the fire exits were blocked, there were no fire alarms and no sprinklers. Kader ignored workers' safety to make toys as cheaply as possible for global companies to

> sell in Britain's toy shops.... The Kader fire is the
> most dramatic example, but worker's health and
> safety is abused every day across Asia in order to
> make cheap toys. (1996, p 1)

In addition to the Kader factory fire, two other high-profile cases
have fuelled the new ethical agenda for global business in the
1990s. The recent attention to the child labour issue is linked to
the political and public outcry following the murder of the 12-
year-old Pakistani child labour activist Iqbal Masih in April 1995.
Similarly, the hanging of Nigerian poet Ken Saro-Wiwa and eight
fellow Ogoni activists in November 1995 brought worldwide
attention to the environmental and social impact of Shell's oil-
drilling activities in the Niger Delta.[10] All three cases have helped
raise fundamental questions about the role of global corporations
in protecting human rights, local communities and ecosystems.

Many other similar stories could be told about the failure of
business to provide acceptable working conditions or to ensure
adequate local community benefits throughout the southern
hemisphere. From coffee, tea and banana plantations to athletic
shoe and clothing factories, the issue of ethical standards is
becoming a growing concern for global companies and high street
retailers alike. Development and human rights groups have
succeeded in raising the media and public profile of a wide range
of social and ethical concerns. This has placed major companies
such as Mattel, Hasbro, The Gap, Nike and Reebok on the
defensive. Some are beginning to respond with codes of conduct,
supply chain audits and partnerships with development and human
rights groups. The latter trend offers scope for businesses and
NGOs working in different sectors to promote the idea of
environmental justice – a key aspect of both third-wave
environmentalism and global sustainability (see Chapter two).

Irresponsible international trade is the main reason why
NGOs and consumers are seeking a changed business response to
social development and environmental justice issues. Many
natural products originating from the South have become part of
everyday life for most consumers in the North – exotic fruits,
vegetables, nuts, fish and oils; fabrics; minerals; and wood, among
others. Increasingly finished products for northern markets are
being manufactured in southern factories. The reason why NGOs
claim that many of these products are unfairly traded is that they
are often grown, mined or manufactured under poor working

conditions and with inadequate financial benefits accruing to the local communities concerned.

Fair trade needs to become central to mainstream business practice. A small but growing number of companies, such as The Body Shop, Ben & Jerry's Ice Cream, and Starbuck's Coffee, emphasise the importance of trading with communities in need in both their home countries and the developing world. In the case of The Body Shop, this means support for both community economic regeneration in inner-city Glasgow (eg Soapworks factory) and for "economically-stressed communities, mostly in the majority [developing] world" (The Body Shop International, 1994. p 12).

In order to begin to address ongoing concerns about unfair trade, growing numbers of northern-based businesses are forming partnerships with development and human rights groups. Four of these initiatives are described below:

- **Migros, Del Monte and Bread for All:** Beginning in 1981 Swiss organisations such as Bread for All vigorously denounced the role of the fruit company Del Monte in the Philippines. As the leading food retailer in Switzerland, with exclusive rights to Del Monte products, Migros faced a public relations crisis. At first the chain contested the criticisms, while sales of the product concerned – pineapples – declined dramatically. In 1982, a meeting was held between Migros, Del Monte and various development NGOs to look into ways of improving working conditions. Together they drew up a clause for suppliers, which Del Monte then ratified. In 1994, concern grew that the clause was not being monitored and that improvements had not been secured. Bread for All called for a permanent and independent monitoring body which was subsequently formed as a commission of five Filipinos, drawn from churches, universities and the diplomatic corps. Bread for All's General Secretary Cristoph Stuckelberger explains: "Our philosophy behind this is partnership and not confrontation. If you want to have confrontation as your basic attitude, then the social clause is not the right instrument for you." Del Monte has agreed to continue to purchase pineapples from endorsed suppliers, even if they are more expensive (see Christian Aid, 1996, pp 26-27).

- **The Gap and human rights groups:** In 1995, the American-based clothing retailer The Gap came under pressure from newspapers and campaigners for the activities of one of its sub-contractors in the Central American country of El Salvador. The manufacturer's management was accused of human rights abuses such as forced contraception, forced lock-ins, sexual harassment and death threats to unionists. When they fired more than 300 unionists campaigning for better conditions, religious, labour, consumer and development groups in the US mounted demonstrations and letter writing campaigns. The Gap's reaction was initially denial and the campaign intensified. The company then changed its position, admitted a problem and stopped purchases from the factory. This was condemned further by campaigners who saw it as doing little to solve the problem. Therefore, in 1995 The Gap met representatives of the human rights group, the National Labour Committee. They agreed that the company should resurrect trade with the factory in El Salvador with the goal of improving conditions there. Subsequently The Gap agreed to allow independent human rights workers immediate access to plants producing Gap clothing. The company also began to work with the Interfaith Centre on Corporate Responsibility, Business for Social Responsibility and the National Labour Committee, to design and implement an independent monitoring system for its worldwide operations (see Christian Aid, 1996, p 27).

- Fairtrade Foundation, Sainsbury's and the Co-operative Wholesale Society: The Fairtrade Foundation is a charity which brings together seven British development and consumer NGOs: CAFOD, Christian Aid, New Consumer, the National Federation of Women's Institutes, Oxfam, Traidcraft Exchange and the World Development Movement. In 1996, Fairtrade launched a pilot project, the Third World Supplier's Charter, to encourage and facilitate the development of effective corporate codes of conduct concerning relations with suppliers in southern countries. The first two companies to agree to work with Fairtrade are the major supermarket chain Sainsbury's and a second business in the food and retail sector, the Co-operative Wholesale Society. Sainsbury's has selected a number of its own-brand products for the pilot study to test the code of conduct and to confirm the ethical principles which Sainsbury's will be required to adopt. Dino Adriano, the company's new CEO and an Oxfam trustee since 1990, explains the company's motivation: "Ethical trading has always been an integral part of our business practice and we are committed to ensuring that our suppliers have comparable standards to ourselves." A Fairtrade spokesperson argues that "retailers [must be] prepared to accept some kind of independent monitoring" in order to alleviate consumer concerns. Sainsbury's long-term aim is to integrate an ethical standard into all supplier audits and specifications for its own-brand products (see Paton, 1996).

- **World Federation of Sporting Goods Industry and Save the Children (UK):** In late 1996, the global sporting goods industry trade association announced that it planned to develop a code of ethical conduct for the production of all sporting goods. The impetus for this move came from growing criticism of the industry by development and human rights NGOs about the use of child labour to produce soccer balls. In addition to the planned code of conduct, the federation announced in early 1997 a new partnership with Save the Children (UK), ILO, UNICEF, the North American Sporting Goods Manufacturing Association (SGMA), the Soccer Industry Council of America (SICA), the Sialkot (Pakistan) Chamber of Commerce and the Pakistan-based Steering Committee on Child Labour. The overall aim of the partnership is to undertake a series of actions to eliminate child labour from the production of soccer balls in Pakistan, the source of more than 75 per cent of the world's billion dollar soccer-ball market. The partnership will oversee an independent monitoring programme to verify local manufacturer efforts to eliminate child labour. It will also support various social development projects to provide improved educational and other opportunities to children who lose their jobs as a result of the programme. Global companies and brands such as Nike, Reebok, Mitre, Umbro, Lotto, Brine, Franklin and Puma (and many other smaller brands) have indicated that they will only purchase Pakistani soccer balls from local manufacturers who join the monitoring programme. By working together, the various partners hope to begin to address some of the underlying causes of child labour in Pakistan (see WFSGI, 1996; 1997).

While these partnership experiences offer hope that business is becoming more proactive on social and ethical issues, the overall global picture remains uncertain. Voluntary codes of conduct have the potential to serve as a catalyst for corporate action, however, a recent example of questionable practice suggests that such codes will only be effective if backed up by ongoing independent monitoring. In late 1996, WDM criticised UK toy companies for their failure to enforce fully the British Toy & Hobby Association's "Vendor and Subcontractor Code of Conduct" adopted earlier in the year. In response to WDM's call for independent monitoring, the association argued that: "We regard that as an invasion" (see Hollinger, 1996, p 7).

Despite the emergence of social and ethical partnerships between business and development NGOs, there is still much that divides the worlds of business and campaigning. The same is true of business–environmental group relations. While there is evidence that partnerships between business and different types of NGOs are both possible and practicable, the above example illustrates that campaigning groups continue to play an important role in critiquing corporate behaviour. For their part, some business people persist in questioning the legitimacy and credibility of NGOs in scrutinising corporations. In the face of ongoing global corporate irresponsibility, it is not surprising that campaigners often still respond with protest. The following chapter on McDonald's relations with the environmental movement illustrates that it is indeed possible to move from protest to partnership and back again.

Notes

[1] Based upon Murphy, 1996b.

[2] DuPont 'Part of Our Lives' billboard advertisement at Heathrow airport, 1996.

[3] WWF-International acknowledges that there has been some progress since Rio on the environmentally sound management of toxic chemicals. In particular, it sees the Intergovernmental Forum on Chemical Safety playing an important role in promoting better integration between Chapter 19 of Agenda 21 and all other relevant chapters (eg freshwater, agriculture, oceans and coasts, etc). The organisation also regards the forum as "the first framework for international chemicals management",

albeit one that needs to be strengthened and formalised through the creation of a legally binding framework convention. A second WWF priority in the toxic chemicals area is the development of public tracking and reporting systems for pollutant release and transfer (WWF-International, 1997b, p 8).

[4] In 1996, Greenpeace USA published a damning report entitled *Dow Makes You Poison Great Things* which concludes that the company's chlorine-based products "are likely to be the world's largest root source of dioxins" (Greenpeace Business, 1995/96, p 5).

[5] In March 1997 European Union commissioners and North Sea fisheries and environment ministers reached a non-legally binding political agreement on the establishment of no-fishing zones and restrictions on individual catches. Specific proposals include: the introduction of selective fishing gear; restrictions on beam trawling; and curtailment of the practice of discarding fish considered to be too small to market. The agreement failed to set any timetables for government action (see Brown, 1997).

[6] McVities (United Biscuit) is the UK's largest manufacturer of biscuits.

[7] Others have argued that the reason these companies announced they would stop buying fish oil from North Sea sources is that Birds Eye Walls (Unilever) had already done so and because of the ready availability of alternative oils.

[8] This project lasted a month and concluded with the report 'Developing economic incentives for responsible fishing: the report of the Marine Stewardship Council preliminary scoping project' (Bendell, 1996). From this project the name Marine Stewardship Council was coined.

[9] In the UK and elsewhere in the industrialised North, ethical issues such as the treatment of animals are also rising up the corporate agenda. From anti-fur campaigns to protests related to the transport of live animals, business is being challenged by animal rights activists to stop certain practices and improve others. The Royal Society for the Prevention of Cruelty to Animals (RSPCA) has taken the partnership route with its Freedom Food programme which offers producers and retailers a mechanism to certify that their food products are from animal-friendly sources.

[10] Following ongoing public pressure about its social and environmental policies, particularly in developing countries, Shell revised its 'Statement of General Business Principles' in March 1997 to include for the first time explicit support for human rights (see Wagstyl and Corizone, 1997). Amnesty International welcomed Shell's move and said that it was now up to Shell to prove its commitment through practical action (see Cowe, 1997).

six

From protest to partnership and back again: McDonald's and the environmental movement[1]

> McDonald's vision is to dominate the global foodservice industry. Global dominance means setting the performance standard for customer satisfaction while increasing market share and profitability through our Convenience, Value and Execution Strategies. (McDonald's Corporation 1995 Annual Report)

Most environmentalists would consider the idea of an environmentally-responsible McDonald's an anathema. The environmentalist critique of McDonald's ranges from basic issues such as the company's massive output of waste to much larger questions about 'cultural imperialism' reflected in its corporate vision of "global dominance". The likelihood of partnership between one of the icons of the throw-away society and a credible environmental group would for most environmentalists seem morally repugnant and quite unthinkable. But in August 1990 that is exactly what happened when representatives of McDonald's and the Environmental Defense Fund signed an agreement to establish a joint task force to address the company's solid waste issues.

In this chapter, we conclude our review of case study material with a look at one of the first business–environmental group formal partnerships – the McDonald's–Environmental Defense Fund Waste Reduction Task Force. In addition to an analysis of this ground-breaking collaboration, we consider past and present relationships between McDonald's and various environmental groups and campaigners. The first part of the chapter provides background material on company history as well as an overview of the major social and environmental concerns which McDonald's has faced in recent years. We then proceed with our examination of the Waste Reduction Task Force. This is followed by a consideration of some of the company's other recent environmental and social responsibility challenges, namely the controversial libel case against two British activists. The chapter concludes with general reflections on the contribution of the global fast-food industry and its standard bearer, the McDonald's Corporation, to both sustainable development and environmental responsibility. McDonald's experience with the environmental movement in recent years demonstrates that environmental group relations with large global corporations remain highly problematic, and that partnership does not mean the end of protest.

McDonald's then and now

The origins of the contemporary fast-food phenomenon can be traced to American roadside restaurants in the 1920s. What began with curb-side meal delivery eventually evolved into large drive-in restaurants where customers parked their cars and were served by car hops – waiters who went from car to car to take and deliver customer orders. The first McDonald's drive-in appeared outside Los Angeles in 1940, and was owned and operated by two brothers, Mac and Dick McDonald.

Although quite successful, by 1948 the McDonald brothers faced growing competition and decided to adopt a new strategy to improve service and attract new customers. Their new format was based upon take-away and self-service which meant that all the car hops lost their jobs. With less staff and overheads, the brothers were able to charge only 15 cents for their hamburgers. Business initially declined because teenagers preferred car hops, however growing numbers of families were attracted by the low prices. The brothers reduced the menu from 25 items to 9 and introduced the Speedee Service System, a standardised food preparation method, which they eventually licensed.[2]

In 1954, the McDonald brothers met Ray Kroc, a Chicago-based salesman who owned the rights to sell Multimixer milkshake machines. Kroc went to California to find out why the brothers needed ten of his machines for only one restaurant. He quickly realised that McDonald's had an excellent product and system which could be replicated elsewhere. Within a week, Kroc signed an agreement with the brothers, which made him their national franchise agent and launched today's largest fast-food chain. In 1961, Kroc bought the rights to the McDonald's concept from its originators for $2.7 million.

According to David Upton and Joshua Margolis (1992), Kroc continued the McDonald's tradition of a limited menu, low prices and fast service, and then went on to out perform all of his competitors with a three-pronged strategy:

- to make sure McDonald's products were of consistently high quality;

- to establish a unique operating system; and

- to build a special set of relationships between the McDonald's corporation, its suppliers and its franchisers.[3]

Today the McDonald's Corporation is the world's largest fast-food firm with over 21,000 outlets in over 100 countries, serving more than 33 million customers every day. Annual global sales are in excess of $30 billion with operating profits approaching $3 billion. Anyone who paid $2,250 for 100 shares when the company was floated in 1965 would now own almost 20,000 shares worth well over $1 million.[4]

Environmental and social challenges

American sociologist George Ritzer describes McDonald's as "one of the most influential developments in twentieth century America" whose "impact is felt far beyond the confines of the United States and the fast-food business." Ritzer sees the company as the "paradigm case" for "McDonaldization" – "a wide-ranging process … by which the principles of the fast-food restaurant are coming to dominate more and more sectors of American society as well as of the rest of the world" (1993, p 1). Novelist Douglas Coupland captures an important dimension of this phenomenon when he uses the term "McJob" to refer to "a low-pay, low-prestige, low-dignity, low-benefit, no future job in the service sector" (1991, p 5).[5] Ironically, McDonald's has had its own McJobs programme to train and hire disabled workers since 1981.[6]

Media coverage of McDonald's is largely divided between radical and conservative viewpoints. Whereas radical magazine *Red Pepper* brands McDonald's as "a portentous example of a new global superpower" (Carey, 1996, p 11), *The Economist* insists that "the scale of the global Mac attack is impressive" (1996a, p 77). The McDonald's numbers are indeed impressive, yet how has its outstanding economic success affected its environmental and social responsibilities?

The McDonald's Corporation buys $7 billion of food, paper and packaging annually worldwide. In the USA, McDonald's is the single largest consumer of packaging. A 1991 estimate placed the company's American daily waste output at 1,000 tons (or 2 million pounds), including 700,000 pounds of food waste. As the company's global reach has grown over the past decade, one of its biggest environmental challenges has been how to reduce and manage its waste more effectively. The main drivers in this regard have not come from legislation or regulation. Solid waste disposal has not been a heavily regulated area in the USA, nor in most jurisdictions where the company operates. Most targets for recycling and waste reduction have tended to be fairly loose with little in the way of teeth on the enforcement side.[7] Public pressure has had a far greater influence on company policy. Concerns about the company's environmental impact have often focused on the ubiquitous 'clamshell', a foam polystyrene container for hamburgers and other hot food items. First introduced in the mid-1970s, McDonald's clamshell eventually became a highly visible target for environmental group protest.

Beginning in the mid-1980s, McDonald's environmental record became the target of extensive media coverage and environmental activism.[8] In 1986, two campaigns on opposite sides of the Atlantic launched a wave of public protest about the company's ethics.

In the UK, the independent London Greenpeace group[9] published 'What's wrong with McDonald's?', a campaigning pamphlet which raised concerns about the health, nutritional, environmental and social consequences of the company's products and operations. The leaflet featured a cartoon of a cigar-chomping American corporate fat cat hiding behind a mask depicting the company's clown mascot Ronald McDonald and invited its readers "to think for a moment about what lies behind McDonald's clean, bright image" (London Greenpeace, 1986).

In the USA, grassroots protests organised by the Citizen's Clearinghouse for Hazardous Waste renamed the mascot Ronald McToxic and encouraged children to mail 'McTrash' back to the company. As a result, some American cities banned polystyrene packaging, forcing local McDonald's franchises to come up with alternatives.

With consumers increasingly choosing products on the basis of environmental criteria, the McDonald's hamburger clamshell packaging gradually became a "symbol of ecological evil" (Gifford, 1991, p 34). Media coverage about solid waste issues raised the spectre of "a nation running out of landfill capacity" and emphasised "eye-catching events like roving garbage barges" (Reinhart, 1992, p 9).

The late 1980s also coincided with McDonald's worst domestic sales slump in its 35-year history. Facing growing consumer pressure, the company announced intentions to spend $100 million annually on recycled products, and invested in a polystyrene-recycling plant. The McRecycle USA programme included the use of recycled products for the construction, renovation and equipping of new and existing restaurants. The programme was boosted when over 500 suppliers agreed to participate, however, McRecycle had many teething problems. Polystyrene recycling proved to be difficult and expensive, and products such as serving trays tended to warp and crack. The in-house recycling programme had success rate of only 30-40 per cent as customers wanted convenience of take-away and throw-away, not diligent sorting. Up to 70 per cent of the clamshells, for example, were simply disposed of beyond the golden arches (see *The Economist,* 1992). "Although some scientific studies indicate[d] that foam packaging [was] environmentally sound, customers just didn't feel good about it" (McDonald's Annual Report, 1990, in Gifford, 1991, p 35).

Around this time, the company also made several overtures to environmental groups, but only the World Wildlife Fund (USA) acquiesced when McDonald's offered to fund a WWF-US rain-forest poster and booklet.[10] While the WWF-US initiative may have been a good public relations move, the company desperately needed credible, independent advice on how to better manage its growing waste problems. In mid-1989, McDonald's vice president Shelby Yastrow appeared opposite Fred Krupp, Executive Director of the New York-based Environmental Defense Fund on a cable television programme. McDonald's suddenly discovered a potential partner.

Enter the Environmental Defense Fund

The Environmental Defense Fund (EDF) was founded in 1967 by a group of scientists to fight DDT spraying on Long Island. Start-up funding came from a memorial fund honouring Rachel Carson. In 1984, Harvard lawyer Fred Krupp became Executive Director and the organisation's membership, staff numbers and budget subsequently grew in leaps and bounds.[11] Under Krupp's leadership, EDF developed greater expertise on technical and legal aspects of environmental issues, and became particularly well known for its research on solid waste. In an influential 1986 Op-Ed piece in the Wall Street Journal, Krupp described EDF's approach as the third wave of environmentalism which recognises a need for market-based solutions. Krupp believes, as we argue in Chapter two, that the third wave builds upon the first wave's nature agenda and second wave's legislative focus, and relies upon diversity and pragmatism:

> We're not ideologues on environmental issues....
> I think environmentalists would become more powerful, more forceful and achieve greater results if we deployed more tools in our tool kit. We should continue to aggressively lobby, aggressively litigate, aggressively criticise corporate malfeasance and promote stricter regulation. We also should be able to problem-solve with corporations. (in Gifford, 1991, p 36)

In early 1989 before the initial contact between the two organisations, EDF staff member John Ruston had proposed a project which could enhance McDonald's solid waste management. Ruston assumed that such a project would almost certainly have to be initiated by EDF without McDonald's cooperation. He was proved wrong.

Following their initial meeting, Yastrow and Krupp agreed that Krupp should visit McDonald's headquarters in Oak Brook, Illinois. In July 1989, Krupp wrote to McDonald's CEO Michael Quinlan to request a meeting on environmental issues. On 10 October, 1989, Krupp told company President Ed Rensi that McDonald's could only become a leader on the environment by changing its operations.[12] Krupp also argued that EDF could assist McDonald's in managing its waste more effectively and efficiently. One year of informal discussions and negotiations followed, including EDF staff visits to several McDonald's locations. This culminated with the two parties agreeing to form a joint solid waste task force.

Upton and Margolis illustrate the risks and opportunities of such a partnership, particularly for McDonald's:

> When McDonald's accepted EDF's suggestion to help assess the company's solid waste stream and explore ways to reduce it, McDonald's was making a bold move. It was engaging a new partner to help address environmental concerns, one aspect of the increasingly complex situation in which the company now found itself. For a private corporation of McDonald's stature to collaborate with an environmental organisation entailed significant risk and required a willingness, by both parties, to consider new ways of thinking about operating practices. (1992, p 10)

There were also major risks for EDF as Krupp notes:

> Most of our members are people who have deep suspicions about corporations' behaviour toward the environment; they give to environmental groups as a way to have a watchdog over the corporations; so it is very risky to take an organization like EDF and work with corporations.... But our product – changing the world – is hard to produce. (in Reinhart, 1992, p 10)

Despite such obstacles, Krupp managed to convince EDF's board of trustees to support the proposed partnership. Krupp then formally notified the executive directors of a number of other environmental groups. The response was mixed. Some expressed cautious optimism. Others were less supportive. Lois Gibbs of the Citizen's Clearing House for Hazardous Waste, which had pioneered the Ronald McToxic and McWaste campaigns in the late 1980s, condemned EDF's move as a sell out and later criticised EDF for not giving grassroots campaigners enough credit for making McDonald's realise that it had a waste problem in the first place. Well-known environmental activist Barry Commoner argued that EDF had been taken over by "business-minded honchos" who had abandoned genuine activism (in Atlas, 1990). EDF nevertheless persevered and prior to the project launch one of EDF's waste specialists held a number of meetings with his counterparts in various environmental groups. This consultative process continued throughout the project, an essential move given the scepticism within the environmentalist community about McDonald's capacity to change its ways.

The Waste Reduction Task Force

On 1 August, 1990, McDonald's Corporation and EDF signed a formal agreement on a joint task force to address McDonald's solid waste issues. The partnership agreement was widely covered by the US media, most of which was extremely positive.

The main points of the agreement were as follows:

- the task force would evaluate McDonald's materials use and solid waste issues, and develop strategies to reduce the company's US-based restaurant solid waste stream;

- there would be no acceptance of any monetary or in-kind support at any time;

- either party could terminate the project at any time if few or no substantive agreements were forthcoming;

- both parties would continue with their ongoing business and advocacy activities;

- if either party disagreed on research findings or conclusions, the final report would consist of separate statements reflecting each party's perspective;

- EDF reserved its right to criticise McDonald's;

- McDonald's required EDF task force members to work in one of its restaurants for at least a day each;

- larger issues such as rainforest destruction, global warming and the high-consumption, highly disposable nature of McDonald's business were strictly off-limits.

Both organisations committed a number of staff to the joint venture. McDonald's assigned operations and environmental affairs specialists, whereas EDF contributed three scientific and economic experts. The environmental affairs director for McDonald's exclusive packaging supplier, the Perseco Company, also joined the task force. During the course of project both organisations brought in additional expertise as required. This also included experts from other environmental organisations.

The partnership process

According to EDF, from the outset the task force "benefited from the willingness of McDonald's and its suppliers to open their doors for a review of their operations" (WRTF, 1991, p 6). In addition to more than 30 task force meetings in one year, the seven-member group also visited two of McDonald's food suppliers, five packaging suppliers, a major McDonald's distribution centre, a polystyrene recycling plant and a facility to convert food waste into garden compost.

The task force's deliberations reveal a delicate balancing act between a range of competing interests (see Box 6.1). The decision to phase out clamshell sandwich packaging, although only one of 42 task-force recommendations, proved to be the most contentious. As the clamshell epitomised both McDonald's speedy service and growing opposition to the fast-food culture, the negotiations and ultimate decision revealed some of the inherent tensions in business–environmental group partnerships.

According to Shelby Yastrow, vice president, McDonald's:

> That clamshell package was the symbol that
> everyone glommed onto. We knew if we got rid
> of that thing, it would be like pulling forty thorns
> out of our paw. (in Gifford, 1991, p 35)

For the EDF members of the task force, the clamshell was clearly
not the best environmental option. For many within McDonald's,
however, the decision to abandon the clamshell represented a
fundamental change in its highly successful operating system. The
polystyrene industry saw McDonald's decision as an ill-founded
move which would have adverse effects on many American
businesses and communities. Initial opposition within McDonald's
also focused on the impact of the decision upon existing suppliers,
two of whom were severely affected. Although McDonald's had
always considered supplier relations essential to its success, these
relations also depended upon the supplier's ability to adapt to
changing consumer demands. As a highly-visible "icon of the
throwaway society", the clamshell simply had to go (Upton and
Margolis, 1992, p 14).

Although the clamshell decision clearly garnered most of the
publicity, the 42 task-force recommendations included many
others which would lead to significant changes to the operational
side of McDonald's. Perhaps most important was the task force's
call for a new McDonald's Waste Reduction Policy designed to
provide a framework for the entire McDonald's system in the
USA, including offices, restaurants, distribution centres and
suppliers. The Waste Reduction Policy subsequently adopted by
the company identified the following key principles:

- effectively manage solid waste by taking a 'total lifecycle'
  approach;

- reduce the weight and/or volume of packaging;

- implement reusable materials where feasible within operations
  and distribution systems;

- make the maximum use of recycled materials in the
  construction, equipping and operations of restaurants;

- conserve and protect natural resources through increased
  efficiency and conservation;[13]

- encourage environmental values and practices in local
  communities by providing educational materials;

- ensure accountability procedures;

- maintain a productive, ongoing dialogue with all stakeholders.

These principles in turn were backed up by the company's Waste Reduction Action Plan which included ten waste reduction goals; nine related to product substitution; sixteen concerning recycling; and seven related to the integration of the action plan into standard operating procedures and product specifications.[14] Two EDF task force members commended the plan for being "comprehensive, incremental and ongoing ... the general characteristics of an effective environmental programme" (Prince and Denison, 1991, p 5).

Beyond the task force

Following the release of the task force report in April 1991, both organisations continued to monitor progress on the implementation of the Waste Reduction Action Plan. After one year, EDF noted that McDonald's were "well along in carrying out the specifics of the Action Plan" and had "developed on its own many new initiatives that go beyond those laid out by the task force."[15] These included the formation of an Optimal Packaging Team to identify opportunities for further environmental improvements and the establishment of an independent company called Triace to work directly with individual franchisers on waste minimisation programmes.

In April 1993, McDonald's informed EDF that the company was using more recycled and chlorine-free paper. The company also reported reductions in the amount of packaging used for a number of products. Another year later, McDonald's reported that in the three years since the task force report, the company had eliminated 7,500 tons of packaging annually. Other major achievements over this timespan included: a doubling of recycled content in packaging (half post-consumer); lighter packaging; and an expansion of its pilot project in composting to include 15 New York restaurants. In the 1993-94 period, the company also introduced new packaging for the Big Mac, which was 10 per cent lighter than the former wrap and which had 40 per cent recycled content and used unbleached paper.[16]

Box 6.1: Waste Reduction Task Force key milestones

September-October 1990: Much of the early discussions focus on the future of the clamshell. Suppliers offer various replacement options including wrappers and boxes. Preferred option becomes insulated polyethylene wrapping paper which had already been field tested.

October 1990: In late October, word reaches EDF that a pro-clamshell group within McDonald's is mobilising. EDF fears that the company will renew its commitment to the polystyrene containers. EDF's Krupp calls McDonald's Rensi and "puts the project on the line", insisting that the task force has found a viable alternative.[17]

November 1990: A few days later Krupp flies to Illinois to meet with McDonald's senior management. Two days later McDonald's agrees to replace the clamshell, where possible, with the new polyethylene wraps.[18] Various American newspapers criticise the McDonald's decision.

December 1990: McDonald's cites a 1990 study which finds that the clamshell life cycle uses more natural resources than the replacement wrap. The study also notes that the new wrap offers significant reductions in pollutant releases and that its volume is only one tenth of the clamshell.

January 1991: McDonald's sweeps an Advertising Age/Gallup poll as the most environmentally responsible fast-food chain.

April 1991: Task force releases report with 42 separate proposals, pilot projects, and testing. Ultimate goal was to reduce waste volume by 75 per cent and to reduce its growing waste disposal costs.[19]

April 1993: McDonald's publishes Waste Reduction Status Report. 23 of 42 task force recommendations already implemented. 17 projects completed.

April 1994: Original 42 initiatives grow to more than 100 solid waste projects, 55 of which are completed.

A number of other initiatives have developed, largely on the impetus of the McDonald's–EDF collaboration. In 1993, McDonald's and EDF were two of the founding members of the Paper Task Force, a partnership to create demand for environmentally preferable paper which also includes Johnson & Johnson, NationsBank, Prudential Insurance and Duke University. In late 1994, McDonald's announced that it planned to collaborate with the Composting Council and the National Audubon Society to launch 'Food for the Earth: a composting initiative for the foodservice industry'.[20]   Then in early 1995, EDF and the Pew Charitable Trusts formed the Alliance for Environmental Innovation to develop joint environmental projects with major American corporations.

While the Waste Reduction Policy initiated by the task force is primarily designed for McDonald's American market, its general principles are considered to be company-wide policy.   Each McDonald's subsidiary is expected to implement the policy, however the company recognises that each country has its own management structure and system.   The degree of implementation, therefore, varies country-to-country.   According to corporate director of environmental affairs Bob Langert, "it is not McDonald's policy to dictate organisational policy on environmental matters to subsidiaries."[21]   For example, clamshell packaging is still used in the UK, but has been replaced in many other countries besides the USA.   Approximately 25 per cent of McDonald's outlets worldwide still use the clamshell.   According to a McDonald's UK spokesperson, concerns remain about the ability of paper packaging to retain food temperature to the same extent as the clamshell.   Any future decision to replace the clamshell in the UK will depend upon consumer acceptance of the alternatives.[22]   Meanwhile, preliminary testing of 'the Earthshell' is underway in Canada and the USA.   This limestone-based packaging is designed to degrade naturally.

Another side of the story

Most analysts of the McDonald's-EDF partnership extol the substantial achievements and spin-off effects outlined above. Many writers emphasise the good news aspect of the story and ignore larger ethical questions about global corporations such as

McDonald's and the drawbacks of the partnership for EDF and the environmental movement. *The Economist* notes that "the partnership has improved McDonald's image" (1992, p 64). Joel Makower insists that "in the end things went better for both parties than either had expected" (1993, p 191). Edwin Stafford and Cathy Hartman conclude that: "Third Wave environmentalists view the McDonald's–EDF alliance as the model for future green alliances to emulate" (1996, p 57).

One of the few exceptions can be found in a Harvard Business School case study by Professor Forest Reinhardt. Although Reinhardt's assessment of the collaboration is generally upbeat, he acknowledges that some critics believed that EDF "was spending too much time in the company of corporate executives" (1992, p 15). Reinhardt cites one anonymous source as saying that:

> EDF feels it has to kowtow [to obtain access to industry decision-makers]; if that's what they have to do, access isn't worth it.

Reinhardt also quotes Barry Commoner's concern that such environmental group collaboration with business could make environmentalists "hostages [who] take on the ideology of their captors" (in Reinhardt, 1992, p 15).

More significantly for EDF, however, the task force attracted attention away from many of its ongoing projects, namely more than 40 EDF active lawsuits (recalling the organisation's informal motto of the 1970s – "Sue the Bastards"). Even though EDF's Richard Denison argued at the time that the organisation's "public image doesn't do justice to the diversity of approaches we use", Reinhardt insists that EDF needs to find a balance when allocating its resources to its diverse range of activities. There are fundamental questions for environmental groups considering similar strategies: Is it possible for EDF to focus on cooperation with business whilst "maintaining the organizational and cultural strengths that had made its first two decades a success?" (Reinhardt, 1992, p 15). What are the opportunity costs? Should EDF have put their task force resources into lobbying for new legislation such as a landfill tax? Or perhaps for new regulations requiring internal and external waste collection and sorting facilities for all fast food outlets? Such ideas may not be the kind of market-based solutions sought by companies such as McDonald's and third-wave environmentalists such as EDF's

Krupp, however they are a necessary feature of a vibrant and diverse environmental movement. Many other strategies are also needed. In the following section, we offer further reflections on the wider impact of the McDonald's–EDF partnership.

The McLibel story

If one of the ultimate goals of collaboration between business and environmental groups is "to create ecologically sustainable corporations" (Hemphill, 1994, p 44), then any assessment of the success of such partnerships must also consider their impact upon the overall social responsibility of the company concerned.

In the case of McDonald's and social responsibility, one could argue that the company has learned very little from its collaboration with EDF. The following story reminds us that big global corporations such as McDonald's seem much more concerned about higher profits and lower costs than any larger sense of social responsibility.

Around the same time as the partnership with EDF was launched in 1990, McDonald's filed a libel suit against five London Greenpeace group activists in relation to the 1986 'What's wrong with McDonald's' leaflet. Three of the activists subsequently went to court, apologised and agreed not to repeat the alleged actions. The other two, Helen Steel and Dave Morris, decided to fight the case through the courts and have come to be known as the 'McLibel 2' (see Box 6.2).

McDonald's decision to file the libel writs was driven by its concern that the allegations in the original leaflet were being widely reported in the media, as well as in schools and churches. According to a McDonald's UK spokesperson the "lies [were] affecting the company's staff, customers and thousands of independent franchisees" (in Vidal, 1996, p 16).[23] The spokesperson says that the company's objective was to stop publication of the leaflet not to go to court. One of the McLibel 2 insists that the company's real aim was to marginalise and suppress public criticism. Helen Steel believes that

> ... a whole way of thinking is on trial.... We've turned the tables and put McDonald's on trial. We have no particular grudge against them. They

stand for practices that take place every day in our society. We're standing for alternatives....
When we criticise McJobs, we're standing up for workers everywhere.... When we criticise junk food and make links between it and degenerative diseases, we're defending nutritionists and the promotion of healthy eating – the whole way people eat. (in Vidal, 1996, p 14)

The McDonald's move against the McLibel 2 was similar to its way of dealing with its critics at the height of the tropical rainforest issue in the late 1980s. John Elkington and Tom Burke note that:

McDonald's has found it hard to shake off persistent – but erroneous – claims that it had been involved in tropical rainforest destruction. Part of the problem was that the company relied on libel law to pursue those who attacked its record, rather than producing and publicising a clear written environmental policy statement. (1989, p 16)

What began as an apparently straightforward libel case has evolved into a messy process where McDonald's "now has the onus to prove that the statements contained within the London Greenpeace leaflet are 'lies' and that the defendants knew them to be so" (see Box 6.2). Even the company's own 300,000 strong leaflet campaign – 'Why McDonald's is going to court' – has not stopped a barrage of negative publicity which has done little to enhance its corporate image.

McDonald's expected to win the case cleanly and quickly. Its £2,000 a day solicitor predicted in December 1993 that the trial would last only three or four weeks. At 313 days of hearings, McLibel has become the longest-running court case in British history. It is estimated that McDonald's has spent more than £10 million on the McLibel case and related activities.

Box 6.2: A brief history of McLibel

1985: London Greenpeace launches a campaign intended to expose the reality behind the advertising mask of the McDonald's Corporation.

1986: London Greenpeace publishes the leaflet 'What's wrong with McDonald's?'

October 1989-September 1990: McDonald's sends undercover private investigators to infiltrate London Greenpeace. They take minutes of meetings and make friends with members of the group.

September 1990: McDonald's issues writs for libel against five members of London Greenpeace considered responsible for distributing the leaflet. Three of the five formally apologise after legal advice is given pointing out that legal aid is unobtainable for libel cases. The two others, Helen Steel and Dave Morris, refuse to apologise and decide to represent themselves. The three others issue a statement pledging support for the so-called McLibel 2.

Late 1990: The McLibel Support Campaign is set up to generate solidarity and financial support.

Late 1993: On behalf of McDonald's, Richard Rampton QC applies to the court for a non-jury trial. McDonald's submit that the scientific evidence necessary to examine the links between diet and disease are too complicated for a jury to understand. The judge agrees. Morris and Steel have the onus of proving that the leaflet statements are true or fair comment. The defendants are also required under British libel law to provide primary sources of evidence to substantiate their case, including witness statements and documentary proof but not press cuttings.

March 1994: McDonald's publishes a leaflet entitled 'Why McDonald's is going to court' and distributes 300,000 of them to customers via its burger outlets. The leaflet claims that: "This action is not about freedom of speech; it is about the right to stop people telling lies."

April 1994: Morris and Steel issue a counter-claim for libel against McDonald's for the company's accusation that they are telling lies. With the counter-claim, McDonald's now has the onus to prove that the statements contained within the London Greenpeace leaflet are "lies" and that the defendants knew them to be so.

September 1990-June 1994: Twenty-eight pre-trial hearings are conducted during which McDonald's places various legal obstacles in the way of the defendants.

June 28 1994: The full libel trial, presided over by Mr Justice Bell, commences in High Court.

Box 6.2 continued

September 1994: Operation 'Send-It-Back' is launched in Nottingham by Veggies, a mobile vegetarian food service.

June 28 1995: First anniversary of the trial. National media report that settlement negotiations between McDonald's and the defendants are under way. The defendants say that McDonald's initiated settlement discussions.

December 11 1995: On Day 199, the trial becomes the longest civil case in British history.

February 16 1996: McLibel Defendants access McSpotlight website for the first time on-line on a laptop connected by mobile phone to the Internet, outside McDonald's in Leicester Square, Central London.

December 13, 1996: After 313 days of hearings over a two-and-a-half year period, the longest-running court case in British legal history ends. A judgement was expected by mid-1997.

Source: The Diary of a Stance, McSpotlight (1996)

Mark Stephens, senior partner in large London law firm argues that

> McLibel is a fleabite which has turned into pustulating boils all over the corporate body. It can only get worse for [McDonald's].... People will say big business has trampled over two individuals exercising the right of free speech. Even Saatchis couldn't get McDonald's out of this one. They are in a no-win situation. (in Vidal, 1996, p 16)

The net result of the McLibel case has been a barrage of negative publicity for the company. Business and Society Review (1995) reports that McDonald's has apparently "learned nothing" from Nestle's experience with two consumer boycotts over its marketing of infant formula in developing countries. The same report cites an item from The Wall Street Journal which sees McDonald's once again a target of public protest:

> Instead of polishing McDonald's squeaky-clean image, the trial seems to have singed it. McDonald's already has felt the heat elsewhere: Finnish environmentalists protested its fortieth

birthday in April, and 400 youths ransacked a Copenhagen outlet in March setting furniture afire. (Business and Society Review, 1995, p 76)

Meanwhile, in the UK the protests launched in 1986 by London Greenpeace continue. A revised version of the original 'What's wrong with McDonald's' leaflet is being circulated to promote the cause of the McLibel 2 as well as a new campaign called 'Operation Send-It-Back'. The latter is organised by a Nottingham-based group and includes actions outside McDonald's UK headquarters as well as mail campaigns where people are encouraged to post McDonald's branded rubbish back to the company.

The McLibel case has also been a catalyst for international protest using new forms of information technology. On 20 February, 1996, McSpotlight, a World Wide Web Internet site (www.McSpotlight.org), was launched by the McInformation Network, an international network of volunteers working from 14 countries around the world. Its 120 megabytes of information contains 21,000 files on different topics, many of them highly critical of McDonald's. In addition to various clippings, cartoons and quotes, there are real audio interviews with the McLibel 2, damning video clips and in 14 languages: 'What's wrong with McDonald's' , the original text of the offending leaflet. In its first week, the site was accessed 174,000 times.

McDonald's has indicated that it is investigating the McSpotlight development, but has not yet decided on possible legal action. In April 1996, McDonald's responded with its own Internet home page (www.mcdonalds.com). The official company site focuses "on the McDonald's System around the world, community involvement, McDonald's food products and nutrition, career opportunities, the environment and McDonaldland, a section for kids" (McDonald's Corporation, 1996, p 9).

Collaboration or conflict?

The McDonald's story raises many questions about sustainable development within the context of the global fast food industry. There are also questions about what constitutes an environmentally responsible business and how environmental groups should best respond in order to influence business behaviour.

What began half a century ago as a small, efficient family-run business has spawned a diverse fast-food industry which is now worth in excess of $100 billion. As the industry leader, McDonald's is looked upon by competitors and customers alike as the model for fast-food retailing. This case demonstrates the complexity inherent in the process of defining best practice in corporate social and environmental responsibility. On its own, the partnership story illustrates the company's willingness to participate in a process of shared responsibility with a major environmental organisation. Both parties conclude that the Waste Reduction Task Force achieved a lot. The McLibel story, however, reveals another side of McDonald's which places the company in a less favourable light. McLibel also illustrates that environmental groups have other tools in their campaigning kit. Will the new forms of protest linked to the McLibel case eventually force McDonald's to seek new environmental group partners to address many of the lingering concerns about its growing global dominance?

Many within McDonald's would respond by saying that the company is in the business of serving quality food at a low price and not in the business of global social equity or environmental change.[24] The bottom line for many of McDonald's critics in the wider green movement, however, is that selling hamburgers is ultimately unsustainable. In addition to worries about the hamburger's disposable packaging, the green critique of meat production and transport includes concerns about: animal welfare; reliance of growth-promoting hormones; pesticide residues in animal feed; and corresponding adverse effects on people's health typified by the British mad cow disease crisis. An alternative vegan Britain would use only 25 per cent of existing agricultural land. When many applauded the collaboration between McDonald's and EDF, a scientist in a rival environmental group argued that "the best thing McDonald's could do would be to get out of the business of marketing meat" (in Gifford, 1991, p 36).

Ironically, eliminating meat is almost what McDonald's has done in its recent move into what one analyst calls "its final frontier" – India. The first outlet in New Delhi opened in October 1996 with a new menu and a redesigned kitchen. All beef and pork products have been deleted from the local menu and all cookers, fridges and staff have been divided into two separate categories – vegetarian and non-vegetarian – with no sharing of utensils. McDonald's would probably describe its Indian strategy as both economically wise and socially responsible. On the horizon, though, McDonald's once again must confront the face of protest. In January 1996, the National Awareness Forum created havoc at a Kentucky Fried Chicken outlet in southern India. Protesting farmers smashed windows and burned KFC chicken in the streets of Bangalore. Forum activists are fighting to protect India's cultural diversity and to stop the factory farming of chickens for fast food consumption. Their next target is McDonald's and they have vowed "to pull down the golden arches too" (Stackhouse, 1996, p A9).[25]

In the end, McDonald's evokes two solitudes. To its critics, McDonald's is by definition the antithesis of the socially responsible corporation, as sociologist George Ritzer reveals:

> In spite of the fast-food restaurant's widespread acceptance, many people have rebelled against, and attacked, it on a variety of grounds. A few communities have fought hard, and at times successfully, against the invasion.... They have reacted against the garish signs and structures, the traffic, the noise, and the nature of the clientele.... Most generally, they have fought against the various kinds of irrationalities and assaults on tradition that the fast-food restaurant represents. (1993, p 163)

The McLibel 2 make much of the low wages and poor working conditions for McDonald's restaurant staff. Echoing novelist Douglas Coupland's description of "McJobs", the London Greenpeace group argues that "the majority of employees are people who have few job options and so are forced to accept this exploitation" (London Greenpeace, 1996).

To the company and its supporters, McDonald's is what a successful and socially responsive company is all about as a recent UK company leaflet on the environment asserts:

> At McDonald's, we believe we have a special responsibility to help protect and preserve our environment for future generations. A business leader must be an environmental leader as well,

which is why we analyse every aspect of our business in terms of its impact on the environment, and take what action is necessary to lead both in word and deed. (McDonald's Restaurants Ltd, 1994)

Although its partnership with EDF represented a bold environmental leadership move at the time, McDonald's continues to be perceived by many within the wider green movement, rightly or wrongly, as an environmental pariah. The McLibel case and the company's vision of global dominance serve to fuel the environmentalist image of McDonald's as an inherently irresponsible and unsustainable corporation. From this starting point, is there any prospect for future dialogue and partnership to address these concerns? Perhaps – but only if the larger sustainability issues associated with fast food consumption and globalisation become part of the partnership agenda. In the following chapter, we analyse the overall impact and wider significance of business–environmental group partnerships in the sustainability transition.

Notes

[1] This chapter is largely based upon a case study written by David F. Murphy for the New Academy of Business. See Murphy, 1996c.

[2] The brothers sold licenses for $1,000 to other entrepreneurs to open their own McDonald's restaurants and use the system. According to McDonald's promotional material, "the brothers were not interested in expanding and making more money and in many ways were of simple means and although they preferred a winning formula they did not have the will or inclination to develop it further." See McDonald's Education Service, 1996.

[3] Kroc's approach contrasted sharply with the norm at the time which saw fast-food companies providing limited support to franchisees and favouring low-cost suppliers. Today more than 75 per cent of McDonald's American outlets are owned and operated by local, independent franchisers. See Upton and Margolis, 1992, p 2.

[4] The increase in share numbers is based upon ten share splits since the initial flotation. See *The Economist*, 1993, p 95. Other figures from *The Economist*, 1996a, p 77.

[5] Coupland adds that a McJob is "frequently considered a satisfying career choice by people who have never held one."

[6] During its first ten years of operation, the programme trained more than 9,000 potential employees, 87 per cent of whom took up employment. See Wood, 1994, p 515–16.

[7] In late 1996, the UK government introduced the Producer Responsibility regulations to meet its obligations under the EC Directive on Packaging and Packaging Waste. The new regulations place obligations on businesses in the packaging chain to meet specific targets for the recovery and recycling of packaging waste. By 2001, businesses will be expected to recover 50 per cent of such waste and to recycle 15 per cent of each material (eg, plastic, metal, glass, etc).

[8] In 1984, BBC television's *Nature* programme criticised McDonald's for its role in the destruction of tropical rainforests. When threatened with libel, the BBC apologised to the company.

[9] Not to be confused with Greenpeace-UK which is also based in London. Set up in 1971, London Greenpeace was the first European Greenpeace group. By the mid-1980s it had become a small, grassroots domain for anarchists and libertarian greens. It continues to campaign on a variety of issues.

[10] Gifford notes that the Sierra Club and other environmental groups "spurned advances by McDonald's." (1991, p 34). McDonald's adopted its first written policy statement related to the tropical rainforest issue in mid-1989 (see Elkington and Burke, 1989, p 16).

[11] By 1990, EDF's membership had tripled to 200,000, staff had quadrupled to 125 and its budget went from $3.4 to $16.9 million (see Stafford and Hartman, 1996, p 55).

[12] Another version of the story says that Krupp first got the idea of a joint EDF–McDonald's project following a visit with his children to one of the company's restaurants where he had been struck by the amount of solid waste generated by the company.

[13] McDonald's Waste Reduction Policy states that the company "will not permit the destruction of rainforests for our beef supply. This policy is strictly enforced and closely monitored." (see WRTF, 1991, p 18).

[14] WRTF, 1991, pp 19-22.

[15] Open letter by the three EDF task force members dated 20 April 1992.

[16] Upton and Margolis (1992) report that a review of the task force by McDonald's managers raised many questions about the initiative. Some managers were concerned that waste management may become another transient issue like the energy crisis of the 1970s. This raised other questions about the place of environmental affairs in the future operations of McDonald's.

[17] This part of the story is offered by Gifford (1991) and is missing from most academic papers on the partnership.

[18] The only exception was the continued use of polystyrene packaging for breakfast meals.

[19] Suggestions included: shrinking napkin size; increasing size of ketchup packets (so customers use fewer); recycled, unbleached paper bags; recycling of all corrugated cardboard packaging; and limited field testing of composting. Ideas rejected included: refillable cups; reusable plates; and straws with smaller diameters.

[20] As of late 1996, the 'Food for the Earth' project was on indefinite hold. McDonald's has found that there is insufficient infrastructure for large-scale composting. While the company continues to support composting in principle, a more supportive infrastructure will be needed before the project can be implemented.

[21] Telephone conversation with B. Langert, 28 October, 1996.

[22] Telephone conversation with B. Fleck, January, 1997.

[23] Only 23 per cent of McDonald's 660 UK restaurants are franchised.

[24] When McDonald's ability to meet its stated mission is threatened, the company can act quickly. In early 1996, when faced with growing public concerns about mad cow disease in the UK, McDonald's suddenly decided to suspend the sale of British beef products in all of its British outlets and replaced its local suppliers with beef imported from The Netherlands. When politicians accused McDonald's of creating public panic, the company insisted that it had not taken the decision lightly and that it saw its move as an act of leadership. However, McDonald's quickly became a target of protest by the British farming community. In the Howe of Angus in Scotland where a new outlet opened in April 1996, a local protester called the McDonald's boycott of British beef "pathetic" and declared: "If they are going to open restaurants here, they should be supporting us, not turning against us" (in Cluston, 1996). This again confirms the struggle to define the essence of corporate social responsibility in a world of competing interests.

[25] See also McKibben (1996).

seven

Finding solutions together: the future of sustainable development

At the beginning of this book, we situated our discussion of business–environmental group partnerships by linking them to the Rio process and the emergence of sustainable development in the early 1990s. The thirty-month Rio process produced 24 million sheets of paper and much bravado about the need for global partnership. Agenda 21, the so-called programme of action for sustainable development, provided a collaborative framework for governments, business and NGOs, yet contained many contradictory messages.[1] The contested version of sustainable development which emerged from Rio, nevertheless, provided a basis for both action and ongoing debate. The post-Rio period has produced millions more sheets of paper and seemingly endless exchanges in cyberspace. The rhetoric of sustainable development continues to ring louder than the limited numbers of success stories about implementation. Most governments and multilateral agencies still struggle to embrace and implement the diverse and complex dimensions of sustainability. Transnational corporations often co-opt the language and would have us believe that we are all environmentalists now. For their part environmental groups and other NGOs remain divided about both the meaning and value of sustainable development as either an organising principle or campaigning tool. Meanwhile most people around the world remain largely oblivious to the activities of the global policy entrepreneurs who continue to dominate the official post-Rio policy process.

Despite such obstacles and divisions, the implementation of the Rio's proposed global partnership for sustainable development has somehow managed to begin. Governments may continue to talk, but non-governmental actors such as business and environmental groups have already started the process with diverse global and local responses. This book has outlined a particular dimension of this new reality – the emergence of new partnerships between business and environmental groups based upon the ethic of finding solutions together.

In this final chapter, we begin with some general reflections about why and how these new partnerships emerged in the 1990s. We outline some of the common causal factors and implementation themes of the various partnerships described in the book. This is followed by a review of the costs and benefits of partnerships, first for business and then for environmental groups. We then address a number of the critiques of such market-based strategies, including questions about the relationship between business–environmental group partnerships, legislation and the democratic process. The chapter ends on a cautiously optimistic note by linking partnerships to the emergence of a new social realism. While we accept that business–environmental group partnerships are no magic sustainability potion, we conclude that new myths such as sustainable development hold the promise of bringing adversaries together to forge more ecologically secure and equitable world futures.

Common themes and lessons learned

Causal factors

Our case studies have demonstrated that environmental awareness and business response does not happen without many years of persistent environmental group campaigning. With the renewed enthusiasm for environmentalism in the late 1980s, the power and influence of environmental groups grew and the focus of environmental group campaigning began to shift towards finding and implementing solutions. This period coincided with the introduction of more flexible government regulation on environmental matters and protracted negotiations between governments leading up to the Rio Summit. The lack of an effective political response has been a major factor in the environmental movement's move to embrace market mechanisms as a potential vehicle for achieving societal change.

As we noted in Chapter two, with the advent of the third wave, environmentalists began to adopt a more pragmatic view of the role of campaigning in finding solutions. Third-wave environmentalists generally agree upon the need to influence market forces, however their tactics cover a wide spectrum – from initial attempts at dialogue with business to direct action protest and from media campaigns and consumer education to formal partnerships with business. The role of direct action protest in forcing reluctant companies to the negotiating table is particularly significant. Most of the partnerships described in this book emerged as a direct or indirect result of many years of environmental group protest. In Chapters five and six, we found that companies such as Dow, Unilever and McDonald's have faced (and continue to face) considerable criticism from various groups within the wider green movement about their environmental, social and ethical credentials. Each of their respective partnership experiences (Dow–EPE, Unilever–WWF-International and McDonald's–EDF) emerged in part as a result of such protest or the threat of future protest. Despite its current image as an environmentally responsible corporate citizen, even B&Q (Chapter four) was originally a target of grassroots protests and boycotts before embarking upon the partnership route through the WWF-UK 1995 Group.

Third-wave environmentalism is encouraging a new consensus between pragmatic environmentalists and idealistic business managers. This process is also being driven by the emergence of a third stage of business response to environmental challenges – the sustainability agenda. Although few, if any, companies worldwide have fully embraced sustainability, key business people are beginning to influence corporate agendas in significant ways. A convergence of this third-stage business response with third-wave environmentalism is perhaps the most significant driver behind the partnerships described in this book (see Figure 5). These new partnerships are founded upon a belief that incremental change is possible in the short term, whilst acknowledging that there must be ongoing negotiations about the longer-term social, economic, political and cultural changes needed for sustainable development.

Figure 5: Some causal factors of business–environmental group partnerships

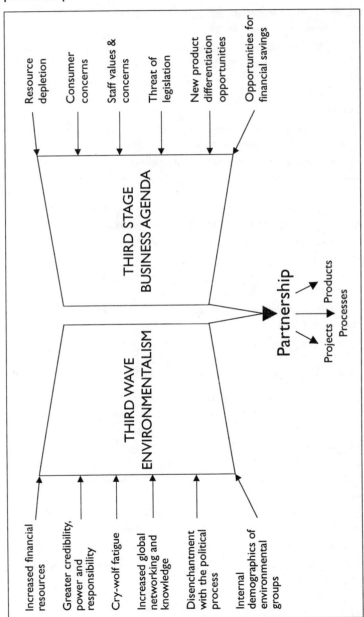

Box 7.1: Prerequisites for partnerships

Environmental issue of high media profile and public concern, largely driven by environmental group campaigning.

Perceived or actual failure of political, governmental, initiatives to achieve improvements relating to environmental problems.

Failure of business initiatives to secure improvements relating to the environmental issue(s); and failure to convince the public of any benefits secured.

Presence of a threat of organised anti-business protest if nothing is seen to be done to alleviate the environmental problem(s).

Existence of a mainstream environmental group(s) with enough financing and commitment to form a partnership without receiving direct finance from business partners for this role.

Adequate communication and understanding within the environmental movement to allow any partnership time to establish itself.

Belief of company directors in the prudence of building formal relationships with environmental groups.

Belief of company directors in the benefits of improving company image for enhanced stakeholder relations.

Presence of committed champions within both companies and environmental groups.

Willingness to take a leap of faith and to accept the ambiguity inherent in ideas such as sustainable development and partnership.

The partners may often disagree about what constitutes a more sustainable future and yet they recognise the value in working together to identify common ground and to take interim steps towards finding solutions. In the following section, we review the key implementation themes emanating from the partnerships described in this book. Box 7.1 summarises the prerequisites for partnership.

Implementation themes

The case studies described in this book reveal a number of common implementation themes. We would like to highlight the following:

- building positive interpersonal relationships;

- establishing achievable goals and appropriate monitoring systems;

- maintaining financial independence;

- promoting transparency and accountability.

We begin with what is the most obvious and perhaps most important feature of business–environmental group partnerships – positive* interpersonal relationships. Business–environmental group partnerships depend upon the commitment of individuals to a process where both partners' needs are effectively met. The partnership process relies upon the cooperation of many committed individuals, particularly from the private sector where competitive rivalry reigns supreme. Environmental groups empower charismatic individuals to seek out credible and cooperative business partners. Many companies respond to the offer of partnership by identifying or appointing environmental champions to represent their interests. For example, much of the success of the 1995 Group (Chapter four) has depended upon people like WWF-UK's Francis Sullivan and B&Q's Alan Knight to lead the process. The 1995 Group has also provided a forum where campaigners, competitors, retailers, suppliers and manufacturers alike could work together towards shared objectives.

Partnerships thrive when participants take the time to build strong relationships with each other. This is not an ideal process without conflict or tension. It is rather about trying to think with each other in order to solve problems together. When disagreements arise, they are often based upon misunderstandings. The partners need to realise that they do not necessarily share the same concepts or even the same vocabulary. Ongoing, open communication between all partners is an extremely important part of the process. In addition, partnerships need to be open to wide participation, indeed joint ownership, as only this will enable the initiative to be accepted by other sectors of society.

Our second key implementation theme is the need to reach agreement on achievable goals, implementation strategies and monitoring systems. This should include open reporting and full compliance with all agreements. Environmental groups and their business partners must aim to develop systems and build capacities to ensure effective ongoing monitoring of the partnership. In developing its own strategies and methods, the WWF-International–

Unilever fisheries partnership (Chapter five) has been able to learn from and improve upon the forest sector partnership approach (Chapter four). The use of external facilitators to assist with partnership implementation is another beneficial model, as illustrated in Chapter five by Dow and EPE's collaboration on the EMAS Plus project. External facilitation and reporting of the process enhanced both the efficiency and credibility of the initiative.

Our third key theme is that the partners should maintain financial independence. Businesses and environmental groups should be clear at the outset about each other's expectations and resource constraints. In particular, environmental groups should be forward looking and establish financially secure means of administering their end of the partnership. This is particularly important where environmental groups assume the role of monitoring the activities of business partners as we described in Chapter four. Similarly, the credibility of the Environmental Defense Fund (EDF) partnership with the much-maligned McDonald's (Chapter six) hinged upon the fact that EDF did not receive any monetary or in-kind business support. Otherwise, the environmental group's independence could be compromised as was the case with Pollution Probe's endorsement of Loblaws' green product range (Chapter five). The partnership may have brought Pollution Probe much needed financial benefits but the net result was a tarnished reputation within the Canadian environmental movement.

Another major implementation theme is that transparency and accountability should be promoted throughout the process. For businesses this means engaging their various stakeholders. For environmental groups this involves communicating with their trustees, members and other parts of the wider green movement. This openness helps to lessen public scepticism of what is a very new phenomenon. The commitment to transparency should involve clear and stated aims from all partners and the publication of non-commercially sensitive data on the performance of the partnership.

Accountability also depends upon ongoing critical monitoring of the process by the environmental group partner and other parts of the wider green movement. For business, this critical monitoring ensures that the partnership is deemed to be credible in the public eye. However, if the business fails to implement its end of the agreement, the environmental group partner or other environmental groups have the option of initiating renewed, overt pressure against the business concerned.

The new partnerships described in this book are facilitating incremental change towards sustainability. By engaging business in more direct and formal ways, mainstream environmental groups have initiated a process which holds much promise for third-wave environmentalism and a genuine third-stage sustainability response from business. However, there are also costs associated with these new partnerships for both business and environmental groups. In the following section, we offer some reflections on the costs and benefits of partnership for business. This is followed by an analysis of the potentials and pitfalls of partnership for environmental groups.

The costs and benefits of partnerships for business

There are many reasons why partnerships with environmental groups are becoming an increasingly popular strategy for companies. As we described in Chapter three, adopting a proactive stance towards environmental challenges is increasingly being seen as good business strategy. Working with environmental groups can help business develop a better understanding of the implications of the third-stage sustainability agenda.

It would be wrong to suggest that partnership with environmental groups and the operation of third-stage management strategies are tried and tested mechanisms for maintaining business profitability. It is too soon to know the full costs and benefits for businesses which adopt such strategies, however, from the case studies a number of themes emerge. We deal with these business benefits and costs in turn.

Benefits of partnership with environmental groups

The benefits of working with environmental groups broadly relate to environmental public relations, eco-efficiency and organisational learning.

For reasons of marketing, recruitment, employee motivation and risk management (preventing store boycotts and protecting share prices) it is prudent to cultivate the public impression of a socially and environmentally responsible business. Credibility with

"perception is everything"

customers and stakeholders is key. Studies by the National Consumer Council (NCC) and Market & Opinion Research International (MORI), among others, repeatedly tell us that consumers do not trust business environmental claims. Most people, nevertheless, believe what environmental groups tell them. In an effort to change public perceptions, business has begun to engage environmental groups in new ways. For example, Dr Peter Scupholme of British Petroleum, who commissioned SustainAbility to perform an assessment of BP's relations with environmental groups, believes that partnership is an effective way of demonstrating his company's public commitment to sustainable development.

By working with environmental groups, companies are also generating a level of interest in their environmental policies which hitherto has only been experienced by the likes of the eco-conscious Body Shop. Campaigning groups have the kind of links with the media that are the envy of corporate PR departments. To have these impressive environmental group PR machines working for business is an attractive bonus. The experience of many companies in the WWF-UK 1995 Group was that partnership with one environmental group helped to reduce the attention of other environmental groups, although this has not been the experience of the McDonald's Corporation. For the most part, however, collaboration with environmental groups helps business to promote an environmentally responsible public image.

Given that the costs of confrontation are so high, especially when boycotts are involved, constructive engagement with environmental groups can prove to be a safer option. In this way business–environmentalist partnerships represent the incorporation of the precautionary principle into core business practice – a key aspect of third-stage sustainability management.

In addition to these fairly intangible benefits, financial and natural resource savings – or eco-efficiencies – can be achieved through partnership with environmental groups. Savings on energy and waste can be identified with the help of external environmental expertise. For example, EDF technologists helped McDonald's determine how to reduce both its waste output and disposal expenditure (Chapter six). Likewise, companies in the 1995 Group saved on expensive consultancy fees by working with WWF-UK. Mike Inchley, of the DIY retailer, Do It All, explains that "the timber sourcing issue was a major business problem which required expert advice. Forest conservationists at WWF-UK were the natural partners to help us solve the problem" (Chapter four). With complex supply chains and often strained buyer-supplier relations, the DIY retailers have benefited greatly from WWF-UK's free advice in implementing their forest product sourcing and certification programmes. In addition, there are many other untapped partnership opportunities available for business to pursue (see Box 7.2).

Costs of partnership with environmental groups

It would be unwise to give the impression that partnerships are purely win–win scenarios for participating businesses. Partnerships place new demands on management time and often bring additional administrative costs. There is also potential for decreased profit margins and conflicts between product performance and environmental quality. For example, adopting environmental criteria for procurement may lead to greater supply chain rigidity with the relinquishing of 'just-in-time' supplies.

Critics on both sides of the political spectrum may challenge green business motives for different reasons. By forming environmental partnerships, business may be accused of buying influence by radical greens. Questions may equally be raised by sceptics in the City and financial press who often argue that time spent on above-compliance environmental management is time taken from traditional profit-related activities such as marketing, product development and sales.

Another concern is that companies may find themselves restricted by the often commercially unaware nature of campaigning groups, as illustrated by certain companies' frustration with the slow, cumbersome nature of the Forest Stewardship Council (FSC) process. These companies have argued that this is preventing them from fully realising the anticipated promotional benefits of the partnership (Chapter four).

In addition to such concerns, some top directors and business analysts would reject the notion that companies have a responsibility to anyone other than their owners. They would argue that an emphasis upon stakeholder relations diverts business from its ultimate purpose in society – the pursuit of profits. For instance, Milton Friedman (1962) insists that the role of business is to create economic wealth by enhancing shareholder value, and that the role of government is to establish laws to guide this process. Friedman's definition of corporate social responsibility does not extend beyond these economic and legal parameters. Another example of this line of argument is offered by Elaine Sternberg who believes that the core purpose and implied responsibility of business is to "maximise owner value over the long term by selling goods or services" (1994, p 32). Both Friedman and Sternberg challenge the use of corporate resources for non-profitable moral purposes. Indeed Sternberg calls this "theft; the unjustified appropriation of the owners' property" (p 41).

The triple bottom line

These ideas seem oddly out of touch with the recent corporate response to social, environmental and ethical concerns. Even though much of this may be driven by enlightened self-interest, growing numbers of business leaders are beginning to recognise the need for a triple bottom line of financial, legal and moral obligations. We believe the moral bottom line will become as significant to core business practice as the financial and legal bottom lines. This is because of a variety of factors: the rising prominence of business globally; the intensifying social and environmental problems facing communities worldwide; and a growing sense that individuals have the right to demand greater responsibility from those who exercise economic power over them.

Partnerships with the wider green movement can assist companies to manage the moral bottom line and not just their environmental impacts. This is demonstrated by the emergence of social development partnerships as described in Chapter five. These new initiatives show how consumers, staff, shareholders and communities are becoming increasingly concerned with a wider range of ethical issues related to business activities. It is no longer a question of solving either ecological damage, cruelty to animals, or human rights abuses. Instead businesses today are being asked to behave responsibly – in all areas and for all issues. Even responsible businesses will never be perfect, but they must endeavour to solve problems over which they have a degree of influence.

Those who dismiss the stakeholder economy are failing to anticipate the future context within which business must operate. This lack of vision may make it far more difficult for business to respond as and when public pressure on any given issue rises to the fore. By working with environmental groups and other NGOs, business is forced to consider new and different ideas. This may mark the beginning of an organisational learning process that has the potential to move business into the third stage (see Chapter three).

Towards a learning organisation

The final and most important benefit for participating businesses relates to organisational learning. There is a new saying that if there is a future it will be green. If profit-making organisations are to meet the demands of green futures, they will need to undergo profound organisational change. Third-stage corporate strategies need to consider fundamental questions such as "who really needs this product?" and "will the community be healthy and prosperous enough to produce and to buy our products in the future?" In order to address such concerns, business needs to work with other sectors of society. A collaborative approach to solving the social and environmental problems caused by business may be the most progressive and relevant organisational learning strategy of all. By embracing partnership strategies, business, environmental groups and other NGOs have the potential to define the future of private enterprise.

The potentials and pitfalls of partnership for environmental groups

Building upon our discussion above, it is still too early to determine all of the potentials and pitfalls of partnership for environmental groups. However a number of themes emanate from the case studies. Partnership with business is a worthwhile strategy for many environmental groups as it can lead to real environmental improvements, greater environmental education and the harnessing of consumer support for environmental goals, as well as 'giving teeth' to voluntary initiatives. However partnership with business also presents a number of strategic problems largely related to organisational independence, particularly the ongoing capacity to criticize and advocate a radical vision of sustainability. We examine the potentials and the pitfalls in turn.

Box 7.2: Business–NGO partnership opportunities

There is a wealth of opportunity for business–NGO partnerships from the global to the local levels. The following partnership ideas are based upon emerging ideas in the business and NGO communities, and the authors' own suggestions:

- Ethical marketing group: environmental groups might work with companies on ways of promoting products and services in a more ethically responsible manner.

- Oil stewardship council: oil companies might work with environmental, developmental and human rights groups to develop independently verifiable codes of conduct which cover oil extraction, oil transport and oil infrastructure lifecycles.

- Clean transport club: a car manufacturer, major service station chain and environmental group might collaborate to provide electric cars, battery swapping facilities and advertising/endorsement, respectively.

- Tourism stewardship council: a major tourism company and environmental group might seek to establish a global accreditation system so holidays could be graded on their total environmental, social and ethical impacts.

- Freedom clothes council: high street retailers might work with social development and human rights groups to develop a clothes labelling scheme for items from worker-friendly factories.

- Human rights accreditation council: a major human rights group might work with transnationals on appropriate human rights policies and the monitoring of subsidiaries and political regimes.

- Ethical investment council: a network of NGOs could work with banks and ethical investment funds on a widely-recognised ethical Dow Jones or FTSE rating.

- Environmental justice lobbying coaltion: responsible companies and NGOs might collaborate to lobby for legislation and directives deemed to be in the interests of an environmentally just world (and against those deemed disadvantageous, such as the WTO technical barriers to trade agreement).

- Lesbigay accreditation council: a major lesbian, bisexual and gay rights group might work with sympathetic companies on anti-sexuality discrimination and responsive equal opportunities policies, leading to a 'pink' logo for products or companies.

The potentials of partnership with business

Partnerships with business provide environmental groups with ways of implementing solutions to the many environmental problems where business has a significant impact. This approach can lead to substantial environmental benefits. For example, several hundred people worldwide can now make a secure and sustainable living from FSC-certified forests (Chapter four), several thousand people living near Dow Europe manufacturing sites are more likely to feel safer about chemical production processes and several million people may yet be able to fish for their livelihoods for generations to come as a result of the MSC (Chapter five).

Partnership with business is also a catalyst for the greater environmental education of society. Managers of corporations, who may have never before engaged constructively with environmental issues are now doing so. These corporations can reach many more people than an individual environmental group. Supplier assessments like those described in Chapter four mean that thousands of supplier companies now have more proactive environmental policies and programmes. By advertising their environmental policies to customers and staff, many people are learning more about environmental and social problems. In addition, the demonstration of workable partnership solutions can be an effective means of promoting a new way forward for government policy makers.

Partnership with business also serves to harness consumer support for environmental goals. Despite its drawbacks, a more sustainable form of consumerism represents one way in which individuals can express their concern for the environment and promote positive change. Research in a number of western countries shows that consumers are now dismissive of many company's green claims, believing them to be largely false (NCC, 1996). By becoming involved in the development of consumer information systems and ecolabelling, we believe environmental groups offer an opportunity to restore consumer confidence in environmental products and hence the consumer's sense of agency. This may help continue to politicise the market in favour of sustainability goals and ensure that consumer concern is translated into real social and environmental improvements.

In a similar way, partnership with business can give 'teeth' to voluntary initiatives. Since Rio, there has been a proliferation of voluntary, industry-led initiatives such as codes of conduct

(UNCTAD, 1996). There is now a growing debate about the efficacy of such initiatives. On the one side, western governments argue that these initiatives "achieve sustainability and growth with the minimum of regulation and the maximum of voluntary action" (Gummer, 1995). One the other side, critics suggest that governments "embrace of the voluntary approach ... amounts to them shifting into neutral and taking their hands off the wheel" (FoE-UK, 1995, p 45). Much of this debate has regarded the division between self-regulation and 'command and control' as being synonymous with a distinction between standards determined by industry and standards determined by governments. However, voluntary mechanisms such as business–environmental group partnerships require industry to accept standards and targets but do not rely upon industry to set the targets. Instead, benchmarks for sustainability are defined in collaboration with environmental groups whose primary goal is achieving sustainability. In this context, environmental groups can play a validating role for voluntary initiatives, giving them added credibility and the necessary 'teeth' to deliver more substantial change in business behaviour.

The pitfalls of partnership with business

There are a number of concerns associated with business partnerships. These relate to the pitfalls of third-wave environmentalism in general, brought on by the growing institutional nature of many environmental groups.

First, there is the question of independence. By becoming partners of business, environmental campaigners should ask themselves whether supporter donations should be used to provide business with free environmental advice. As we noted above, by charging for their services, environmental groups would lose their independent status. Instead environmental groups should protect their one major strength – their understanding of environmental problems and the conservation principle – and seek to advise and endorse organisations who already charge business for environmental consultancy or certification services, with the stewardship council model described in Chapters four and five.

Another concern related to autonomy is that single-issue partnerships may prevent environmental groups from publicly criticising its business partner on other social or environmental matters. The worry, therefore, is that partnering groups may lose their edge as industry watchdogs.

Successful NGOs of the twenty-first century will be the ones who manage to demonstrate that professionalism is compatible with ideological clarity. A key reason why businesses works with environmental groups and other NGOs is because of the respect they have in society. It is therefore in everyone's interest not to undermine this public confidence. A successful strategy for environmental groups, for example, may be to become more specialised. As a result, the environmental movement as a whole could more effectively fulfil the roles of both facilitator and watchdog. Dowie believes that major American environmental organisations will only remain relevant if they stop imitating each other:

> Environmentalists need to agree that, say, the Sierra Club takes book publishing and eco-tourism.... Greenpeace takes mammals and Izaak Walton saves fish. The Legal Defense Fund litigates in State Courts, the National Resources Defense Council takes the federal cases, and the Environmental Defense Fund negotiates. (1995b, p 36)

A limited amount of specialisation has already occurred between and within environmental groups. While this is welcomed, we do hold reservations. Organisational specialisation may restrict innovative thinking and undermine the awareness of alternative strategies. For example, work portfolios may become increasingly narrow, with staff developing a set of skills that relate to the operation of a business partnership rather than meeting specific and measurable environmental goals.

In most of the partnerships described in this book, almost no attempt was made to develop systems to evaluate the partnership's direct contribution to the achievement of environmental goals. Today the main quantitative analyses of an environmental group's success is based upon membership levels and the extent of media coverage. In the new solutions era, third-wave environmentalists need new ways to judge performance. Indicators such as 'the percentage reduction in waste per dollar spent', or 'the acres of forest saved per pound invested' are required if we are to truly know the full costs and benefits of business partnerships for participating environmental groups.

This leads to another concern with business–environmental group partnerships – the opportunity costs. With an increasing amount of time and finance spent on working with business, other means of achieving environmental goals, such as litigation or park management, may be compromised. In addition, media work may focus increasingly on the general public's role as green consumers rather than on conservation-minded citizens. Stephen Corry of Survival International explains:

> The message ... will become: don't worry about lobbying your Member of Parliament, or the timber importers, or writing to governments, the press or companies, don't worry about ... hard-hitting international campaigns – just eat more Brazil nuts. (1993, p 9)

This makes it even more imperative to have measures of performance in order to assess business partnership campaigns alongside more traditional environmental campaigns.

Partnerships and the solutions agenda

A final area of contention related to partnerships is the associated emphasis upon the new solutions agenda. Although we welcome this development, we attach some caveats to our support.

First, there is the question of funding. A vibrant membership base is essential for the survival of environmental groups. Experience thus far shows that conflict between environmental groups and business or government attracts media attention and stimulates new membership. Mark Gilden of the UK's leading direct marketing provider for environmental groups notes that:

> *In 1995, WWF-UK's direct mailing to potential new members came hot on the heels of the Brent Spar confrontation between Greenpeace and Shell. WWF obtained the highest number of new members from a mailing in 8 years.*

Another problem with the emphasis upon solutions, is that problems and solutions are relative. The environment is open to a variety of interpretations based on an individual's value base. It can be said that something is not a problem or an issue until someone describes it as such. Before *Silent spring* pollution was occurring yet it was not a major global problem or issue as people did not generally recognise it as such. Until recently environmental groups have been solely concerned with identifying, describing and promoting environmental issues (Hannigan, 1995). As they focus more on solutions to the problems already defined, their ability – and desire – to identify emerging issues may be lost in the process. Some would argue that society needs problems if it is to continue evolving: before solutions must come problems.

Environmentalists who advocate the solutions agenda need to ask themselves: Who is going to champion new problems in the future? The concern is that as the solutions agenda becomes the vogue then those who wish to raise new problems will be increasingly ostracised. This marginalisation of creative and provocative thinking might become the 'final solution', as those who do the provoking are identified as the problem.

In order to address the various concerns about partnerships and the solutions agenda, environmental groups should:

- specify their strategic role within the wider green movement;

- develop improved internal performance indicators;

- foster networks with other groups; and

- encourage innovative thinking and problem identification within their own organisations and in interactions with others.

These actions would help to strengthen the long-term efficacy of business–environmental group partnerships. They would also help to answer a lingering question about market-based mechanisms: can the market really deliver sustainable development?

Dealing with critiques of market-based approaches

We recognise that there are many environmentalists who would be inclined to reject partnership with business and the pursuit of incremental change as a form of 'false consciousness'. These critiques, along with questions such as the relationship of business–environmental group partnerships to globalisation, legislation and the democratic process, need to be addressed. Partnerships must respond to these challenges if they are to contribute to our understanding of sustainability and environmental justice.

Deep green concerns

Those with a deep green or ecocentric perspective (Chapter two) have serious concerns about the capacity of the market to deliver sustainability. They dismiss the anthropocentric assumption that the value of goods and services primarily comes from consumer preference. Corry begs the question "are we really only going to conserve those wildernesses which can pay their way?" (1993, p 13)

There are two answers to this concern. First, a focus on using market mechanism to promote conservation represents a political choice rather than a philosophical perspective on the intrinsic value of nature. For example, FSC board member Yati Bun believes that certification of sustainable forest products may be culturally alien to forest peoples yet their immediate need is to diversify incomes, receive a better price and realise a consistent demand for their work. Second, as we described in Chapter two, ecohumanism is a far more honest way of describing our relationship with nature because, even if we accept that we are just part of nature, we will always value it from our own perspective, as humans.

Box 7.3: Aquarian partnerships

A strong theme in radical green thought is that called the New Age. As the year 2000 dawns, this concept will to take on an increased millennialist hue. New Ageism maintains that the Age of Aquarius, which includes ecological consciousness, is about to dawn. Astrologers say that we enter a new age every 2000 years, establishing new civilisations and cultures. The Earth is currently emerging from the Age of Pisces – an age initiated by Jesus and his teachings, which, arguably, has put few of them into practice. Pisces has been dominated by polarisation and conflict – between cultures, religions, races, and within western consciousness – including the mind–body split, the masculine–feminine and society–nature polarities. The notion of duality is embodied in the Piscean symbol, of two fish swimming in opposite directions. By contrast, Aquarius symbolises harmony, holism, balance and high moral and spiritual awareness – it will be an age when human consciousness is not split from nature. In this way, Aquarius may already be ushering in an age of collaboration and partnership. Source: Pepper (1996)

A second concern for deep greens relates to the understanding of wealth. Most of the damage caused by the industrial economy to the planet, its people and communities is linked to the operation of the global economy and the northern middle-class way of life: TV, shopping, and wanting to be richer than others. Deep greens believe that we must redefine need and wealth in our society. Marshall Sahlins describes how this might be done:

> [T]here are two possible courses to affluence. Wants may be 'easily satisfied', either by producing much or desiring little. The familiar conception ... [is that] man's [sic] wants are great, not to say infinite, whereas his means are limited.... But there is also a Zen road to affluence; human material wants are finite and few, and technical means unchanging but on the whole adequate. Adopting the Zen strategy, a people can enjoy unparalleled material plenty – with a low standard of living. (in Wall, 1994, pp 24-5).

Surprisingly these ideas are beginning to be considered by companies committed to the third-stage sustainability transition. As part of this shift in the area of product development, many large corporations are beginning to ask the question: *Who needs it?* (see SustainAbility, 1995b). Collaboration with environmental groups helps the related process of organisational learning. This aspect of partnerships could be welcomed by deep greens.

One of the gurus of ecocentrism, Arnie Naess (1988) believes that there is value in all perspectives and points of view, and that educational information exchange is a fundamental prerequisite to bringing about a sustainable and just society. This too suggests dialogue between business and environmental groups is compatible with deep green philosophy.

Ecofeminist concerns

Another perspective on the partnership process is provided by ecofeminists. Ecofeminism suggests that in a society dominated by men, the 'male' approach mediates what we value as knowledge. Patriarchal society views nature as a commodity instead of an integral part of its existence. Ecofeminists argue that economic solutions will not solve our present problems. Rather they suggest that male-dominated modes of thinking, knowledge and ways of exercising power need to be transformed for real sustainability to be achieved. Business–environmental group partnerships, especially product-oriented partnerships, could be open to ecofeminist critique as they represent an increasing commodification of nature.[2] This does not necessarily mean that there are insurmountable obstacles to collaboration between the ecofeminist and the business person. In practice there may be more common ground than not. For example, each may share concerns about the implications of Malay sweatshops for the welfare of women textile workers, even though they may have different ways of looking at the problem. The business person may view it as a threat to worker welfare, product quality or consumer confidence, whereas the ecofeminist may interpret it as another symptom of patriarchal subjugation. However, when both embrace "the partnership way", they are committing themselves to a mutual learning process. In the words of Eisler and Loye, they are acknowledging that "we have to understand what lies behind our symptoms and that this understanding is a prerequisite for any real change" (1990, p 2). The partnership way offers the possibility of finding short-to-medium term solutions whilst maintaining dialogue about the need for longer-term social, economic and environmental change.

Socialist concerns

Those who hold an ecosocialist perspective (Chapter two) may also challenge any approach which is founded upon market demand for environmental protection.

Ecosocialists believe that valuing environmental assets through the market is unjust, as value is determined by those with economic power.[3] In this way Corry asks: "Are we really only going to stand up for the dispossessed if they start producing something we want?" (1993, p 13). A better question would be: "Can we change the market so that individuals can stand up for the dispossessed in the market place as well as at the ballot box?" We strongly believe that politicising the market offers individuals other important ways of expressing their values.

This ecosocialist critique does remind us how the capitalist market has thus far served to reduce what are fundamentally social and environmental interactions to impersonal financial transactions. Most of us do not think about whether our sweatshirt was made in an Asian sweatshop or whether our wooden toilet seat was 'stolen' from indigenous peoples in the Amazonian rainforest. The green consumer and corporate social responsibility movements are serving to make us more aware of the non-utility credentials of the products we buy. By supporting this process, business–environmental group partnerships might be providing one solution to ecosocialist critiques of the market. For example, partnerships focusing on product endorsement, such as FSC, mean that consumers can now obtain accurate information about wood-product sources and production processes.

The socialist critique of capitalism has a number of limitations but it does reveal a lot about why business continues to exploit communities and environments. The growth of the shareholder phenomenon has created a pressure for companies to externalise as many costs as possible and increase dividends. Making money out of money independent of productive activity, the satisfaction of needs and the stewardship of nature has become a debilitating virus, infecting most if not all industrial economies.[4]

Perhaps only the abolition of shareholder capitalism and the adoption of cooperative economic policy will provide the policy context for bona fide corporate social responsibility. And perhaps only a major reinvention of liberal democracy that divorces financial power from the ability to communicate political ideologies and influence political leaders will allow the marginalised to exercise their rights. However, an increase in the number of employee-owned firms and an overhaul of liberal democracies is not likely in the near future. Instead it is more likely that by increasing the ethical awareness of the owners of capital, the market may begin to exert a more progressive influence. The emergence of a number of ethical investment funds, often in collaboration with environmental groups, is one factor which may give business managers the mandate to examine the moral bottom line more closely.

Another ecosocialist concern relates to the North–South divide. If consumption is the way individuals can exercise power in the modern world economy then this presents major problems for citizens of the South, whose purchasing power is currently low. The inability to express political power through control over production or consumption may be an underlying factor in the growth of ecoterrorism, sabotage and grassroots activism in nations of the South. In the absence of radical changes in the global economy, sympathetic groups in the North may be a more effective mechanism to enable southern groups to exercise their rights. This is illustrated by the way WWF-UK has asked timber companies to consider the effects of the trade on forest dwellers and how WWF-International is also attempting to make the MSC responsive to the needs of indigenous fishing communities.

Partnerships and globalisation

Touted as both obstacle to and opportunity for sustainability, globalisation, perhaps the dominant trend of our times, seems irreversible. Global acceleration in the form of commercialization, communications and conferencing is often predicated upon the proliferation of American popular culture and other northern influences (Miller, 1990; Featherstone, 1990). This face of globalisation, argue its critics, not only promotes unsustainable consumption patterns, but also undermines self reliance and threatens cultural integrity. Globalisation has been widely criticized for its homogenizing, controlling and harmful effects within regions, nation states, societies and communities (Barber, 1992; Sklair, 1991; Chomsky, 1988).

Globalisation can also be viewed optimistically. The corporate, free market argument states that breaking down national and regional boundaries is a prerequisite for a viable world economy. This formula for overcoming poverty, increasing employment, promoting fair pricing and generating wealth, is founded on principles of competitiveness, individualism and sustained growth. For transnational corporations (TNCs), this form of globalisation sustains their raison d'être and ensures their power and influence (Cox, 1992).

Opponents of globalisation and TNCs criticise the unfettered global growth model and the "increasing remoteness of decision-making in a globalised economy" (*The Guardian*, 1996). Critics argue that a much more equitable and balanced vision of globalisation is necessary. The emergence of a global civil society is one of the alternatives – alliances and networks of NGOs that create new political space apart from nation states, TNCs and multilateral agencies.

By entering into partnerships with NGOs, some businesses are calling for a broader interpretation of global civil society. Under attack as the 'bad boys' of globalisation, TNCs are seeking out NGO partners to help global business enhance its image and contribution to sustainable development. When NGOs enter into partnerships with TNCs, they are often accused of colluding with the agents of 'global economic imperialism'. For example, some critics would argue that Unilever should simply stop purchasing from southern fisheries, or that B&Q should cease the sale of tropical timber. By working with such companies, environmental groups are seen to be legitimising a fundamentally unsustainable global trading system. However, we believe that such partnerships have the potential to 'civilise' multinational capital, promote positive change in the short-to-medium term and provide a catalyst for more radical change in the future.

Partnerships and the democratic process

Disenchantment with the political process in western industrialised countries is identified as a key factor in the development of third-wave environmentalism and the subsequent growth of partnerships. With business and environmental groups beginning to develop and implement policies in areas traditionally associated with politics and government, we are seeing the emergence of new political agents and structures. A BBC Radio 4 programme (Davies, 1995) on the WWF-UK 1995 Group commented that:

> [Voluntary market based initiatives, such as business-environmentalist partnerships, are] replacing the cog whirring at the heart of political change. Out goes the voter, in comes the consumer. Broad based political philosophy is superseded by target driven and expedient single issue politics.... If the price of consumer power is the devaluation of voter power we may all end up losers.

One concern is that this DIY form of politics is reactionary, as issues of current concern to consumers and environmental group supporters determine the political agenda. Many would question whether business and environmental groups should be the catalyst for political change, and the market the forum for political principles and ideas related to social justice and human rights, for example. In Chapter five, we mentioned how the Fairtrade Foundation is calling on retailers to adopt codes to safeguard workers' rights in southern countries. Inalienable rights; to be determined by the shopper?

It is true that relying upon business–environmental group partnerships to protect these fundamental rights is a contentious issue. Society cannot rely on Adam Smith's "invisible hand" of the market to deliver social and environmental justice. However, given the growing inability of national governments to protect individual and community rights in a globalised economy, we need to find new and additional ways of promoting social and environmental justice.

Partnerships, policy and legislation

We believe that business–environmental group partnerships are not necessarily an obstacle to improved environmental policy and legislation. Although it is too early to analyse their impact upon the legislative and regulatory processes, there are already differing views on the relationship between partnerships and government policies. Dr Alan Knight of B&Q, a partner of WWF-UK, believes the role for legislation is a limited one:

> The role of legislation is to set the lowest standard below which no business should ever stoop ... what voluntary initiatives can do is set a lot higher standards than legislation could ever do, and then the market will choose to buy into or not buy into those standards. (in Davies, 1995)

The notion that legislation will always lag behind voluntary mechanisms is, however, debatable. We agree that there are advantages for companies which exceed regulatory standards, but we do not see this as a justification for further deregulation. We also challenge the idea that the market alone should set benchmarks for best environmental practice. Rather we believe that independent indicators are required for sustainable development. We recognise that such indicators must be developed through wide consultation with all interested stakeholders. The partnership model may offer governments new ways of developing relevant regulatory standards for industry and sustainability indicators for all sectors of society.

Some companies have called for the setting of a legislative level playing field for environmental performance. At the conclusion of a 1994 Business and the Environment seminar, senior executives from over 30 major UK corporations:

... [rejected] the notion that market forces alone could achieve the transition to a genuinely sustainable economy.... [They urged] governments to set out a much clearer vision for a sustainable future, and to put in place a transparent framework for regulation, incentives and ecologically driven taxation within which they could operate.

Similarly George White of the UK retailer J. Sainsbury's believes:

> *It would be a great testament to the vision of the managers here at J. Sainsbury Plc if legislation [related to the impacts of our purchasing] were to be agreed at the national or international level over the next five years. By setting new and higher environmental standards, we establish targets for both our competitors and the Government to aim for.*

We believe that the development of business–environmentalist partnerships based upon market activities should have a mutually supportive relationship with international, national, regional and local policies. Partnerships are compatible with calls for enhanced intergovernmental and governmental regulation and enforcement. Whether business–environmental group partnerships will act as catalysts for future environmental regulation, or serve to replace it, will depend in part on which business view achieves the ascendancy – the hands-off approach or the raising of standards model. In the meantime and in light of the political obstacles to effective regulatory structures, it is imperative that businesses and environmentalists act together in those areas where mutual advantage exists.

Lingering sustainability questions

Going down the partnership road has not diminished the wider green critique of business. Larger sustainability questions continue to plague all companies. The experience of McDonald's as outlined in Chapter six aptly demonstrates that partnership does not equal the end of protest. As described in Chapter five, both Dow and Unilever continue to face challenges from the environmental movement although not nearly as pronounced as those experienced by McDonald's. For the many businesses engaged in the partnerships described in Chapter four, the forest product sourcing and certification activities have arguably introduced new corporate pressures and challenges. Most of the companies concerned are still a long way from the revised end-of-decade target of 100 per cent certified wood and paper products on store shelves. Even as leading retailers such as B&Q make progress, radical environmental groups continue to demand more substantial changes in the way the forestry industry manages the world's forests.

The new social realism

Throughout this book, we have described how former adversaries with very different philosophical, ideological and political backgrounds have begun to find common ground and a way forward. The inherently ambiguous language of sustainable development has allowed people with very different perspectives to communicate and find solutions together. Our case studies suggest that the value in finding common cause is gaining momentum as we approach the new millennium. Indeed partnerships between business and environmental groups are helping to formulate a new philosophy, ideology and politics about society and its relationship with the environment.

We advocate a move beyond left and right towards a new consensus: beyond ecocentrism vs homocentrism to a philosophy of ecohumanism; beyond anti-industrialism vs modernism to an ideology of post-modern ecologism; and beyond socialism vs neo-liberalism to a politics of new social realism. This new social realism is founded on combining the left's social ethic with the right's pragmatic realism (see Figure 6).

The new social realism is about finding short-to-medium term solutions to global–local problems while beginning a longer term learning process about the causes of such problems. In this way, it is reformist yet radical, incremental yet structural.[5] We have described how this new consensus has emerged between non-state actors in part because of their disenchantment with the political process. The outstanding question must therefore be: What is the role of government in a society which appears to be embracing a new philosophy, ideology and politics?

Figure 6: Beyond left and right towards a new social realism

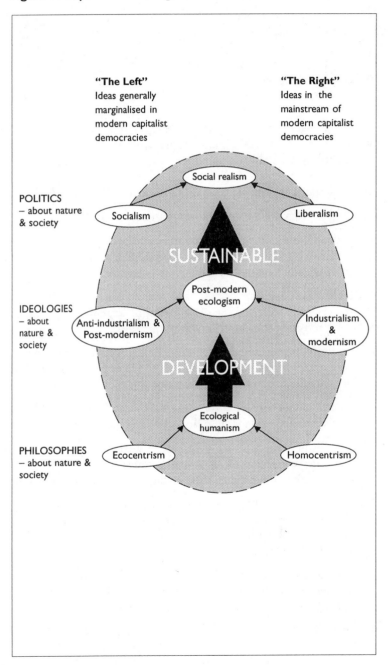

Policy implications

It is not within the scope of this book to explore fully the policy implications of business–environmental group partnerships; however, the partnership experience and the ideas of new social realism do suggest a new policy framework for governments and multilateral agencies to pursue. This policy framework would recognise the role that political bodies can play in facilitating, rather than imposing, more sustainable and just societies. The following suggestions incorporate ideas on stakeholding and the new centrism that have become popular in western societies in the late 1990s, yet expands upon them to encompass sustainability concerns.

New social realism suggests that political bodies should:

- seek to work with nature rather than against it;

- make the most of existing resources and promote less resource intensive – even non-material – needs and wants, rather than striving to increase natural resource consumption;

- build neither a 'me' or a 'we' society but a 'me and we' society, by fostering an awareness of community without compromising the entrepreneurial spirit;

- promote appropriate local, regional and international trading networks, while abandoning the ideological pursuit of uncontrolled and unaccountable global trade;

- create more space for creative thinking in liberal representative democracy, by checking the dominance of financial centres over political power;

- promote collaboration between interest groups in society when setting standards or introducing new legislation;

- move from command-style regulation to commitment-style regulation, where companies commit to improvements and agree to work with other sectors of society to determine how this might be achieved;

- embrace market mechanisms as an additional tool for social and environmental control without losing sight of the need for appropriate legislation and enforcement;

- reward companies that engage a wider range of stakeholders;

- provide an impetus for alternative company ownership and profit-sharing models, including support for greater employee ownership of companies.

Similar to the idea of sustainable development, this new social realism may mean many different things to many people. We believe, however, that it offers governments and multilateral agencies a more inclusive philosophical and political framework for the future.

In the foreword to this book, John Elkington describes how people who were used to throwing bricks at each other are now trying to build together. Ultimately, because of the structural problems with shareholder capitalism, the initiatives we describe in this book may fail to deliver environmentally secure and just societies. However, even if the new structures built between business and environmental groups do crumble, at least we will have learnt more about the architecture of human societies. We agree with Elkington that the process of trial and error or trial and success, are prerequisites to finding a sustainable society.

Rio+ 5 and the future of sustainable development

Five years on from Rio, governments, UN agencies and other major groups are reviewing the implementation of Agenda 21 and other Earth Summit-related agreements and initiatives. Earth Summit II has offered an opportunity to take stock of efforts to promote sustainable development to date and to re-energise the sustainability transition as we approach the new millennium.

Given that Agenda 21 and the other Rio agreements left many issues unresolved and indeed contained many contradictions, the various participants in the post-Rio process need to renew their efforts to find a better way forward. There is much in the way of practical experience with both partnership and sustainable development to draw upon. The case studies in this book offer examples of exemplary practice as well as ongoing problems and disagreements. Similarly there are many discontinuities at the international policy level. For example, Agenda 21 empowers local communities to participate in the process of finding global–local solutions and yet endorses a global free trade system under the auspices of an unaccountable World Trade Organisation (WTO).[6]

The WTO is increasingly being seen as the most powerful and influential of the multilateral agencies. Designed to eliminate the fragmentation of the global economy, the WTO promotes free and open access to markets worldwide. In contradiction with the spirit of Agenda 21, the WTO decided in early 1996 to exclude NGOs from any direct involvement in the organisation's work or its meetings. Then at its Singapore Ministerial Meeting in December 1996, WTO member governments rejected the use of trade measures to enforce labour rights and standards. This decision "killed once and for all the possibility of WTO involvement in labour issues" (Williams, 1996, p 4). Such discontinuities raise serious questions about the capacity of Agenda 21 and the UN system to promote sustainability, and undermine the potential of partnerships to effect change in the short-to-medium term.

As we argued in Chapter one, sustainable development has reached a crossroads at the dawn of the new millennium. Many priorities identified at Rio and beyond have yet to be implemented (see Box 7.4). In order to reduce the contradictions of Agenda 21 and the various post-Rio institutions, the various stakeholders in the future must all be allowed to participate more fully in the decision-making process. Unresolved issues and competing interests will not be eliminated, but this does not preclude learning how to work together more effectively. The future of sustainable development depends upon universal commitment to manage diversity more competently and to search for solutions together.

Box 7.4: Examples of sustainability priorities

- strengthen the integration environment and development policy;
- place greater emphasis upon social sustainability issues;
- address unsustainable patterns of production and consumption;
- evaluate market-based instruments;
- negotiate a code of conduct and compliance measures for transnational corporations;
- improve the accountability and representation of the intergovernmental process of the Commission on Sustainable Development;
- enhance government regulation and global governance (see Bigg and Muecke, 1996).

The search for solutions

Just as the climate of sustainable development has helped to bring together traditional enemies, the resulting cross-pollination of ideas and knowledge may plant the seed for new ways of thinking and grow to produce robust solutions to unsustainable development. The mythic power of sustainable development provides a platform for exploring new models of society. Whether this new myth will endure and foster long-term change remains to be seen.

This book has demonstrated that one of the most resonant sustainability themes is that individuals in business or environmental groups are capable of imagining new ways of working outside the restrictive roles society has given them. That is what partnerships are all about. The individuals described in our case studies are not merely company managers and environmental campaigners; they are people who are constrained by their own roles, responsibilities, and fears but liberated by their preparedness to listen. By listening to each other, the partners may gain new insights into problems that face us all.

Long-time direct action protester, Angie Zelter,[7] demonstrates that dialogue with business is both possible and necessary:

> *I think the major thing is that you have to be willing to listen and to make some adjustments.... Quite simply if you're willing to go in and smile and shake hands, then that's the first step. Some NGOs are only confrontational. Now I think there's a role for being confrontational and I think people in industry see me as fairly aggressive in some ways. But at the same time if you're willing to sit down and talk to them and see their viewpoint to some extent, then I think there's a way forward.*

Perhaps we are on the verge of something bigger. People are beginning to recognise their small part in the wider world. People are beginning to think of the implications of their actions and people are beginning to listen to each other. Indeed, people are beginning to consider the needs of a 'we society' and not just a 'me society'. If these changes help to breakdown some of the alienation and competition we feel in work, in the street, in academia, even in our personal lives, then we may just stumble across a new way forward and reinvent the future.

Notes

[1] For example, *The Ecologist* criticised Rio's emphasis upon global management and free trade as a perpetuation of northern cultural imperialism and economic dominance over the peoples of the South. However, Rio's endorsement of open markets was also linked to southern government and business demands for unrestricted access to northern markets. In this sense, sustainable development was challenged by the South as giving unfair competitive advantage to green business/industry in the North.

[2] An ecofeminist analysis of the partnership process might also question whether equal collaboration and consensus is really possible across cultures. If the consultation process is driven by northern-owned global companies and western environmental groups, can indigenous cultures be truly represented? For example, the FSC describes itself as fully participatory, involving a variety of groups and cultures in the standard setting process. But take a certification assessment. For certification there needs to be a written management plan. 'Writing', 'management' and 'plan', are western terms and they need to be used carefully. Traditional forms of knowledge and social organisation are not always easily transposed into a "written management plan".

[3] Another criticism of voluntary business–environmental group partnerships might be that they are based on an incorrect assumption about the power of the consumer. Pepper argues that "the idea ... green consumers can greatly influence decisions about what is made, and how, is a re-emergence of the myth of consumer autonomy, exposed by Galbraith (1958), who showed how demand is stimulated and led by producers" (1996, p 83).

[4] The question of ownership and control was a not adequately dealt with at Rio. According to *The Ecologist* "[the question was] not *how* the environment should be managed but *who* will manage it and in *whose* interest" (1992, p 122). As business engages greater numbers and kinds of stakeholders, there may be more potential for natural resource management to be shared with local communities.

[5] Gareth Porter and Janet Welsh Brown suggest three alternative strategies for creating and strengthening global sustainability: incremental change; global partnership; and global governance (1991, pp 145-56). Their categorisation appears to imply that incrementalism is incompatible

with the partnership and governance models. We argue that new social realism embraces incremental change, global partnership and global governance. By helping business take incremental steps toward the sustainability agenda, environmental groups have the potential to radicalise business gradually. Business–environmental group partnerships represent only one aspect of the global partnership approach. Furthermore, these voluntary partnerships also need to be backed up by effective global–local regulation and governance.

[6] There is a growing body of literature on the greening of the WTO and WTO–NGO relations. See for example Charnovitz (1996), Hundall (1996) and Smith (1996).

[7] Zelter is a veteran activist who has been involved in direct action protests since the early days of the Greenham Common women's protest against nuclear weapons. Other affiliations include the Citizens' Recovery of Indigenous Peoples' Stolen Property Organisation, Reforest the Earth, the Women's Negotiating Team and most recently the East Timor Ploughshares campaign. The latter resulted in Zelter and three other women protesters being charged with causing £1.5 million of damage to a British Aerospace Hawk military jet destined for Indonesia. All four were acquitted in July 1996 (see Craig, 1996).

Annex – a guide to the development and implementation of business–environmental group partnerships

The partnership models described in this book offer a wide range of approaches to business–environmental group collaboration. We accept that partnership will not be an appropriate method for all issues and contexts as it is still too early to determine whether this new pattern of business relations will endure. However, if planned and implemented appropriately, partnerships can offer both business and different kinds of NGOs useful tools to discuss and promote global sustainability.

Although each partnership is different there are some common themes. Accordingly some common lessons can be learned for the successful management of the partnership process. Partnerships can be understood as moving through three phases:

- partnership initiation: involves the initial contact between those who will form the core participants. Usually an agreement to cooperate is signed, which outlines the goals of the partnership, along with the respective roles and responsibilities of the partners;

- partnership implementation: follows the initiation phase and deals with practical issues rather than conceptual or process issues. Agreements are implemented, with participants learning from the partnership experience and adjusting goals in light of this experience;

- partnership evolution: the end of the partnership often leads to a new form of process, product or project-orientated partnership.

Partnership checklist

We now present a checklist for the successful management of partnerships. These suggestions are based on the material presented in the case studies and additional reflections on the management of business–environmental group partnerships.

Partnership initiation

General suggestions:

- identify partnership purpose: process-orientated, project-orientated or product-orientated;

- define the problem, the common ground and the opportunity;

- define clear and defensible objectives and action plans;

- identify key people to lead the partnership process;

- engage critical stakeholders in the process and decide on mechanisms for their future input;

- establish equitable and open decision-making procedures;

- launch the partnership in an open public forum;

- establish a basis for continued collaboration.

Suggestions for business:

- inform contacts in trade associations and other professional bodies;

- consult those involved in similar initiatives in order to assess the practicality of the proposed goals;

- find out the levels of expertise held by the proposed environmental group partner, assess their campaigns and identify the benefits they could offer;

- involve departmental managers who will be substantively affected by the partnership;

- be open with the environmental group partners about problems;

- recognise the implications for core business practice;

- do not use the partnership as an endorsement of your company by the environmental group partner.

Suggestions for environmental groups:

- inform counterparts in environmental groups working on similar issues;

- identify and target those sectors of the industry with the greatest capacity to act quickly;

- assess your organisational capacity to perform the required tasks;

- encourage companies to embrace broad principles relating to corporate responsibility for the issue at stake;

- seek corporate disclosure of information to the environmental group and the public;

- be open about the potential pitfalls of working with business.

Partnership implementation

General suggestions:

- support participant needs and interests with an emphasis on personal contact;

- be adaptive and revise goals if necessary;

- resolve disputes quickly;

- think creatively about new management systems to facilitate the developing partnership;

- do not allow partnership managers to act with complete autonomy from senior management;

- lobby government to support the initiative.

Suggestions for business:

- promote the vision of the partnership to key stakeholders;
- define responsibility for day-to-day liaison with the environmental group;
- invest in the necessary information technology and training;
- prepare research reports on the partnership to ensure that lessons may be learned;
- see the initiative as a pilot project with potential implications for the future.

Suggestions for environmental groups:

- coordinate trading, investment, corporate fundraising and campaigning branches of the organisation;
- develop a policy on relations with business if one is not already in place;
- consult external experts to analyse the implications of the partnership;
- seek feedback from business partners about your organisation's role and contribution to the partnership;
- don't let financial, resource and skills limitations restrict the growth of the partnership;
- don't take money for partnerships which involve a public endorsement of participating businesses.

Partnership evolution

General suggestions:

- celebrate the success and share the credit;
- evaluate acheivements against initial goals;
- examine the potential to formalise achievemnets;
- publish summaries of successes and failures;

- support research into the initiative in order to identify lessons learned and new initiatives to be supported.

Suggestions for business:

- communicate successes and limitations to key stakeholders;
- utilise the knowledge and skills learned;
- attempt an assessment of costs against benefits.

Suggestions for environmental groups:

- attempt an assessment of the financial efficiency of the partnership;
- assess expenditure against environmental gains and more abstract goals.

These are the rudiments of a complex process. For more information contact David F. Murphy at the New Academy of Business or Jem Bendell.

David F. Murphy is a Research Fellow with the New Academy of Business (London). The New Academy is an independent educational organisation which brings together the best in values-led business practice with progressive management thinking. David has also undertaken various assignments for a number of international organisations working in the fields of environment, development and social responsibility.

Jem Bendell is a researcher, writer and consultant on corporate social and environmental responsibility. He is founder of The Values Network, which is sponsored by The Body Shop, C&A and other organisations. The network aims to promote dialogue between business and NGOs on voluntary responsibility standards and certification. He is currently at Eco-Sourcing International, an information service on ethical products.

List of contacts

Organisation	Phone	Internet/e-mail
B&Q	44-1703-256256	www.diy.co.uk
Body Shop International, UK	44-1903-731500	www.the-body-shop.com
BP, UK	44-171-496-4800	www.bp.com
Dow Europe, Switzerland	41-1-728-2111	www.dow.com
ESI, UK	44-7000-560876	www.ecosource.co.uk
EDF, USA	1-212-5052100	www.edf.org
EPE, Belgium	32-2-771-1534	www.epe.be/epe/epe.html
FSC, Mexico	52-951-46905	http://antequera.antequera.com/FSC
FSC UK Working Group	44-1686-412176	hannah@fsc-uk.demon.co.uk
FoE, UK	44-171-490-1555	www.foe.co.uk
Greenpeace International, Netherlands	31-20-523-6222	www.greenpeace.org
Loblaws Corporation, Canada	1-416-922-2500	www.loblaw.com
MSC, UK	44-171-350-4000	106335.77@compuserve.com
McDonald's Corporation, USA	1-630-623-5252	www.mcdonalds.com
McSpotlight Information Network, UK	44-171-713-1269	www.mcspotlight.com
Milieudefensie, The Netherlands	31-20-622-1366	www.dds.nl/~mildef/mildef.html

New Academy of Business, UK	44-181-563-8780	www.new-academy.ac.uk
Pollution Probe, Canada	1-416-926-1907	www.web.net/pprobe
Responsible Care, CEFIC, Belgium	32-2-676-7302	www.cefic.be
School for Policy Studies, UK	44-117-974-1117	www.bris.ac.uk/Depts/SPS
Shell International, UK	44-934-1234	www.shell.com
SustainAbility, UK	44-171-937-9996	www.sustainability.co.uk
UNED-UK, London	44-171-839-1784	www.oneworld.org/uned-uk
Unilever, UK	44-171-822-5252	www.unilever.com
WBCSD, Switzerland	41-22-839-3100	www.wbcsd.ch
WFSGI, Switzerland	41-27-775-3570	www.wfsgi.org
WWF-International, Switzerland	41-22-364-9111	www.panda.org
WWF-UK	44-1483-426444	www.wwf-uk.org

References

Adams, P. (1992) 'Third World tactics at Rio: soak the West', in *The Globe and Mail*, Toronto, 4 June, p A19.

Adams, W.M. (1990) *Green development*, London: Routledge.

Adams, W.M. (1993) 'Sustainable development and the greening of development theory', in F. Schuurman (ed) (1993) *Beyond the impasse*, London: Zed Books.

Aina, T. and Salau, A. (1992) *The challenge of sustainable development in Nigeria*, Ibadan, Nigeria: Nigerian Environmental Study/Action Team (NEST).

Alverson, D.L., Freeberg, M., Murawski, S.A. and Pope, J.G. (1994) 'A global assessment of fisheries by catch and discards', FAO Fisheries Technical Paper 339, p vii.

Aspinwall, R. and Smith, J. (eds) (1996) *Environmentalist and business partnerships: a sustainable model?* Cambridge: The White Horse Press.

Atlas, T. (1990) 'McDonald's, critic takes aim at trash', in *Chicago Tribune*, 2 August.

Aydin, Z. (1994) 'Agenda 21 and the Commission on Sustainable Development', Paper presented at Global Forum 94, Manchester, 26 June.

Bailey, I. (1996) '"Disgusting" tape phoney: sealers', in *Evening Telegram*, 7 February, St John's, Canada.

Bailey, R. (1993) *Eco-scam: the false profits of ecological apocalypse*, New York: St Martin's Press.

Barber, B.R, (1992) 'Jihad vs McWorld', *The Atlantic Monthly*, vol 269, no 3, March, pp 53-63.

Barbier, E.B., Burgess, J., Bishop, J. and Aylward, B. (1994) *The economics of the tropical timber trade*, London: Earthscan.

Barrett, S.M. and Murphy, D.F. (1995) 'The implications of the corporate environmental policy process for human resources management', in *Greener Management International,* issue 10, April, pp 49-68.

Barrett, S.M. and Murphy, D.F. (1996) 'Managing corporate environmental policy: a process of complex change', in W. Wehrmeyer (ed) *Greening people,* Sheffield: Greenleaf.

Beckerman (1995) *Small is stupid: blowing the whistle on the greens,* Oxford: Duckworth.

Bendell, J. (1995) *Can't see the wood for the trees? Corporate green consumerism in the UK timber market and its potential for combating rainforest deforestation,* Unpublished BA dissertation.

Bendell, J. (1996) *Developing economic incentives for responsible fishing: the report of the Marine Stewardship Council preliminary scoping project,* WWF-International internal paper, unpublished.

Bendell, J. and Sullivan, F. (1996) 'Sleeping with the enemy? Business–environmentalist partnerships for sustainable development: the case of the WWF 1995 Group', in R. Aspinwall and J. Smith (eds) *Environmentalist and business partnerships: a sustainable model?*, Cambridge: The White Horse Press.

Bhargava, S. and Welford, R. (1996) 'Corporate Strategy and the environment: the theory', in R. Welford (ed) (1996b), *Corporate environmental management: systems and strategies,* London: Earthscan.

Bigg, T. and Mucke, P. (1996) 'Synthesis paper on NGO priorities and concerns for the 1997 General Assembly Special Session' prepared for the CSD NGO Steering Committee, 24 May.

Bingham, D.A. (1973) *The law and administration relating to protection of the environment,* London: Oyez Publications.

Body Shop International, The (1994) *Values & vision 94,* Littlehampton: The Body Shop International.

Booth, D. (1993) 'Development research: from impasse to new agenda', in F. Schuurman (ed) *Beyond the impasse,* London: Zed Books.

Boston Globe (1990) 'McDonald's bids to clean up its reputation' [by H. Schattle], 2 August.

Bowcroft, O. (1996) 'McDonald's "triggered panic with hasty ban"', in *The Guardian*, 2 April.

Brandt Commission (1980) *North–South: a programme for survival*, London: Pan Books.

Brandt Commission (1983) *Common crisis: North–South cooperation for world recovery*, London: Pan Books.

Brenton, T. (1994) *The greening of Machiavelli: the evolution of international environmental politics*, London: Earthscan and the Royal Institute of International Affairs Energy and Environment Programme.

Brown, L. (1995) *State of the world*, Worldwatch Institute, New York; W.W. Norton.

Brown, M. (1992) 'The way of the world', in *GQ* (British edn), July, no 37, pp 66-73.

Brown, P. (1992) 'Long and troubled road to Rio', in *The Guardian*, 3 June, p 6.

Brown, P. (1997a) 'Ministers agree fish blueprint', in *The Guardian*, 15 March, p 14.

Brown, P. (1997b) 'Ministers agree fish blueprint' in *The Guardian*, 15 March, p 14.

Buckley, N. (1993) 'Weeding out the weakest links in the chain', in *Financial Times*, 26 August.

Buckley, N. (1994) 'Suffering in a saturated market', in *Financial Times*, 15 September, p 24.

Buitelaar, W. (1995) 'Environment, sustainability and industrial relations', in *European Participation Monitor*, no 11, pp 12-18, Dublin: European Foundation for the Improvement of Living and Working Conditions.

Business and the Environment (1994) Report of the First Annual Senior Executives Seminar, *Sustainability and profitability: conflict or convergence?*, Cambridge, organised by Business and the Environment, September.

Business and Society Review (1995) 'McDonald's', no 94, p 76.

Business Wire (1995) 'Scientists warn of disruption from global warming', 18 September.

Cairncross, F. (1991) *Costing the Earth*, London: Business Books and The Economist Books Ltd.

Cairncross, F. (1995) *Green inc*, London: Earthscan.

Campbell, J. with Moyers, B. (1988) *The power of myth*, Anchor Books edition, July 1991, New York: Doubleday.

Capra, F. and Pauli, G. (eds) (1995) *Steering business toward sustainability*, Tokyo: United Nations University Press.

Carey, J. (1996) 'McDonald's unmasked', in *Red Pepper*, no 25, pp 11-13.

Carson, R. (1962) *Silent spring*, Boston: Houghton Miflin.

CASA (1996) *Annual Report 1995*, Edmonton: Clean Air Strategic Alliance.

Castle, S. (1996) 'Now burger giant bans British beef', in *The Independent on Sunday*, 24 March, p 1.

Centre for Our Common Future (1992) *Rio reviews*, Geneva: Centre for Our Common Future.

Charnovitz, S. (1996) 'Participation of Non Governmental Organizations in the World Trade Organization', in *University of Pennsylvania Journal of International Economic Law*, vol 17, no 1, pp 331-57.

Charter, M. (1992) *Greener marketing*, Sheffield: Greenleaf.

Chatterjee, P. and Finger, M. (1994) *The Earth brokers: power, politics and world development*, London: Routledge.

Chemical Industry Association (1996) *Responsible care: the UK indicators of performance 1990-95*, London: Chemical Industry Association.

Chomsky, N. (1988) *Language and politics*, Montreal: Black Rose Books.

Christian Aid (1996) *The global supermarket*, London: Christian Aid.

Chryssides, G. and Khaler, J. (1993) *An introduction to business ethics*, New York and London: Chapman and Hall.

Cluston, E. (1996) 'Scots protest at McDonald's Dutch choice', in *The Guardian*, 30 April, p 7.

Colborn, T., Myers, J.P. and Dumanoski, D. (1996) *Our stolen future*, London: Little, Brown and Company.

Cook, R.M., Sinclair, A. and Stefβnsson, G. (1997) 'Potential collapse of North Sea cod stocks', Nature, no 385, 6 February, pp 521-22.

Corry, S. (1993) *Harvest moonshine taking you for a ride: a critique of the rainforest harvest its theory and practice*, A discussion paper, London: Survival International.

Cotgrove, S.F. and Duff, A. (1981) 'Environmentalism, values and social change', *Bristol Journal of Sociology*, vol 32, no 1, pp 92-110.

Coupland, D. (1991) *Generation X: tales for an accelerated culture*, New York: St Martin's Press.

Cowe, R. (1995) 'Green onslaught may sink chlorine', in *The Guardian*, 17 February, p 39.

Cowe, R. (1996a) 'Sainsbury labels itself as first store with ethical trade terms', in *The Guardian*, 20 May, p 17.

Cowe, R. (1996b) 'Tesco and IKEA join Greenpeace attack on the dangers of PVC', in *The Guardian*, 18 June.

Cowe, R. (1997) 'Amnesty chief's challenge to Shell', in *The Guardian*, 15 March, p 14.

Cox, R.W. 'Multilateralism and world order', in *Review of International Studies*, no 18, pp 161-80.

Craig, O. (1996) 'Wild, wild wimmin', in *The Sunday Times*, 4 August, p 15.

Daly, H. (1996) *Beyond growth: the economics of sustainable development*, Boston: Beacon Press.

Dauncey, G. (1989) *After the crash*, London: Merlin Press.

Davies, S. (1995) 'Breaking the log-jam', *Agenda*, BBC Radio 4, 2 September.

Davison, D.J. (1978) *The environmental factor: an approach for managers*, New York: John Wiley & Sons.

Denison, R.A. et al (1990) *Good things come in smaller packages – the technical and economic arguments in support of McDonald's decision to phase out polystyrene foam packaging;*

why and how the environmental benefits, 6 December, Washington, DC: Environmental Defense Fund.

Department of the Environment (1994) *Partnerships in practice*, London: DoE.

Desai, N. (1994) 'Linking UNCED with forthcoming United Nations conferences', in *CSD Update*, no 2, p 1, New York: UN Commission on Sustainable Development.

Dibb, S. (1995) 'Swimming in a sea of oestrogens: chemical hormone disrupters', in *The Ecologist*, vol 25, no 1, pp 27-31.

Dodds, F. and Bigg, T. (1997) 'The UN Commission on Sustainable Development', in F. Dodds (ed) *The way forward: beyond Agenda 21*, London: Earthscan.

Douglas, M (1970) *Natural symbols*, London: Barrie & Rockliff The Cresset Press.

Dow (1995) *EH&S requirements: building toward a sustainable future*, May, Midland, Michigan: The Dow Chemical Company.

Dow (1996a) *Shared priorities for success: 1995 Annual Report*, Midland, Michigan: The Dow Chemical Company.

Dow (1996b) *Continuing the Responsible Care journey: steps toward sustainability – 1996 Progress Report on Environment, Health and Safety*, Midland, Michigan: The Dow Chemical Company.

Dow Europe (1992) *Dow Europe environmental strategy: environmental pressures are unmet needs*, Horgen, Switzerland: Dow Europe.

Dow Europe (1995) *Environmental Progress Report 1994*, Amsterdam: Dow Information Centre.

Dowie, M. (1995a) *Losing ground: American environmentalism at the end of the 20th century*, London: The MIT Press.

Dowie, M. (1995b) 'The fourth wave', in *Mother Jones*, March/April, pp 34-36.

Drummond, J. (1997) 'Tribes who won't see the forest for the sleaze', in *The Independent*, 4 January, p 13.

Dudley, N. (1995) 'Certification in farm and forest: a comparison of organic standards and timber certification', in *Ecology and Farming (IFOAM)*, September.

Dudley, N., Jeanrenaud, J. and Sullivan, F. (1995) *Bad harvest? The timber trade and the degradation of the world's forests*, London: WWF-UK and Earthscan.

Earle M. (1995) 'The precautionary approach to fisheries', in *Responsible fisheries*, Development Education Exchange Papers, October, Rome: Food and Agriculture Organisation.

The Earth Times (1996) 'How modern commerce abuses the oceans' [by K. Winiarski], 15 February.

The Ecologist (1992) 'The Earth Summit débâcle', vol 22, no 4, July/August, p 122.

The Ecologist (1992) 'Whose common future?', vol 22, no 4, July/August.

The Ecologist (1995) *Overfishing: causes and consequences* (special double issue), vol 25, no2/3, March/April, May/June 1995.

The Economist (1992) 'Management brief: food for thought', 29 August, pp 62-64.

The Economist (1993) 'Big Mac's counter attack', 13 November, p 95.

The Economist (1996a) 'Macworld', 29 June, pp 77-78.

The Economist (1996b) 'Toxic shock', 3 August, pp 77-79.

ECRA (1996) Ethical Consumer Magazine Research Supplement, no 44, November/December.

Edelman, M. (1971) *Politics as symbolic action*, Chicago: Markham.

Ehrlich, P. (1972) *The population bomb*, London: Ballantine.

Eisler, R. (1996) 'Creating partnership futures', in *Futures*, vol 28, no 6/7, August/September, pp 563-66.

Eisler, R. and Loye, D. (1990) *The partnership way*, San Francisco: Harper.

Ekins, P. (1992) *A new world order: grassroots movements for global change*, London: Routledge.

Elkington, J. (1996) 'Building sustainable production and consumption patterns', A paper for *Towards Earth Summit II*, the UNED-UK Annual Conference, 18 November, London.

Elkington, J and Burke, T. (1989) *The green capitalists* (revised edn), London: Victor Gollancz.

Elkington, J. and Hailes, J. (1988) *The green consumer guide*, London: Victor Gollancz.

Elle (American edn) (1992) 'The Rio Summit: Rx for the planet' [by M. Schapiro], June, pp 64-68.

ENDS (Environmental Data Services) (1994) 'CBI bids to revive environment forum', *ENDS Report*, March, London: ENDS.

ENDS (1996) *Ends Report*, April 1, London: ENDS.

Enloe, C.H. (1975) *The politics of pollution in a comparative perspective*, London: Longman.

EPE (1994a) *EPE info service*, no 1, Brussels: European Partners for the Environment.

EPE (1994b) *The EPE sustainability laboratory report*, 26-27 October, Brussels: EPE.

EPE (1994c) *Towards shared responsibility* (2 vols), Brussels: EPE.

EPE (1996) *Building trust through EMAS: what can we learn from Responsible Care?*, Dow Europe/EPE EMAS Stakeholder Pilot Project Proposal, Brussels: EPE.

EPE (1997) *Building trust through EMAS: what can we learn from Responsible Care?*, Report of the Dow Europe/EPE Workshop, 31 October-1 November 1996, Brussels: EPE.

Esteva, G (1992) 'Memories of underdevelopment: Mexicans finding new dignity by rejecting development', *Utne Reader*, no 53, September/October, pp 137-38.

The Evening Standard (1996) 'Peril of the pesticides' [by D. Cooper], 11 December, pp 20-21.

FAO (1993) 'Marine fishes and the law of the sea: a decade of change', FAO Fisheries circular 853.

FAO (1995a) *Responsible fisheries*, Development Education Exchange Papers, October, Rome: FAO.

FAO (1995b) *The state of world fisheries and aquaculture*, Rome: FAO Fisheries Department.

Featherstone, M. (ed) (1990) *Global culture*, London: Sage.

Finger, M. and Chatterjee, P. (1992) *Ecocurrents*, vol 2, no 2, May.

Fishing News International (1997a) 'Fishing in fashion for the protesters', February 1997, p 2.

Fishing News International (1997b) 'Industry questions eco-label scheme – can it work for a complex business?', February 1997, p 4.

Flavin, C. and Young, J. (1994) 'Shaping the next industrial revolution: an environmentally sustainable development', March, vol 122, no 2586, p 48.

FoE-UK (1988) *Good wood guide*, London: FoE-UK.

FoE-UK (1991a) 'Stop the chainstore massacre', Press Release 8 November 1991, London: FoE-UK.

FoE-UK (1991b) 'Friends of the Earth brings DIY stores into line', Press Release 11 December 1991, London: FoE-UK.

FoE-UK (1992) 'Timber agreement under fire', in *Earth Matters*, issue 17, winter, p 5, London: FoE-UK.

FoE-UK (1995) *A superficial attraction: the voluntary approach and sustainable development*, December 1995, London: FoE-UK.

Frank, A.G. (1967) *Capitalism and underdevelopment in Latin America*, London: Monthly Review Press.

Friedman, M. (1962) *Capitalism and freedom*, Chicago: University of Chicago Press.

Friedman, T. (1996) 'Turning swords into beef-burgers', in *The Guardian*, 19 December (originally published in the *New York Times*).

Galbraith, J.K. (1958) *The affluent society*, Harmondsworth: Penguin.

Gallon, G. (1991) 'The green product endorsement controversy: lessons from the Pollution Probe/Loblaws experience', in *Alternatives*, vol 18, no 3, pp 17-25.

Gallup (1992) *The health of the planet survey: a preliminary report on attitudes toward the environment and economic growth measured by surveys of citizens in 22 nations to date,* New Jersey: George H. Gallup Memorial Survey, June 1992.

Ghosh, R. (1992) 'Environmental push born at Stockholm', in *The Globe and Mail,* Toronto, 16 June, p A10.

Gifford, B. (1991) 'The greening of the golden arches', in *Rolling Stone,* 22 August, pp 34-36.

Gorz, A. (1989) *Critique of economic reason (Metamorpheses du travail* translated by G. Handyside and C. Turner), London: Verso.

Gosling, P. (1996) 'Green goods get the red card', in *The Independent on Sunday,* 21 April, p 7.

Gray, B. (1989) *Collaborating: finding common ground for multiparty problems,* San Francisco: Jossey-Bass.

Gray, T. (1997) 'The politics of fishing', Briefings number 12, Global Environmental Change Programme, University of Sussex, March.

Green Magazine (1993) 'Making sense of the movement', vol 4, no 7, April, pp 34-36.

Greenpeace Business (1992) 'Rio fiasco', no 8, August/September, p 1.

Greenpeace Business (1995/96) 'Dow Chemical – a leading dioxin source', no 28, December/January, p 5.

Greenpeace Business (1996/97) 'Manufacturers and retailers reject Monsanto's genetically altered soya beans', no 34, December/January, pp 2-3.

Greenpeace-International (1992) *UNCED undone: key issues Agenda 21 does not address,* Amsterdam: Greenpeace-International.

Greenpeace-International (1996a) *Greenpeace principles for ecologically responsible fisheries: preliminary document,* Amsterdam: Greenpeace-International.

Greenpeace-International (1996b) *Taking back our stolen future: hormone disruption and PVC plastic,* April, London: Greenpeace-International.

Greenpeace-UK (1995) *Greenpeace Annual Review 1995,* London: Greenpeace-UK.

The Guardian (1996) 'Buchanan's quack cure wins' [editorial], 22 February.

Gummer, J. (1995) Quoted in the Advisory Council on Business and the Environment Seminar Proceedings, *Environmental reporting: what the city should ask*, London: Department of Trade and Industry.

Habermas, J. (1979) *Communication and the evolution of society*, London: Heinemann Educational.

Hannigan, J. (1995) *Environmental sociology: a social constructionist perspective*, London: Routledge.

Hardie, D.W.F. and Davidson Pratt, J. (1966) *A history of the modern British chemical industry*, Oxford: Pergamon Press.

Hardin, G. (1968) 'The tragedy of the commons', *Science*, no 162, pp 1243-48.

Harris, P.G. (1996) *Letter to WWF*, 19 April, London: Timber Trade Federation.

Hart voor Hout (1997) *Report on Heart for Wood campaign – 1996 results*, Amsterdam: Hart voor Hout.

Hawken, P. (1994) *The ecology of commerce*, New York: HarperBusiness.

Helvarg, D. (1996) 'The big green spin machine: corporations and environmental PR', in *The Amicus Journal*, summer, pp 13-21.

Hemphill, T. (1994) 'Strange bedfellows cozy up for a clean environment', *Business and Society Review*, no 90, pp 38-44.

Hill J.A. (1994) 'Working with suppliers to reduce waste and environmental pollution', in B. Taylor et al, *The environmental management handbook*, London: Pitman.

Hirsch, F. (1977) *Social limits to growth*, London: Routledge & Kegan Paul.

Hirsch, J. and Roth, R. (1986) *The new face of capitalism: from Fordism to post-Fordism*, Hamburg: VSA-Verlag.

HMSO (1996) *Fish stock conservation and management*, London: HMSO.

Hoffman, A. (1996a) 'A strategic response to investor activism', in *Sloan Management Review*, vol 37, no 2, winter, pp 51-64.

Hoffman, A. (1996b) 'Trends in corporate environmentalism: the chemical and petroleum industries, 1960-1993', in *Society & Natural Resources*, no 9, pp 47-64.

Hollinger, P. (1996) 'Toymakers "ignoring factory code"', in *Financial Times*, 4 December, p 7.

Holmberg, J. (ed) (1992) *Policies for a small planet*, London: Earthscan and IIED.

Holmberg, J. et al (1993) *Facing the future: beyond the Earth Summit*. London: Earthscan and IIED.

Hundall, S. (1996) 'Towards a greener international trade system – mulitlateral environmental agreements and the World Trade Organization' in *Columbia Journal of Law and Social Problems*, vol 29, no 2, pp 175-215.

Hunt, L. (1997) 'Why today's man is losing his virility', in *The Independent*, 6 January, p 13.

Hutchinson C. (1995) *Vitality and renewal: a manager's guide for the 21st century*, London: Adamantine Press Limited.

IISD (1992) *Business strategy for sustainable development: leadership and accountability for the '90s*. Winnipeg, Canada: International Institute for Sustainable Development.

The Independent (1995) 'Sainsbury shows a way ahead', 26 January, p 33.

Ingelhart, R. (1977) *The silent revolution: changing values and political styles among western publics*, Princeton, NJ: Princeton University Press.

IUCN (1978) 'The strategy gets a warm welcome', in *IUCN Bulletin*, vol 9, no 10/11, p 64.

IUCN et al (1980) *The world conservation strategy*, Geneva: IUCN, UNEP and WWF.

IUCN et al (1991) *Caring for the Earth*, Published in partnership by IUCN, UNEP and WWF, London: Earthscan.

Jacobs, J. (1990) 'Profit from "green" products isn't shocking', in *The Montreal Gazette*, 11 April.

Jacobs, M. (1996) *Politics of the real world: a major statement of public concern fron over 30 of the UK's leading voluntary and campaigning organisations*, London: Earthscan.

Jetter, M., B&Q *Timber Purchasing Policy*, Research Working Paper, Newcastle: New Consumer.

Keating, M. (1993) *The Earth Summit's agenda for change*, Geneva: Centre for Our Common Future.

Kenny, B. (1992) *The Greenpeace book of greenwash*, Amsterdam: Greenpeace-International.

Khor, M. (1992) 'What to do, now it's over', in *Third World Resurgence*, August/September, no 24/25, pp 4-5.

King, A. and Schneider, B. (1991) *The first global revolution: a report by the Council of The Club of Rome*, New York: Pantheon Books.

King, P. (1995) 'This panda means business', *WWF News*, Autumn, Godalming: WWF-UK.

Kleiner, A. (1992) 'The three faces of Dow Chemical', in *Business and Society Review*, no 80, winter, pp 28-35.

Knight, A. (1992) *B&Q's timber policy towards 1995: a review of progress*, Eastleigh, Hampshire: B&Q plc.

Knight, A. (1996) 'A report on B&Q's 1995 timber target', in R. Aspinwall and J. Smith (eds), *Environmentalist and business partnerships: a sustainable model?* Cambridge: The White Horse Press.

Korten, D. (1990) *Getting to the 21st century*, Hartford, Conn.: Kumarian Press.

Korten, D. (1995) *When corporations rule the world*, London: Earthscan.

Korten, D. (1996) 'Development is a sham', in *New Internationalist*, no 278, April, pp 12-13.

Krakauer, J. (1991) 'Brown fellas: Ron Arnold and Alan Gottlieb have money, muscle and something to say to millions of angry Americans. Uh-oh ... there goes the biosphere', in *Outside*, December.

Lamb, R. (1996) *Promising the Earth*, London: Routledge.

Lascalles, D. (1995) 'Antagonists clear the air', in *Financial Times*, 27 September, p 16.

Law, S. (1992) 'Land use guru finds developers adding to Oregon's 1000 Friends', *Portland Business Journal*, 6 January, p 12.

Lean, G. (1995) 'Greener on the other side', in *The Independent on Sunday*, 31 December, p 21.

Lean, G. (1996) 'Bigger, richer and duller: Friends of the Earth at 25', in *The Independent on Sunday*, 5 May, p 5.

Lean, G. (1996) 'Sex-change chemicals in baby milk', in *The Independent on Sunday*, 26 May, p 1.

Lee, K. (1993) *Compass and gyroscope: integrating science and politics for the environment*, Washington DC: Island Press.

Lewis, P. (1992) 'Storm in Rio: the day after – pursuing the portents of new global politics', in *The New York Times*, 15 June, p A1.

Ljunggren, D. (1996) *Unilever, WWF unite in bid to save fish stocks*, Reuters Ltd, 22 February, 01.14.

London Greenpeace (1986) *What's wrong with McDonald's?* London: London Greenpeace.

London Greenpeace (1996) *What's wrong with McDonald's?* revised summary leaflet, London: London Greenpeace.

Lovelock, J. (1979) *Gaia: a new look at life on Earth*, Oxford: Oxford University Press.

MacNeil, J. et al (1991) *Beyond interdependence*, New York: Oxford University Press.

McCormick, J. (1989) *Reclaiming paradise: the global environmental movement*, Bloomington: Indiana University Press.

McCoy, M. and McCully, P. (1993) *The road from Rio: an NGO action guide to environment and development*, Utrecht, The Netherlands: International Books and World Information Service on Energy (WISE).

McDonald's Corporation (1996) *The annual: McDonald's Corporation 1995 annual report*, Oak Brook, Illinois: McDonald's Corporation.

McDonald's Education Service (1996) *The history and background to McDonald's*, London: McDonald's Restaurants Ltd.

McDonald's Restaurants Ltd. (1994) *Environment: facing the challenge*, London: McDonald's Restaurants Ltd.

McGrew, A. (1993) 'The political dynamics of the new environmentalism', in D. Smith (ed) *Business and the environment: implications of the new environmentalism,* London: Paul Chapman Publishing.

McInerny, J. (ed) (1996) *Sustaining developments since the Rio Summit,* proceedings of the UNED-UK 1995 Annual Conference, 27 November.

McKibben, B. (1996) 'Chicken sutra: KFC and the battle for India's soul', in *Utne Reader,* no 77, September/October, pp 11-12.

McKinsey and Co (1992) *Building successful environmental partnerships: a guide for prospective partners for the President's Commission on Environmental Quality,* New York: McKinsey and Co.

McSpotlight (1996) *McSpotlight web site,* www.mcspotlight.org/, Amsterdam: McInformation Network.

Maitland, A. (1996) 'Unilever in fight to save global fisheries', in *Financial Times,* 22 February, p 4.

Makower, J. (1993) *The E Factor: the bottom line approach to environmentally responsible business,* New York: Times Books.

Makower, J. (ed) (1996) 'Beyond regulations: why regulators are taking bold steps toward corporate self-enforcement', in *The Green Business Letter,* April.

Maltby, J. (1995) *Setting its own standards and meeting those standards: voluntarism versus regulation in environmental reporting,* A paper presented at the 1995 Business Strategy and the Environment Conference, 20-21 September, University of Leeds, UK.

May, T. (1996) 'Kingfisher appeases city with do-it-yourself rejig', in *The Guardian,* 25 March, p 14.

Meadows, D.H., Meadows, D.L., Randers, J. and Behrens, W. (1972) *Limits to growth,* London: Earth Island.

MEB (Management Institute for Environment and Business) (1995) *The power of environmental partnerships* (F. Long and M. Arnold eds), Fort Worth, Texas: Dryden Press.

Merchant, C. (1992) *Radical ecology,* New York; Routledge.

Miller, L.H. (1990) *Global order: values and power in international politics*, Boulder, Colorado: Westview Press.

Moffatt Associates (1996) *The 1996 UK business and the environment trends survey*, London: Moffatt Associates Partnership.

Moore, E. (1997) 'Beanz meanz geanz', in *The Guardian Education*, 7 January, p 10.

Murphy, D.F. (1992) *Are people around the world beginning to think alike? Feedback from the UNCED process*, unpublished MSc dissertation, Bristol: School for Policy Studies, University of Bristol.

Murphy, D.F. (1996a) *DIY-WWF alliance: doing it together for the world's forests*, research working paper series on corporate social responsibility, Bristol: School for Policy Studies, University of Bristol.

Murphy, D.F. (1996b) *Dow Europe: responding to environmental pressure through dialogue and partnership*, research working paper series on corporate social responsibility, Bristol: School for Policy Studies, University of Bristol.

Murphy, D.F. (1996c) *From protest to partnership and back again: social responsibility and the McDonald's Corporation*, unpublished case study, London: New Academy of Business.

Murphy, D.F. (1996d) 'In the company of partners – businesses, NGOs and sustainable development: towards a global perspective', in R. Aspinwall and J. Smith (eds), *Environmentalist and business partnerships: a sustainable model?* Cambridge: The White Horse Press.

Myers, N. (1992) *The primary source: tropical forests and our future*, London: W.W. Norton.

Naess, A. (1988) 'The basics of deep ecology', in *Resurgence*, 126, pp 4-7.

Nash, R. (1977) 'Do rocks have rights?', in *The Center Magazine*, November/December, pp 1-12.

National Consumer Council (1996) *Green claims: a consumer investigation into marketing claims about the environment*, London: NCC.

National Consumer Council (1996) *Green consumers: a consumer investigation into marketing claims about the environment*, London: NCC.

Newhouse, J. (1992) 'The diplomatic round: Earth Summit', in *The New Yorker*, 1 June, pp 64-78.

Nikiforuk, A. (1990) 'Sustainable rhetoric', in *Harrowsmith*, no 93, September/October, pp 14-15.

NLRTEE (Newfoundland and Labrador Round Table on the Environment and Economy) (1995) *The report of the partnership on sustainable coastal communities and marine ecosystems in Newfoundland and Labrador*, St Johns: NLRTEE.

Patey, T. (1996) 'Experts must tackle crisis in fish stocks', in *The European*, 8 February.

Paton, N. (1996) 'Sainsbury's makes first ethical monitoring move', in *SuperMarketing*, 24 May.

Paul, C.S. (1996) 'Environmental purchasing requires green partners', a paper presented at the 1996 Business Strategy and the Environment Conference, 19-20 September, University of Leeds, UK.

Payoyo, P.B. (1994) *Ocean governance: sustainable development of the seas*, New York: United Nations University Press.

Pearce, F. (1991) *Green warriors: the people and politics behind the environmental revolution*, London: The Bodley Head.

Pepper, D. (1996) *Modern environmentalism: an introduction*, London and New York: Routledge.

PETA USA (1994) *Companies that test on animals*, January 1, USA: PETA.

Phillips, R. (1996) 'No quick fix from Unilever', in *The Independent on Sunday*, 3 November.

Ponting, C. (1992) *A green history of the world*, London: Penguin.

Porter, G and Welsh Brown, J. (1991) *Global environmental politics*, Boulder, Colorado: Westview Press.

Prince, J. and Denison, R.A. (1991) 'Launching a new business ethic: the environment as a standard operating procedure at McDonald's and at other companies', A paper for the Ariel

Halpren Memorial Symposium, *Business ethics and the environment*, Amos Tuck School of Business Administration, Dartmouth College, Hanover, New Hampshire, 21-22 November.

Real World (1992) 'What went unsaid at UNCED', in *Real World: The Voice of Green Politics*, pp 4-6, London: The Green Party.

Reid, D. (1995) *Sustainable development: an introductory guide*, London: Earthscan.

Reinhart, F (1992) *Environmental defense fund*, Harvard Business School Case Study N1-793-037, Boston: Harvard Business School.

Repetto, R. and Gillis, M. (1988) *Public policies and the misuse of forest resources*, Cambridge: Cambridge University Press.

Rietbergen, S. (ed) (1993) *The Earthscan Reader in tropical forestry*, London: Earthscan.

Rietbergen, S. (1995) *Tropical forestry handbook*, London: Earthscan.

Riggs, R. and Plano, J. (1988) *The United Nations: international organization and world politics*, Pacific Grove, California: Brooks/Cole Publishing Company.

Ritzer, G. (1993) *The McDonaldization of society*, London: Pine Forge Press.

Robbins, N. and Trisoglio, A. (1992) 'Restructuring industry for sustainable development', in J. Holmberg, (ed) *Policies for a small planet*, London; Earthscan.

Roberts, P. (1995) *Environmentally sustainable business: a local and regional perspective*, London: Paul Chapman Publishing.

Roddick, A. with Miller, R. (1991) *Body and soul*, London: Ebury Press.

Roddick, J. (1994) 'Second Session of the Commission on Sustainable Development', a paper presented at 'Towards a sustainable future: promoting sustainable development', Global Forum Academic Conference, Manchester, 1 July.

Rowell, A. (1996) *Green backlash: global subversion of the environment movement*, London: Routledge.

Rowland, W. (1973) *The plot to save the world*, Toronto: Clarke, Irwin & Company Ltd.

Royal Dutch Shell Group (1969) 'Policy on environmental conservation', in *Quality: the Bulletin of the Shell Committee for Environmental Conservation*, no 1, December, p 1.

Royston, M.G. (1979) *Pollution prevention pays*, Oxford: Pergamon Press.

Sachs, W. (1979) 'Ecodevelopment: a definition', in *Ambio*, vol 8, no 2/3, p 113.

Sachs, W. (ed) (1992) *The development dictionary*, London: Zed Books.

Sancassiani, W. (1995) 'Dow Europe: effective, proactive environmental communication', in *EEMA Review*, May, pp 12-15.

Sandbrook, R. (1983) 'The UK's overseas environmental policy', in *The conservation and development programme for the UK: a response to the World Conservation Strategy*, London: Kogan Page.

Schumacher, E.F. (1973) *Small is beautiful: economics as if people really mattered*, London: Abacus.

Schuurman, F. (ed) (1993) *Beyond the impasse: new directions in development theory*, London: Zed Books.

Scmidheiny, S. (1992) *Changing course: a global business perspective on development and environment*, London: The MIT Press.

Seager, J. (1993) *Earth follies*, London: Earthscan.

Shell Briefing Service (1969) *Environmental conservation*, a management information brief for the staff of the companies of the Royal Dutch/Shell Group, September, London: Shell Briefing Service.

Shell-UK (1995) *Brent Spar*, internal newsletter produced by Barkers Trident Communications on behalf of Shell UK Ltd, London.

Simon, J. (1981) *The ultimate resource*, Princeton: Princeton University Press.

Sklair, L. (1991) *Sociology of the global system*, London: Harvester Wheatsheaf.

Smart, B. (ed) (1992) *Beyond compliance: a new industry view of the environment*, Washington: World Resources Institute.

Smith, A.D. (1996) 'Executive branch rule-making and dispute settlement in the World Trade Organization – a proposal to increase public participation', in *Michigan Law Review*, vol 94, no 5, pp 1267-93.

Smith, Z.A. (1995) *The environmental policy paradox*, (second edn) Englewood Cliffs, NJ: Prentice Hall.

Spaargen, G. and Mol, A.P.J. (1992) 'Sociology, environment and modernity: ecological modernisation as a theory of change', *Society and Natural Resources*, no 5, pp 323-44.

Sproul, J.T. (1996) *Green fisheries? Linking fishery health, practice and prices through eco-certification, labeling and crediting* (first draft), unpublished.

Stackhouse, J. (1996) 'Maharaja Mac set to invade India', in *The Globe and Mail*, Toronto, 12 October, pp A1, A9.

Stafford, E.R. and Hartman, C.L. (1996) 'Green alliances: strategic relations between businesses and environmental groups', in *Business Horizons*, vol 39, no 2, pp 50-59.

Sternberg, E. (1994) *Just business*, London: Little Brown & Company.

Stewart, M. and Snape, S. (1996) *Keeping up the momentum: partnership working in Bristol and the West*, An unpublished study for the Bristol (UK) Chamber of Commerce and Initiative.

Stone, P. (1973) *Did we save the Earth at Stockholm?* London: Earth Island.

SustainAbility (1994) *SustainAbility News: review of 1994*, no 6.

SustainAbility (1995a) *EPE participant questionnaire survey results*, January, London: SustainAbility.

SustainAbility (1995b) *Who needs it? Market implications of sustainable lifestyles* (a SustainAbility business guide), London: SustainAbility.

Sustainability (1996) 'Strange attractor: Business–ENGO partnership. Strategic review of BP's relationships with environmental non-governmental organisations', Summary of findings, July.

SustainAbility and Tomorrow (1994) *The green keiretsu: an international survey of business alliances and networks for sustainable development*, Stockholm and London: Tomorrow Media and SustainAbility.

SustainAbility, NEF and UNEP (1996) *Engaging stakeholders*, London: SustainAbility.

Taylor, B., Pollock, S., Hutchinson, C. and Tapper, R. (1994) *The environmental management handbook*, London: Pitman.

Third World Network (1992) 'The "Sustainable Council for Business Development"' in *Third World Resurgence*, August/September, issue 24/25, p 22.

The Times (1997) 'Bigger Mac means 5,000 jobs to be filled in 1997' [by S. Cunningham], 3 January, p 23.

The Toronto Star (1995) 'Battled child labour, boy, 12, murdered', 19 April.

United Nations (1993) *The Global Partnership for Environment and Development*. New York: United Nations Publications.

UNCED (1992) *Agenda 21: the United Nations programme of action from Rio*, New York: UN Department of Public Information.

UNCTAD (1996) *Self-Regulation of environmental management*, Geneva: UN Conference on Trade and Development and UN Publications.

Unilever plc (1996) Environment report: our worldwide approach, London: Unilever Environment Group.

Unilver plc (1997) *Unilever Annual Report 1996*, London: Unilever plc.

Upton, D. and Margolis, J. (1992) *McDonald's Corporation 1992: operations, flexibility and the environment*, Harvard Business School Case Study 1-693-028, Boston: Harvard Business School.

Vanclay, J.K. (1993) 'Saving the tropical rainforests: needs and prognosis', *Ambio*, vol 22, no 4, pp 225-31.

Viana, V., Ervin, J., Donovan, R., Elliot, C. and Gholz, H. (1996) *The forest certification handbook*, Washington, DC: Island Press.

Vidal, J. (1996) 'You and I against the world', in *The Guardian Weekend*, 9 March, pp 12-16.

Vincent, J.R. (1992) 'The tropical timber trade and sustainable development', *Science*, vol 256, pp 1651-55.

Waddock, S. (1991) 'Typology of social partnerships', in *Administration & Society*, February, vol 22, no 4, pp 480-575.

Wagstyl, S. and Corizone, R. (1997) 'Rights and wrongs', in *Financial Times*, 18 March, p 24.

Wakker, E (1995) *Recent developments in the Dutch tropical timber market*, Amsterdam: Mileudefensie.

Wall, D. (1994) *Green history: a reader in environmental literature, philosophy and politics*, London: Routledge.

Wallace, D. (1995) *Environmental policy and industrial innovation: strategies in Europe, the US and Japan*, London: Earthscan and the Royal Institute of International Affairs Energy and Environment Programme.

Wallerstein, I. (1974) *The modern world system* (vol 1), New York: Academic Press.

Ward, B. and Dubos, R. (1972) *Only one Earth*, Harmondsworth: Penguin Books.

Warty, M. (1997) Centre for Business and Economics Research (CEBR), personal communication, 10 January.

Waterman, P. (1991) 'There is an alternative to international relations – a global civil society', in *Z Magazine*, July/August, pp 99-110.

WBCSD (World Business Council for Sustainable Development) (1996) *Trade and environment: a business perspective*, Geneva: WBCSD.

WBCSD (1997) *Signals for change*, Geneva: WBCSD.

WCED (1987) *Our common future*, Oxford: Oxford University Press.

Weber, P. (1994) Net loss: fish, jobs and the marine environment, Worldwatch Paper 120, USA: Worldwatch Institute.

Welford, R. (1995) *Environmental strategy and sustainable development*, London: Routledge.

Welford, R., (ed) (1996a) *Corporate environmental management: systems and strategies*, London: Earthscan.

Welford, R. (1996b) 'Hijacking environmentalism', paper presented at the 1996 Business Strategy and the Environment Conference, 20 September, 1996, Leeds, UK.

Welford, R. (1997) *Hijacking environmentalism: corporate responses to sustainable development*, London: Earthscan.

Welford, R. and Jones, D. (1996) 'Beyond environmentalism and towards the sustainable organization', in R. Welford (ed) (1996b), *Corporate environmental management: systems and strategies*, London: Earthscan.

Welford, R. and Starkey R. (eds) (1996) *The Earthscan Reader in business and the environment*, London: Earthscan.

Wells, P. (1995) *Unilever: integrated rural development programme in India*, The transnational corporation in a host country: policy practice in developing countries, Research working paper series, Newcastle, UK: New Consumer.

Westley, F. and Vredenburg, H. 'Strategic bridging: the collaboration between environmentalists and business in the marketing of green products', in *Journal of Applied Behavioral Science*, vol 27, no 1, pp 65-90.

WFSGI (1995) *The way forward*, proceedings of the Conference on Human Rights held in Verbier, Switzerland, 3 November 1995, London: Brassey's Sports for the Committee on Ethics and Fair Trade, World Federation of the Sporting Goods Industry (WFSGI).

WFSGI (1996) *Sporting goods industry to develop global code of conduct and programme to end child labour*, press release, 22 November, Verbier, Switzerland: WFSGI.

WFSGI (1997) *Sporting goods industry partners with children's and human rights groups to end child labour in Pakistan's soccer ball industry*, press release, 14 February, Verbier, Switzerland: WFSGI.

Wheeler, D. and Sillanpää, M. (1997) *The stakeholder corporation*, London: Pitman.

White, M. (1995) 'Does it pay to be "green"? Corporate environmental responsibility and shareholder value', Paper presented at the 1995 Business Strategy and the Environment Conference, 20-21 September, University of Leeds, UK.

Whitelaw, J. (1996) *The international chemicals agenda: relax - there is a plan*, Geneva: UNEP.

Williams, F. (1996) 'WTO refuses to link trade measures to labour rights', in *Financial Times*, 13 December, p 4.

Williams, R., (ed) (1994) *The forestry industry yearbook, 1993-1994*, London: Forestry Industry Committee of Great Britain.

Williamson, R. (1996) 'Anti-sealing lobby targets salmon', in *The Globe and Mail*, Toronto, 8 February.

Willums, J.O. and Golücke, U. (1991) *WICEM II Second World Conference on Environmental Management: conference report and background papers*, Rotterdam: WICEM.

Willums, J.O. and Golüke, U. (1992) *From ideas to action: business and sustainable development*, London: ICC International Environment Bureau.

Wood, D. (1994) *Business and society* (second edn), New York: HarperCollins.

Worcester, R. (1994) 'Public opinion on environmental issues', in B. Taylor et al (1995) *The environmental management handbook*, London: Pitman.

World Bank (1990) *World Bank Development Report 1990*, Oxford: Oxford University Press.

World Development Movement (1996) *Fair play for toy workers: a briefing on the UK toy campaign*, October 21.

WRTF (1991) *Executive summary of Waste Reduction Task Force final report*, April, McDonald's Corporation and Environmental Defense Fund.

WWF-International (1991) 'Business and environment: the problem and the opportunity', in J.O. Willums and U. Golücke (eds), *WICEM II Second World Conference on Environmental Management: conference report and background papers*, Rotterdam: WICEM.

WWF-International (1994) *WWF's global priorities to the year 2000*, Gland, Switzerland: WWF-International.

WWF-International (1995) *Forest for life: WWF's 1995 forest seminar proceedings,* Godalming: WWF-UK.

WWF-International (1996) Marine Stewardship Council Newsletter, no 1, Godalming: WWF-International.

WWF-International (1997a) *Forests for life: WWF's global forest annual report 96,* Godalming: WWF-International.

WWF-International (1997b) *Spotlight on solutions: recommendations to the 1997 review process, February 24-March 7,* Gland, Switzerland: WWF-International.

WWF-UK (1991) *Truth or trickery?,* Godalming: WWF-UK.

WWF-UK (1996) *The WWF 1995 Group: the full story,* Godalming: WWF-UK.

Young, S.C. (1993) *The politics of the environment,* Manchester: Baseline Books.

Index